CRICKET
ON THE AIR

CRICKET ON THE AIR

A selection from fifty years of radio broadcasts

David Rayvern Allen

British Broadcasting Corporation

To Lindsay and Briony

Published by the British Broadcasting Corporation
35 Marylebone High Street, London W1M 4AA

First published 1985
Selection, arrangement and linking material © David Rayvern Allen 1985
Details of other copyright material are on p. 10

ISBN 0 563 20343 9

Set in 10/12 pt Times Roman by Phoenix Photosetting, Chatham
Printed in England by Mackays of Chatham Ltd

Contents

Illustrations

Acknowledgements

The choice for inclusion was, to some extent, dictated by what is now available, particularly the cricket talks from pre-war. So much has been trampled by the march of time, notably tantalising offerings from D. J. Knight, Norman Riches, Stephen King-Hall, and Hugh de Sélincourt. Even post-war pieces have conceded to lack of space and short-term expediency; who, for instance, would not have wished the chance to savour Arlott's Report to South-East Asia on the technique of George Tribe and Sonny Ramadhin. However, many of the scripts that were still gathering dust in tightly-packed shelves would not have seen natural light again, but for the inestimable help so readily given by Amanda Mares and her colleagues at the BBC's Written Archives Centre at Caversham. My grateful thanks to them all and to the Sound Archives staff at Broadcasting House where a large selection on disc is housed.

Appreciation is also more than due to Tony Kingsford of BBC Publications for commissioning the book in the first place, to Valerie Buckingham for her benign assistance with editing and copyright clearance, to Ann Routledge for the design, and to the staff at the Hulton Picture Library for the sifting of the photographs.

Lastly, a resounding cheer for all the writers and broadcasters whose love of cricket transmitted such enjoyment over the air.

Picture Credits
Allsport/Adrian Murrell 139 above left and below; BBC Hulton Picture Library 113, 114, 115, 116, 118, 119, 120, 137, 138 above, 139 above right, 140, 141 above, 142 above and below left, 143, 144 below; BBC Picture Publicity 141 below right; Colorsport 142 right; Illustrated London News Picture Library 117; Storrington Cricket Club 138 below.

Text Credits
The author and publishers would like to thank the following for permission to reproduce text material: John Arlott, O.B.E. for his interview with Brian Johnston; Don Bradman for his interview with Brian Johnston; André Drucker for 'Cricket Through Foreign Eyes'; Ettinger Bros for Clive Lloyd's interview with Paul Wade; P. G. H. Fender for 'Australia *v.* England, Third Test Match, 1937' and 'B. J. T. Bosanquet – An Appreciation'; Mrs Margaret Gilligan for 'This Test Match Business' by Arthur Gilligan; Michael Green for 'My Grandfather Nearly Bowled W.G.'; Sir Harold Hobson, C.B.E. for 'It Isn't Cricket'; Margaret Hughes for 'A Hundred Up' and 'Cricket in Australia' by Neville Cardus; Major-General The Viscount Monckton of Brenchley, C.B., O.B.E., M.C., D.L. for his father's interview with Freddy Grisewood; Rudy Narayan for his interview with Steve Cape; Bill O'Reilly for 'A Hundred Up'; Steven Pagdin for his interview with Steve Cape; A. D. Peters & Co. Ltd for 'Cricket at Lord's' by Patrick O'Donovan; Lord Scarman for his interview with Steve Cape; Philip Snow, M.B.E., J.P., M.A., F.R.S.A., F.R.A.I. for 'Cricket in the South Seas'; E. W. Swanton, O.B.E. for 'With the MCC in South Africa' and 'Meet E. W. Swanton'; Mrs E. Warner for 'West Indian Cricket and Cricketers' and 'Australia's Greatest Batsman' by Sir Pelham Warner; Neville Webber for 'Brighter Cricket'; Mrs Ruby Whitaker-Wilson for 'The Earliest Days of Cricket' by Cecil Whitaker-Wilson.

The publishers have endeavoured to trace all copyright holders but if we have unwittingly enfringed copyright, we apologise and shall be pleased to hear from copyright holders.

Introduction

The best radio defies accurate description. Although it is a truism to say that the essence of the medium lies in its ability to activate a personal, indeed private, mental picture for each listener, there can be generated an imaginative force which is not to be contained by just words. And yet words enlarged by sounds are the microchips for those fanciful flights by which we all elude the unwanted present.

This is particularly true of broadcasts on cricket. Cricket, by its very nature, conjures an image of contentment; the sky is never cloudy, the grass never blown, the creaking deckchairs supporting wistful memories of waistlines now distended by hampers of chicken or cheddar and the pleasingly flawed white of clapboards in the Pavilion and flannels on the green, helping to reflect the pretence that nobody cares too much or is trying too hard, make for comfortable inertia . . .

Therefore, to marry so captivating an evocation to such a compelling medium is, borrowing a phrase from wireless's ambitious cousin, television, to be on a 'starter for ten'. Why was it, then, that the barons of the emerging 'Beeb' were so tardy in recognising the potency of cricket on the air? Or were they? Was it just the live commentary of cricket that, in the 1920s and early 1930s, seemed to present insurmountable problems? The trials of the first 'live' BBC broadcasts on the game, given in 1927 by 'Plum' Warner and then the Rev. Canon Frank Gillingham, who, incidentally, must be the only one-time Essex wicket-keeper to have been born in Tokyo and die in Monaco, are told by John Arlott in a comprehensive chapter on the history of commentated cricket in Brian Johnston's diverting *Armchair Cricket 1966*. Perhaps it is sufficient to realise that the case for cricket on radio, in whatever form, was not helped when, in his first spell from the Oval with raindrops literally falling on his head and no cricket to report, Gillingham started to give details of the advertisements on the hoardings around the ground.

This book concentrates not on commentary but rather on talks and discussions that portray the game in its primitive form on islands in the South Seas, in settings of rustic charm, in India, South Africa the West Indies and England, as played with scientific sophistication in international stadia. Unconventional characters are seen in conventional surroundings, vice versa, and personalities reminisce about the past and opine about the future. Some of cricket's finest practitioners on the field and fluent talkers off it create these pages. No other game stimulates so much discourse, such immediate contact from strangers of disparate background, and such friendly enmity from those in close communion. No other game produces similar fecundity on printed page or in earnest conversation at local pub and light-hearted debate within Maharajah's palace. Whether cricket is being played on the village green by the theatre critic of the *Daily Telegraph* or whether members of the judiciary knock ball with wood in downtown Brixton the result is the same.

Cricket is not only the great leveller but the great communicator. The most eminent fall to the most humble. Grace was bowled by a schoolboy with a sorbo-rubber ball. What they offered and have to say is, in the end, equally important.

*After all, one has to start somewhere and if a talk for the old Empire
Programme on the derivations of cricket seems a touch convenient and
obvious . . . well, even grizzled inveterates of the games ancient and
modern should find a mild surprise or two worth savouring in the
author's exposition. Cecil Whitaker-Wilson was a radio writer and actor
who came from the Midlands. He had trained as an organist at Chester
Cathedral and it was at the Console that he first broadcast in 1924.
History does not easily reveal whether he was acting or playing on the
three occasions that he went on the air from the tower of Big Ben, though
having taken the part of Haydn in his own play on Mozart, presumably
the chiming was impeccable! Extraordinary. I have just been told that
Whitaker-Wilson lived a road away from where this is being written . . .*

The Earliest Days of Cricket
C. Whitaker-Wilson

Empire Programme, August 1934

First of all, what does the word *cricket* mean? I can only give you my own
opinion. In Anglo-Saxon there existed a word *Cricc* which meant a staff. I
am inclined to think this is at least part of the origin of the word, because
there is distinct evidence that the game was at one time played with a club or
a staff.

I must also point out that in the days of Plantagenet London, the days of
King Richard the Lionhearted, the game – or at least a similar game – was
called *Hondyn* or *Hondoute* which seems to mean *Hand in* or *Hand out*. The
actual word cricket did not appear until about 1550. Now a cricket is a *stool* –
the wicket in other words. There also existed an old word – Old French as a
matter of fact – spelt *wiket* derived from a still older word in Scandinavian
spelt *vik*. This word meant an inlet.

The connection in the Plantagenet stage of the game is that the batsman
stood in a large hole. Possibly he had one stump placed at the back of the
hole. I think the inlet idea comes out in this fact. I *do* know that the ball had
to be placed or else thrown into the hole to run the batsman out. After this,
the wicket really did have the appearance, not only of a *stool* but of a *gate*. I
think the whole derivation is a mixture of ideas. Let us sort them out. *Cricc*
meant a staff – the bat in other words; a cricket is a stool; a wicket is a gate,
and is also connected with *vik*, an inlet. I think the real derivation of the
name of our national game comes out of these combined ideas. This is only
my opinion, of course. I cannot state it as a *fact*.

Judging by various pictures I have seen, the wicket has undergone many
changes since Plantagenet days. I saw one painting of medieval times

13

showing two stumps about a foot high and set at least two feet apart. A third stump was laid across the other two which, again, rather bears out the gate idea. The three stumps came into vogue certainly not before the year 1800. The height was then raised to twenty inches. Bails were probably introduced later.

In an early engraving in a manuscript of the thirteenth century there is a quaint and grotesque delineation of early cricket in which two men are seen playing. One of them is the batsman who holds his weapon – you could hardly call it a bat – in his right hand but with the handle downwards. The other figure is obviously catching the ball although the ball itself is not visible. There is also a manuscript in the Bodleian Library, dated 18 April 1344, where fielders appear. All the players are monks. On the extreme left of this picture, a monk, with his cowl up, poises his right arm which is nearly horizontal. The batsman does not seem quite far enough away, but the whole perspective is a trifle out of drawing. The batsman's cowl is down. His bat, a rough-looking affair, is held in his *left* hand. Perhaps he is a left-handed batsman? I am inclined to think the artist may be at fault, though I have read arguments that the bat was always held in the left hand at this period. I cannot, however, think it was so. At all events, I have found no *contemporary* evidence. There are four fielders in this picture; two have their cowls up and two down. There does not seem to be a wicket-keeper but I don't think the artist could very well have got him in the picture.

Like most games – football especially – cricket came in for censure under Edward III. King Edward deplored these 'worthless pastimes', as he called them, because they 'interfered with the proper practice of archery'. In any case, His Majesty considered it a game 'for the lower orders only'. On the other hand, I have found entries in the King's Wardrobe Account which seem to prove the game of *creag* was becoming regrettably popular amongst the nobility.

Edward IV was a soldier to his backbone. The victor in the Wars of the Roses was hardly likely to patronise a babyish game of ball, for that is how he regarded it. He went further than Edward III. He definitely made cricket, or whatever it was called in Yorkist London, illegal. So that if you had lived in those times and had allowed anyone to play cricket in a field of your possession, it ran you in for a twenty-pound fine and three years' imprisonment. As for the players, they got off with two years and a ten-pound fine. Perhaps this is the severest law ever passed in England against a game.

In the reign of Elizabeth, an innkeeper at Guildford thought he would run a cricket club of his own. So he enclosed a piece of waste land in the parish of Holy Trinity in that city. He was pounced upon and ordered to disenclose the ground again and let it lie waste. What sort of turf he had got there I have never found out, but the evidence of John Derrick, gent, who was one of Her Majesty's coroners, is worth reproducing. He said he was fifty-nine years old, and that he had known that ground for fifty years. It was always used for 'crickett and other plaies when he was a scholler in the free school of Guildford'. However, the case went against the innkeeper – and that was that.

I was amused at Stow's account. He is a great historian, Stow, to my way of thinking, and remarkably accurate. He says the game was not played by gentlemen. The ball 'was used in the tennis courts by *them*, but cricket was played by the meaner sort in the fields and streets'. A regular old snob, John Stow!

As a school game, cricket seems to have begun at Winchester in 1651. I am rather surprised at that because those were the early days of the Commonwealth. It is a wonder the Puritans did not have something to say about it, but I see there is a reference by Dugdale to Cromwell having played it himself. Evidently Dugdale had no opinion of people who played it because he says Cromwell 'threw himself into a dissolute and disorderly course by playing cricket and football'. At all events, they did begin a cricket season at Winchester school in 1651, but why they chose January for the beginning of the season is more than I can tell you. I should have thought the ground would have been hopeless; perhaps it was frozen hard!

Shocking things went on in Maidstone in 1653. I regret to have to inform you that Maidstone was considered 'a very profane town. There were morris dancing, cudgel-playing, stoolball, *crickets*, and many other sports openly and publicly indulged in on the Lord's Day?' Dreadful wasn't it!

We have to thank Queen Anne for repealing the acts against cricket. She considered it a 'manly game, and not bad in itself, but only in the illuse made of it by betting more than ten pounds on it'. There is no doubt there was a good deal of betting over cricket.

The old Artillery Ground at Finsbury was the scene of many a cricket match in 1700. During Anne's reign the London Club was formed and played its matches. By this time there were popping-creases, bails, overs – in fact most things we have in these days. One of the earliest full scores kept in the modern fashion seems to have been at a match on the Finsbury ground where Kent played All England on 18 June 1744. The famous Hambledon Club was formed in 1750 and ran for forty years. They played their matches on Broadhalfpenny and Windmill Downs. Many of these matches were against All England. The chief players were often retainers of country gentry. This thoroughly established cricket and it became the custom to begin the season with a big match on Good Friday.

About 1780, the old Artillery Ground players migrated to White Conduit Fields and became the White Conduit Club. In 1787 they moved their club to Lord's which was then where Dorset Square is now. Lord's was called after the Club's groundsman, Thomas Lord. The Club's name was now the Marylebone Cricket Club – better known as the MCC – and Lord put down turf of a fine quality in Dorset Square. In 1811 he moved it to Regent's Park, not far from where St Dunstan's now stands. In 1814 he took it all up again and laid it on the west side of what is now Wellington Road, St John's Wood, so named after the battle of Waterloo the following year. You all know where Lord's Cricket Ground is – at least those of you who have visited London. It is just opposite St John's Wood Road, Metropolitan Station. While Lord was working at his cricket ground, Hardwick was busy building the church of St John on the other side of the road. There is history here also. The grounds of this church cover one of the principal plague pits of 1665. Also, the religious fanatic of the time of George III – Joanna Southcott – lies buried in its grounds. There are all sorts of mystic inscriptions on her tomb . . . how she would return again with great power. During the war, application was made to the vicar of St John's to have the grave opened because it was honestly believed there were prophetic writings which would forecast the end of the war. There was quite a strong feeling at the time. The vicar would not allow the grave to be touched, in which I strongly supported him. I was organist of that church for ten years.

So these were the early days of cricket – our national game. Rudyard Kipling may have called us flannelled fools, but at least we have seven hundred years of history behind our Test matches, even if we exclude the history of bodyline bowling. Goodbye.

*   *   *

The Church has maintained a continuous if occasionally stormy love-affair with cricket, begun even before that day in the seventeenth century when the parishioners of Boxgrove in Sussex were berated for breaking the stained-glass windows during a game in the churchyard on the Sabbath. Patrick O'Donovan would have relished that episode. Born of a strict Roman Catholic family, well versed in ecclesiastical history, he wrote on religious affairs for the Observer, *besides having a reputation as a flamboyant foreign correspondent who had a 'Trollopian sense of fun' and an engaging gift for self-mockery.*

O'Donovan came to the microphone in 1952 for the series 'Special Correspondent' to give his impressions of a day's play in the second Test match between England and India.

Cricket at Lord's

Patrick O'Donovan

Home Service, June 1952

Lord's Cricket Ground is a sort of crater that has been formed in a highly respectable residential district in London. It stands in a no-man's-land between the aristocratic splendour of Regent's Park and the small shops, the carved and painted pubs, the cheerful noise and muddle of Maida Vale.

Here are factories with fat, black chimneys; here are yards where people store things behind locked gates; here are tall blocks of flats. It seems to have no shops, no cinemas, no park, just a network of calm streets. There is a splendid white church standing at the top of a gentle hill and, beside it, the long brick wall that surrounds the cricket ground.

You can scarcely have failed to notice that recently they played here the second Test match between India and England. I went there on one of the five days set aside for the match – with some thirty thousand other people. There was a small, disappointed crowd round each gate in the brick wall. There were mounted policemen looking noble but with little to do. When I stood on the pavement for a moment wondering which entrance to use, a middle-aged man in young man's clothes walked past and, without stopping, asked if I wanted to buy a good ticket. At the entrances, men who looked like long-established estate workers examined my pass. It was pleasantly easy and informal.

Inside, you were at once confronted with the bleak backs of stands that gave no hint at all what was on the other side. People in an obvious holiday mood were sauntering towards their places or queueing for orangeade. Though you could see no great crowd as yet, the place was filled with an enormous buzz of talk, a sound of thousands of voices in reasonable

17

conversation that made a solid chord of sound. Every now and again, it quickened and rose, and there was a swift and brief burst of clapping. It sounded as if someone were giving away prizes. And underneath each burst, there was also a sort of moo of pleasurable excitement.

But still the crowd, almost all of them men, went on strolling behind the concrete backs of the stands. There were printed cards by some of the doors that gave the names of those who had been given boxes for the match – Colonel this and Commander that. That, too, somehow increased the feeling that this was a local affair and that the size of the crowd and the fame of the ground made no real difference to the traditional way of running a cricket match.

Then the road turned a corner and there was this wide oval of green with white figures, bending and moving, far away in its centre. There were hundreds of people standing here. In front – the cricket, and behind – a balconied building called the Tavern. Its verandah was jam-packed with men, standing with glasses of beer in their hands, watching and discussing the game. In front of them was a gently sloping expanse of concrete, and here for the first time, you could really see the Lord's crowd. This was clearly an important place. Everyone lingered here a little on the way to their seats. Many of the men looked as if they had just come back from the Far East or Africa and had come here to recapture something they had often remembered and desired. They stood, some of them a little lonely perhaps, watching the cricket almost hungrily, absorbing the scene which would make as good a symbol as any of a regretted mother country. Their faces were brown. Their ties tended to be regimental. Their clothes looked well cared for and good. They did not wear bowler hats. In a few weeks, no doubt, they would be off back to their plantations or their mess and when asked about their leave at home, they will say that they're not really sorry to get back, that this country is in pretty bad shape, but that they had a couple of days' cricket at Lord's and that the place hasn't changed much.

Now I don't mean to say that this was a crowd composed of a single class or type. I suppose it was as typical a cross-section of the men of this country as you could find anywhere. There were all sorts – excited small boys, young men in sports jackets and open-necked shirts, old men in cloth caps and watch chains, African students with partings cut into their hair like topiary, Indians in Congress caps or city suits, a few Americans with cameras, bearded men, men with clipped moustaches brushed outwards, bald men whose heads were capped with a knotted handkerchief to keep off the sun, elegant men with silver flasks and sandwich cases, families with string bags and Thermoses. Indeed, you couldn't pin them down at all. They filled the stands; they sat in a wide belt on the grass all the way round the ground; they walked behind the stands, peering between the buildings, meeting friends, buying each other bottled beer, consulting their match cards and talking cricket.

The road round the ground at Lord's meanders like a village street avoiding ancient property rights. Big stands look over little stands. Men with cigars lean over exclusive balconies and shout to men with umbrellas underneath. Waitresses serve tea furiously. There are lawns for people to picnic on, places for the press to have lunch in, memorials to the great names of cricket. And then there is the *Pavilion* which is the Vatican, the Kremlin, the Westminster of cricket – a tall, bony Edwardian building, hung about with flimsy balconies, full of men who mind about cricket almost more than anything else and, on this day, quite impossible to enter unless you have the right to wear the bright and ugly tie of the MCC.

There were discreet gentlemen with white flowers on their sober suits standing just inside its door to see that no strangers got in. There was also, naturally, a knot of little boys just standing and looking in. They were waiting perhaps to get a glimpse of Evans, or Hutton, or Mankad – to watch them walking over the Turkey carpets – and perhaps waiting to ask one of them to sign their match cards.

Then there's the Mound which is a low, grassy bank. Once, I'm told, people used to use it as a casual stand where they could recline like Georgian poets to watch the game. But progress, even in Lord's, has intervened and there's now a low stand in front of it which holds more but which hasn't much pleased the people for whom this place is an institution and therefore unchangeable.

My place was in the grandstand. I sat on a numbered bench under a heavy concrete roof and from out of the shadow looked at the great spread of green at the centre.

Now I don't know if you were expecting some cool post-mortem on the game. But then very few international conferences are so efficiently reported and explained as a Test match at Lord's. All that sort of thing has been done by experts elsewhere. But I was fascinated by the decorum and the dignity of the place and the occasion. The game itself had, emotionally, nothing in common with one of those swift rugby matches where you must stand and shout as the line of three-quarters breaks like a wave on the other team. Some Indian women, with crimson caste marks on their foreheads and long filigree ornaments in their ears, were shouting with excitement whenever they thought an English wicket might fall; but the people round me looked at them with surprise and smiled at each other, not blaming them, rather liking their enthusiasm in fact, but certainly finding it surprising.

Occasionally, one of the batsmen smacked a ball towards the boundary, and then the small boys would rise to their knees and dive for it and make a clot of bodies over it and, after a brief struggle, the ball would come lobbing out of the middle of them in the rough direction of one of the fielders. Once a great hit went soaring across the field and a man stood up from off the grass and caught it with a hand held up over his head. They clapped him too and all through the day the bursts of applause kept breaking over the fielders and batsmen. Every time it happened, pigeons who had been feeding on the grass, rose in panic into the air and went flapping and sailing round in a wide circle and then they settled back just where they'd started from.

Really, the spectators sat there doing two things. They had to preserve in their minds a sort of intellectual tension, comparing the time left for play with the scores made and the number of wickets to fall. There was also an endless series of incidents to watch. An Indian fielder stopped a ball just short of a boundary and threw it in almost casually. It rose in a wide arc and then came down and knocked a stump out of the ground. A brief burst of applause for his skill. England's score went up to another half-century. More applause. Evans scored a century and they clapped and clapped and he just stood by his wicket and raised his bat two or three times and looked at the ground. It all seemed so simple. The batsmen just spooned the ball away at odd angles and one slim figure in white would go racing away after it. The ball seemed to stop dead in the fielders' hands with a mechanical precision. And it was all so unpretentious. There was no dominating athleticism, no display of physical strength for its own sake; the better the player, the more easy he made it look. People went there to admire a rare skill, almost an artistry. They wanted to know which way the balls were breaking. There was no violent partisanship. I think they would have been delighted to see the Indians win, as long as it was a good game. All of them were hoping for that slow, burning excitement that comes occasionally in cricket, when the batsmen are fighting the clock as well as the bowlers, when every ball bowled is a dangerous adventure and when all the clichés about cricket being dull and slow become nonsense.

Of course, they were delighted and perhaps they were proud, too, to have seen Evans's brisk century, rather as people will boast of having heard, say, Toscanini at Milan or having seen Pavlova dance. They'll talk about it every now and again when they meet someone who feels the same way as they do. Then, a few runs after his century, Evans was caught and bowled by Ghulam Ahmed (who threw the ball up into the air with a sort of boyish pleasure). Evans began the long walk back to the Pavilion and everyone stood up and clapped and clapped him the whole way, until he had run the last few paces, through the wicket-gate, up the steps between the members and disappeared behind the plate-glass windows of the Pavilion.

It continued like that all day, a succession of incidents that made a satisfying whole. Some of the spectators came and went all through the match. They dropped in for a few hours' expert pleasure. But most arrived and sat firmly in their seats hour after hour. It had a sort of mesmerising quality. How pleasant to sit and sit, unworried, conscious perhaps of knowing a little more about this one subject than most other people, comparing this near-perfection with the hundreds of games that they had played at schools, on village greens, for works teams and small clubs. And then the game, with all its deceptive simplicity, was beautiful to watch.

No one could claim that Lord's itself is an architectural masterpiece. Yet it fits and it's right. The buildings with their lacy balconies of white-painted iron, the trivial decoration, the pleasant English huddle of it all were exactly right. Behind the stands were the factory chimneys, the tops of trees, the suggestion of a great city. But here in Lord's, we were apart. We had stepped out of the ordinary boredoms and excitements of life. We had stopped worrying about ordinary things and time was only important when it affected the game. But then Lord's is an enclave, set apart by custom and affection. The game is not like anything else in the world; nor is this place.

[*For the record, England beat India by eight wickets.*]

*   *   *

INDIA

R.B. Van Wart worked for twenty years in India. During that time he was State Scout Commissioner for Jodhpur and also Guardian to the Maharajah of Vizianagram's son – the same 'Vizzy' who captained the Indian side to England in 1936, sent Lala Amarnath home for 'alleged' indiscipline and who later became a broadcaster and administrator of the game.

Van Wart's talk, timed to correspond with the MCC visit under Jardine, illustrated the hazards players had to contend with away from the 'Mecca' of cricket

Cricket in India
R. B. Van Wart

National Programme, February 1934

I don't suppose any of you've ever had a cricket match stopped by a couple of tigers trotting into the middle of the pitch. It happened to me once – though it's true they were only cubs about the size of cats belonging to a Maharajah and even in India it doesn't happen often. But in one hill station we used to get monkeys looking on at matches and once, in another, a cloud of little blue butterflies fluttered slowly round and round the pitch and held up play for about five minutes.

Which all helps to show that cricket in India is often very different from cricket at home. Even the MCC team will have found that out, though they've naturally played on the pick of the grounds and under the best conditions. As a matter of fact – except for Bombay, Calcutta and Madras – there are very few grounds that are good enough for county cricket at home. The trouble is that grass in India depends on the rains and if they fail – as they do sometimes – there isn't any. But besides the lack of grass, there are a lot of other little things which help to put a man off his game to start with. When I first went out, I found the strong sun and glare very trying and I could hardly make a run until I got used to it. Then again, playing first on grass, then on matting and then back to grass again makes it very difficult to settle down. Matting wickets take a bit of getting used to, anyway, for bowlers and batsmen, and the ball comes off differently. I used to hate at first having a chalk mark to pat instead of a block. I know it sounds absurd, but it's just those little things which put you off. Worst of all, though, I always thought was playing in a sun-helmet; the brim catches your eye in front and the back gets you awkwardly between the shoulders, especially if you're fielding in the slips, or anywhere where you have to bend down; or when you're in the deep, say, and running for a catch, if you aren't careful it is apt to come off – in spite of the chin-strap – with disastrous results.

There's another drawback about matting wickets and that's their tendency to work loose and wrinkle up. I think it's probably what's been responsible for the low scoring in more than one of the MCC matches. You see the matting is only fixed by long nails driven into the ground at intervals on each side and at the ends so it is very apt to work loose and then you can't get a proper foothold and the ball plays all sorts of tricks.

I'm not trying to find excuses for the MCC. I think they've done very well, but as they're out there and you've probably been watching their progress in the newspapers, I thought it worth trying to describe the conditions under which they've been playing.

Cricketers at home are inclined to grouse at having to travel from Leeds to Taunton but in India twelve hours is looked on as a short journey, and then you may have to start your match within two or three hours of your arrival. Perhaps it's been a long, night journey, with swarms of blanketed coolies getting in at every station mistaking your first-class carriage for a third and then leaving the door open, so that somebody has to get out of bed to shut it; or at the best you're roused at every station by the drone of people selling sweets, hot milk, soda and lemonade. It sounds like '*Puri mittai, gurm dudh, sora-lemnad*', and a bit of that goes a long way towards spoiling a night's rest, I can tell you. Some of the trains have baths – which fill you with hope, but they're a delusion, at any rate in the cold weather; I used to find it was either too cold or the water was full of sand or the coolie had forgotten to fill the water-tank at the last station. I suppose it sounds funny to talk of being too cold in India but I can assure you it can be, and that is another trap for a visiting team; at Delhi, for instance, in January it's hot enough in the daytime but after sunset you need a heavy overcoat and rug out of doors if you want to avoid a chill. Then, to keep fit you mustn't drink water or milk unless it's boiled and you mustn't take cold baths for fear of fever, and so it goes on. And you *have* got to be careful, I assure you. It may have been all right being happy-go-lucky in the old days but in 1934 Indian cricket is the genuine article and our men have had to fight for every run and wicket. The All-India team's tour over here two summers ago and the present MCC visit make this clear enough. We may have introduced cricket to India but it's the Indian's own aptitude for the game that's made him the player that he is.

But we certainly have helped because wherever there's a military, educational or railway centre of any size, such as Secunderabad, Bangalore or Lahore, with its leaven of Europeans, there, and almost only there, you will find cricket. Look what a lot of men like General Poore and Colonel Greig, the old Hampshire cricketers, did for the game; and Tarrant, too, the old Middlesex Australian who went to live in India and has been umpiring the present MCC tour; and of late years the big business firms of Bombay and Calcutta have been attracting a lot of Oxford and Cambridge blues;

among the princes, the Maharajah of Patiala, a really good cricketer, not only ran a good team in his state but did better service still by getting men like Hirst, Rhodes and Kilner out to coach in the cold weather.

Unfortunately, in spite of the training at the Chiefs' Colleges, few of the princes are really interested in the game; polo appeals more to them. The trouble is that few states have more than one real town and that probably has only two or three teams capable of putting up any show at all, so the Maharajah's team has to go long and expensive journeys for every match and he soon loses interest.

I remember one well-known ruler who was a most enthusiastic supporter of cricket, though a very poor performer. I shall never forget his bringing a team to play the Mayo College for Chiefs at Ajmer – where the MCC recently played Rajputana. He was barely five feet high and wore an enormous turban and it was a funny sight when he went out to bat followed to the wickets by a small army of retainers. One took off his coat, two rolled up his sleeves, two put on his pads, two more his gloves and one handed him his bat. Word had gone round the College team that he must make sixteen runs, which he did by swinging round on one leg after slow long-hops; there were a few accidents in the way of chances, of course; but somehow they failed to go to hand and when a careless bowler hit the wicket a quick-witted umpire 'no-balled' him at once. Later, His Highness insisted on trying to take a wicket with slow and very harmless throws and was nearly killed by a hot return which he only just dodged; luckily, the batsman fell on his wicket in the excitement and the Maharajah, having done enough for honour, took himself off in the middle of the over and retired to the Pavilion.

But he, good little man, was an exception; all the other cricketing princes I have seen play the game; it is only the men who hope to curry favour with them who drop their catches for them and that sort of thing.

One can't, of course, even mention Indian cricket without thinking of Ranji; but for one thing he stands alone – and I'm not forgetting Duleep – and for another his cricket heart was in England rather than India.

There's one thing that you won't find in India and that is village cricket. Most Indians live in little villages far from any railway and stay there or thereabouts all their lives; heaps of them have never even heard of cricket or, if they have, haven't the foggiest idea what it is; if they wanted to play they couldn't afford matting, bats and balls – all of which wear badly in that climate, apart from being eaten by white ants – but it is in the scattered up-country towns where you get the real humour of cricket.

That is where the player wears his shirt-tails outside and tucks them between his legs before every ball and where – stout fellow – he plays in bare feet and takes a full toss on them or stops a hot drive without turning a hair.

Sometimes you see the whole field duck like one man and crouch while a swarm of bees crosses the ground; at others, you find wild pigs have rooted up most of the pitch the night before a match; or perhaps you unroll the matting and out pops a nasty little krait – one of the most dangerous snakes there is. One tournament, according to its home-made rules, was played on the knock-down system; as a matter of fact it was in one game; I think there was a blood-feud or something of the kind – ah, yes, and I remember a man once applying to me for the post of games instructor at a big school and ending up, 'At football I am marvellous; at cricket also I am equal, for which I can show a scar mark on my forehead.' A scar mark may have been a striking testimonial, but I didn't give him the job.

Another worthy instructor of youth wrote out some hints for batsmen among which was a real gem: 'On going in, block for a few minutes until your eye is in; the fielders will then come in close; you then lash out a few boundaries which will cause the fielders to spread out, whereupon you resume your blocking tactics.' It sounds beautifully simple, doesn't it?

At one school, I found a couple of sides, boys of eighteen or so, playing with a set of stumps and bats like those you buy in a toyshop for a child of six; one boy seemed to be bowling at both ends. I asked why. 'He is the only one who knows how, sahib,' I was told – and he was bowling underhand grubs all along the ground. But all the same, there were plenty of natural cricketers among them and before long, with a bit of coaching, they had turned into quite a useful side; nearly every one of them had a good eye and supple limbs, and there was a left-hand slow bowler with an action which Rhodes might have taught him. But he, poor lad, went to Palestine with the Jodhpur Lancers and never came back.

As for grounds up-country, they are mostly fair to real bad; sometimes there is grass, sometimes grass at intervals and on one ground there was none at all; we had to make that ground by clearing jungle scrub, laying a broken stone foundation in the sand, putting a layer of kankar on that and then a coating of clay on the top – there wasn't a blade of grass, of course – and I can tell you it was no ground for sleepy fielders; the ball came at you before you could say knife.

Naturally, the pleasantest cricket from an English point of view is at a hill station, provided you take it easy for the first few days; at 9000 feet up or so you soon begin to wonder what has happened to your wind if you try short runs or chase one or two to the boundary before you have got acclimatised.

Down in the plains in the hot weather, it's too hot to play unless you like to do it before nine in the morning or after half past five in the afternoon, and I never could get up any enthusiasm over the game at the unholy hour of six a.m. In the rains you can't play at all in most places so that the real cricket season is in what India calls the cold weather, roughly mid-November to March, with a little extension at either end. Which reminds me – it's very easy to be critical, but why on earth give the MCC the hottest part of the tour in the South, including a Test match at Madras, at the end of the tour, instead of getting that over in December when it is comparatively cool and working up to the cooler north in February?

25

On the whole, football and hockey are more popular in India than cricket, even in Calcutta; the excitement has more appeal; but where Indians are keen on cricket they *are* keen; look at Bombay; in the Test match there were over 16,000 people ringing up to know the score! There's no doubt they are good sportsmen; they play the game and we're proud to have introduced them to it.

*   *   *

The personality of Indian cricket will for ever be indelibly linked with that of 'Ranji'. Ranji attracted purple prose: 'He moved as if he had no bones. One would not be surprised to see brown curves burning in the grass where one of his cuts had travelled, or blue flames shimmering round his bat as he made one of his strokes.'

Here are some extracts from a tribute to K. S. Ranjitsinhji, H. H. The Jam Sahib of Nawanagar, on the hundredth anniversary of his birth, by people who remembered him. The tribute was devised and presented by the Chief Producer of Features in All-India Radio, Melville de Mellow.

A Hundred Up

All-India Radio, September 1972

de Mellow: . . . H. S. Malik, sportsman and diplomat, played for Sussex as Ranji did.

Malik: When I started to play for Sussex and in the Pavilion at Brighton which was the home ground of the County, they had some easy chairs instead of the usual stiff chairs and the legend was that those chairs were brought in by the members at the time when Ranji and C. B. Fry were playing for Sussex, because the members had to get accustomed to sitting long hours in the Pavilion while C. B. Fry and Ranji made their hundreds.

de Mellow: What made Ranji a great cricketer?

Malik: The outstanding thing about him was that he had the eye and the skill to score off any kind of bowling whether it was good length, fast or slow. He was very quick on his feet and very quick with his hands. The great difference between today and the cricket during that time is that today, if you have good-length bowling the batsmen seem to be able to do nothing against it and they can score only off the bad balls. In those days, the great cricketers like Ranji and C. B. Fry and later Bradman – they could score off any kind of bowling . . .

de Mellow: Vijay Merchant, one of the greatest Indian opening batsmen of his day and former chairman of the selection committee of the Board of Control for Cricket in India, analysed the Ranji style thus.

Merchant: He played the ball more late than any known batsman who has graced the game. That means he had tremendously sharp eyes and was able to see the ball right until it came on to his bat. The blind area which all batsmen experience was thus narrowed down and with his flexible wrists he could divert the ball at the last possible moment. He was a great driver of the game but rarely employed the hook stroke. He did not much relish the lob cut but he was a beautiful glancer of the ball. Even a ball on the middle stump, he could glance to leg safely . . . he was known to put in tremendously hard practice and batted in the nets as he would have done in a proper match. That is how he developed his tremendous area of stroke play and concentration. He did not bat at the nets as most of us did for fifteen or twenty minutes but sometimes even for a couple of hours. He used to keep a sovereign on the stumps so that anyone who bowled him out could claim that sovereign. He felt it would be a tremendous incentive to a professional cricketer to bowl at his best against him.

de Mellow: We asked Berry Sarbadhikary, eminent sports critic, author and commentator, to dig into his scrapbook of memories.

Sarbadhikary: When I called on an ailing Sir Stanley Jackson our conversation of course perhaps inevitably steered round to Ranji. Said Sir Stanley, 'He's a perfectionist – he'd settle for nothing less – Ranji practised at the Fenner's for hours on end against Lockwood and Richardson. They were about the fastest in England then – and it was a treat.' Talking about the leg glance, the Surrey and England fast bowler, Bill Hitch, had this to say, 'I had heard about Ranji's fantastic leg glance and was determined to explore the myth. Surrey are playing Sussex. The moment Ranji comes in, I bowl full blast, good length and on the open middle, and what do you think happens? Why, he comes

27

slightly forward, turns the ball with the flick of the wrist down to the deep fine-leg boundary like lightning. I say to myself, "Bill my boy, that's the novice's luck, a big, big fluke." But blimey, when at the fag end of the day with the second new ball, I bowl flat out, Ranji's still doing these flukes to drive me crazy.' Then Bill, strong as an ox, his rugged features wreathed in smiles, said with an air of resignation, 'Come to think of it now, I was a greenhorn – the novice Ranji, the master, the magician.'

de Mellow: Bill O'Reilly of Australia, nicknamed 'Tiger' because of the power and sting of his bowling, pays his tribute to Ranji.

O'Reilly: Even though he scored many, many brilliant centuries for England, he really and truly scored them for India, there's no doubt whatever about that. And I know that he was a tremendous player because Clem Hill, the finest Australian of the same time, was a very good friend of mine in his old age and Archie MacLaren of England, who was a very great friend of Ranjitsinhji's, and Hanson Carter, our famous wicket-keeper, all three of those men spoke of him in almost the same terms of reverence as an Australian speaks of Victor Trumper. They used to feed me with the garbage that the game is greater than the player. Now, I have always said that is utter nonsense, the game can only be great if the fellows playing it are great. Now, occasionally a great man appears on the scene. We had one whom cricket will know for ever. We had another, Victor Trumper, each of those two men stamped the era of his time in the game as his age, the Bradman age, the Trumper age, Ranjitsinhji stamped it on his. These are men, these are names that live for ever. We haven't got one in the game anywhere at the moment.

de Mellow: Ranji loved all forms of sport but excelled at tennis and cricket and loved angling. Seventy-eight-year-old Susinghi Jadeja of Rajkot related an incident that took place while Ranji was at his angling castle in Ireland.

Susinghi: Once during his stay at the castle, Jam Ranjitsinhji wanted to entertain all his Irish gillies with a lunch party. An Englishman called Mr Seaman, who was the household controller, was asked to arrange for that party. Seaman, being an Englishman, hated the Irish like poison so he told Jam Ranji politely, 'Sir,' he would arrange for it, of course, but he, Seaman, feared that, before the lunch began, no Irishman would get up to drink the toast of His Majesty. Jam Ranjitsinhji replied, 'Don't worry, I will see to it.' The lunch party was arranged. When all the Irish gillies came, Jam Ranjitsinhji addressed them with a glass of beer in his hand and said, 'Gentlemen, we have in India a custom that before any party like lunch or dinner starts, we drink to the very best health of the Emperor of India.' Immediately, the whole congregation stood up and shouted, raised their beer glasses and said, 'Here is to the Emperor of India.' These poor Irishmen did not have any idea the King of England and the Emperor of India were one. Thus, with this instantaneous tact he averted an unpleasant incident with grace. Another incident in connection with Jam Ranjitsinhji's old friend Commander C. B. Fry was when Jam Sahib helped in his parliamentary election campaign at Brighton in 1925. In order to help his friend, Jam Ranjitsinhji took us to Brighton where he was to attend one election meeting held in a theatre. When Jam Ranjitsinhji entered the theatre, the Brighton public, who wanted to have a glimpse of their favourite cricket hero, all stood up and shouted, 'Ranji, hurrah, welcome Ranji,' and clapped. Such was Jam Sahib's popularity, years after he left cricket.

At Cambridge he played most frequently on Parker's Piece and it was here on the vast ground where many cricket matches were played simultaneously, here he performed a feat of endurance that has gone down in the history of cricket. One day, Ranjitsinhji's score was 132 before noon. After lunch he walked over to watch another match and finding one team a man short offered to bat for them. In a short time he had scored a century and carried his bat. Returning to his original match, he found his side still batting, whereupon he joined another game and made 120 runs. Thus, Jam Ranjitsinhji had made three centuries in one day and claimed another world record. When Ranjitsinhji joined Trinity College, Cambridge, he got a cricket blue, the first Indian to get that honour in the history of cricket and Cambridge University.

de Mellow: How shall we remember this great man? Shall we remember his great scores and glides and fierce cuts through the slips? Or shall we remember his departure from cricket as a great cliff falling into the sea? Let's turn to Neville Cardus, who wrote of Ranji,

Reader: 'He was a remarkable instance of the power and scope of cricket, to express not only the style that is the man but also the style that is the race. The game was English through and through when he came to it, almost Victorian, in fact. The straight bat and the length ball, first principle or what might be called an ethically sanctioned technique, open and palpable and honoured by long, respectable use. A strange light from the East flickered in the English sunshine when he was at the wicket. "He's no batsman," said the Australian George Giffen, "he is a conjuror." When he turned an approved science upside down and changed the geometry of batsmanship to an esoteric legerdemain, we were bewitched to the realms of rope dancers and snake charmers. This was a cricket of Oriental sorcery, glowing with a dark beauty of its own, a beauty with its own mysterious axis and balance. Bowlers threw up their hands to high heaven as he made his passes of flexible willow and they saw their thunderbolts enchanted from the middle stump to the fine-leg boundary. It was like a shooting star all wrong in our astronomy but right and splendid in some other and more dazzling stellar universe.'

*   *   *

Sixty years after Ranji last played for Sussex, Somerset engaged India's prodigious run-maker Sunil Gavaskar for 1980 on a one-season contract, as a temporary 'star' substitute for Viv Richards who was needed by the West Indian tourists.
Paddy Feeny interviewed Gavaskar for Sports International.

Sunil Gavaskar

Eastern Service, June 1980

Feeny: What about the difference as far as the general standard and style of cricket is concerned, because in India you have the Ranji trophy, here we have the County game. Have you found a terrific difference on your first venture into the County game?

Gavaskar: Yes, there is a big difference, because I think the first thing that you notice here is the superb physical fitness of all the professional cricketers. Then the attitude. I think the attitude over here is a lot different than the one in India because of the various rules like, for example, the over-rate. A County side has to maintain an over-rate and you have different rules as far as the point system is concerned. So there is a lot more urgency about cricket here than in India. And of course in India if you play for a side which comes into the Ranji trophy finals, you have about seven first-class games. Here you might play seven first-class games in six weeks.

Feeny: Seven first-class games throughout the whole season?

Gavaskar: Throughout the season.

Feeny: Which goes on for how long?

Gavaskar: Well, it goes on from, say, November to April.

Feeny: So keeping fit must be quite a problem because obviously you've got this tremendous gap between the games.

Gavaskar: That's right, yes. But you see when you have Test series at home, you have the Test matches in between all these Ranji matches, then there's a Zonal Tournament, so in fact it's seven plus three, ten first-class games, and if you're lucky to be picked for India you get another five Test games.

Feeny: What about this business of fitness as far as you're concerned playing for Somerset? Have you found that you've had to go in for a special kind of exercises, or that you had to take up some weight-training or anything like that?

Gavaskar: No, actually I was fortunate because I came down to Somerset after having just finished a season in India and I think that meant that I didn't really have to do anything extraordinary. In fact, when it comes to doing exercises I really never have been able to do much. I prefer to bowl a lot in the nets, and keep myself fit that way or, you know, do a bit of batting in the nets or do exercises in the dressing-room to keep myself fit. But so far I haven't felt the need to do anything extra and the only thing which I'm concerned about and the only thing which I'm very keen to do before I leave Somerset, is to throw myself at the ball, which is dive as I see the other team-mates in the Somerset team do. And I'm sure when I do, when I really do dive, I'm going to get a big applause from the rest of the team-mates.

Feeny: Because presumably diving is not a thing that you'd do on a hard wicket in India. Is that right?

Gavaskar: That's right, the grounds over there are harder, but I think the most important thing about diving is that when you see the kids in England, they have no fear of diving because the grass is lush green, it's softer. In India I think the maidans where you start playing your cricket when you're a kid, I think the maidans are rough, very rough, so you know when you dive round there you're likely to get seriously injured. So I think the kids in India really wouldn't be in the habit of diving. So perhaps when you get into first-class cricket you'll find that diving becomes a little difficult. But I suppose that if you really try and maybe with a little more practice I should think it's not all that difficult.

Feeny: Well, with my limited experience of fifth-rate cricket, I can tell you one thing, that first time you do dive is a marvellous sensation, because you feel that you're almost flying parallel with the ground. It really does feel great.

Gavaskar: I must try that before the end of the season, for sure.

Feeny: As far as the batting is concerned you're up against an entirely different kind of bowling aren't you, mostly seam, whereas at home in India it would be mostly spin.

Gavaskar: Well, the picture in India is also changing . . . the emphasis is shifting from spin to seam. The only difference is that in India the ball won't move in the air once the first ten or fifteen overs have gone. Whereas in England you might be batting, maybe seventy, eighty and the ball is forty-five, fifty overs old but still the ball moves in the air or off the wicket and that's a thing which is so different, that's a thing which you've really got to guard against in England. You really can't say that you're in all the time because the ball can be moving.

Feeny: Does that take some of the fun out of it?

Gavaskar: No, it doesn't, because I think it makes you sharper, your concentration I think gets stronger, because you can't relax, whereas in India once you've passed forty, fifty, I think you can relax a little bit because the ball isn't going to do anything much either in the air or off the wicket, so you can play down the line and hope to get away with it.

Feeny: Of course, you've got this tremendous variety of styles of cricket as well that you've got to come to terms with, haven't you? Because you've got the three-day game, then you've got 55-over matches, 60-over matches. I think you had a little bit of a problem to start off with in some of the one-day stuff, didn't you?

Gavaskar: No, I didn't. In fact, I was surprised, because when I started off it was a one-day game that I had to play for Somerset before I played the three-day game and it came as a surprise to me, because I hadn't really considered myself a one-day player; being an opening batsman I've always found it a little difficult because I think by nature an opening batsman is a very cautious type of a player and what has happened is that I suddenly found myself playing shots. I found that there were no slips, nobody in catching positions near the bat and that meant that you could afford to throw your bat at the ball without risk of being caught in the slips, and when I started throwing my bat at the ball I found that I was stroking the ball that much better. And, you know, I think that helped me, because I started playing a lot more shots, started enjoying the one-day game and I haven't really had as much difficulty in changing over as I thought I would.

*   *   *

WEST INDIES

Adapting to British conditions, whether on the cricket field or not, has sometimes been an insuperable problem for those not indigenous to these shores. Several months after the Brixton riots in London during 1981, a game of cricket took place at Kennington Oval between the local inhabitants and the police.

Steve Cape conducted various interviews for the Today *programme.*

Brixton *v.* Police

Radio 4, September 1981

Cape: It was a stark difference from the riot conditions of Brixton earlier this year. Instead of Molotov cocktails and bombs, cricket balls were flying and the only weapon was a cricket bat. Lord Scarman took time off from the inquiry into the Brixton riots to watch the match and in a way it put the official seal of approval on the game.

Scarman: It's all a matter of getting on with each other, doing things together, that's all I can say. It's civilised, and it's cheerful, it's fun, and a bit of competition just adds spice to it. It's all so simple. Of course, I want to see grounds available too and it's marvellous to have the use of the Oval, but you can't always get the Oval.

Cape: Of course, you don't have facilities like this in Brixton?

Scarman: Well, I know, that's one of the troubles.

Cape: The game started with a police Crime Prevention Officer as one of the umpires and a Constable in the police team. Their captain was PC Steve Pagdin who was sure the match was doing a lot to repair community relations.

Pagdin: I get to meet people I don't meet every day 'cause as a Home Beat Officer I have my own area and don't get to all parts of Brixton, only on occasions, but I'm meeting a lot of old faces again today.

Cape: It must feel strange to you in a way that only a few weeks ago there were riots in Brixton and now you're all friends and you're playing a game of cricket.

Pagdin: I don't think these chaps were in the riot. These are good, hard-working lads who we've known for a long time and they don't cause any trouble.

Cape: There were some, though, like Brixton barrister Rudy Narayan, who organised the very first police cricket match against the West Indians in England several years ago, who had reservations about the ability of the game to improve relations that much.

Narayan: Undoubtedly a game like this is only symbolic. The real work has to be done in the back streets of Brixton. But, I suppose, an occasion where the police are saying officially, we want to be friendly and certain parts of the Brixton community are saying, well, we want to be friendly too, so it's important in that respect.

Cape: It's noticeable that although there are a number of people here, there aren't that many young West Indians.

Narayan: That's right. And also, there aren't really that many West Indians who make the difference in a riot situation. The West Indians who are here today are not the West Indians who threw petrol bombs or attacked police or fought with police in Brixton in the riots. What you're seeing here is the respectable element of the West Indian community who always get on well with the police, so that in a way it can be rather naïve to use this occasion as saying that everything in Brixton is lovely.

Cape: Well, the atmosphere remained festive and it was clear that the Brixton Police Cricket Club were no match for the fast West Indian bowlers. With wickets falling in quick succession, in the end the West Indians won by 57 runs. There were no hard feelings though and everyone wants another game.

First Spectator: As far as I'm concerned, it is very good, it is very good for the community and things like that, you know. What I'd like to see really, then we could get to talk and things like that. If we've got to live together, things like this got to happen. You don't only capitalise, you've got to socialise.

Second Spectator: I just hope there's more people, you know, especially in the younger age group, who'll see this on the telly or hear it on the radio and come to realise – right, that's what the spirit is all about, you know. It's not a thing of we hate the police or the police hate us, the police is there to do a job. We all live together, you know.

*　　　*　　　*

Clive Lloyd has captained a Test side more times than anyone else. The trademark of his leadership has been a quiet, unassuming sense of authority often conveyed on the field by a soothing gesture of the hand like a wise old warrior chief calming his restless tribe.

He was interviewed in July 1980 by Paul Wade during the West Indies tour of England.

Clive Lloyd

Wade: You're always regarded as a very easy-going nice sort of a guy and yet you're very keen on discipline in a side.

Lloyd: Yes, actually I can't change my nature. I've never been regimental in any way. I respect the players, they respect me. I suppose I can be swayed a bit, that's all, but it's obvious that I don't like being taken for granted and I let them know when I'm being taken for granted, and I suppose that's when they know that they've overstepped the line.

Wade: You seemed to have learned an awful lot. You were surprised and rather horrified at some of the senior players when you were a youngster and I think you determined never to let senior players get away with murder at the expense of younger players. Has this been important to you? Just learning from experience?

Lloyd: Yes, well, I suppose I've put a few things into practice that I've picked up. It's obvious that I think that the senior players have a role to play because whatever they do a young player thinks, well, that's the run of things and he can get out of hand. Now I try and instil certain things in the younger players so that they can pick up the important things for team spirit and I try to let them understand that that is the right thing to do. So, I've had very good rapport with all my young players. Sometimes the senior players tend to get a bit out of line but not in the sense that I have to do anything drastic. They've been good over the years and I'm quite happy with the way they've conducted themselves.

Wade: A lot of people look at the talented sides that you've had over the years and they say, well, it can't be difficult to captain a side that's got so much talent. Is it easy in fact?

Lloyd: Well, a lot of people seem to think so. We have four fast bowlers but you still have to change them around, you've got to put the right field and then you still have to bat. You've got to instil confidence in your side. We had a very good side in the fifties and the sixties but we still got beaten . . .

Wade: If there's a youngster listening to the programme now who's captaining his thirteen-year-old side, what do you think is the most important thing he should be doing? Should he be worrying about tactics, talking to the players, or what?

Lloyd: Respect. Players have got to have respect for him and respect for his authority as captain. He's got to instil discipline, see that they are physically fit and they are genuinely interested in what they are doing and that they are interested in playing the game as a team. And he's got to lead by example.

Wade: So really you've got to be a good batsman, a bowler or wicket-keeper to be a captain.

Lloyd: Oh, you don't have to be the best performer. You've got to have the know-how of running a side. You've got to be able to do something. You don't then necessarily have to be the best batsman or the best bowler but you've got to hold your own in their company.

Wade: Everyone keeps on saying that this is your last series. Can you tell us if it's your last series or quite what's happening?

Lloyd: Well, they seemed to have retired me for quite some time now . . . when your legs go, when your reflexes go and your eyes go and your friends go. That's the time to go.

[*Clive Lloyd finally retired from the West Indies captaincy at the end of the 1984–5 tour of Australia.*]

In 1966, the year that Clive Lloyd made his Test début, Neil Durden-Smith spoke to Wesley Hall for the programme 'Champion's Choice'. Hall, that fearsome yet eminently fair fast bowler whose long run-up to the wicket was one of the aesthetic joys of cricket during the sixties, later became a Senator in the Barbados Parliament, Personnel Manager of a brewery and Manager of the WI side to Australia in 1984–5.

Wesley Hall

Light Programme, October 1966

Durden-Smith: Well, people see you now, Wes, as a giant six feet, two inches. You're a great favourite with all the crowds. How did it all start for you?

Hall: Well, actually, I started bowling fast at the age of eighteen. Before that I used to keep wicket and bat at school. Of course, all boys in Barbados usually begin their cricket on the beaches or on the roadside. You know, in Barbados, a small island twenty-one miles by fourteen, one has got to start that way because the better positions are reserved for the great players in the Saturday afternoon clubs, but I am thrilled to have come such a long way.

Durden-Smith: What about your family? Did they help you in cricket?

Hall: Well, yes. My mother, she was very kind to me. She used to buy my cricket clothes as a little boy and encourage me when I failed and that was very important.

Durden-Smith: You were saying that you were first of all a batsman/wicket-keeper. How did you first start bowling then?

Hall: Well, when I left school I was playing in the first division – schoolboys in Barbados play against the international stars which is very beneficial to them and I went and worked with the cable office as an operator there, and we had an intermediate side which is, of course, a low grade. I was playing one day and the captain, he thought I looked big enough to be a fast bowler and he asked me to bowl a few balls which I did and I've been doing it ever since.

Durden-Smith: In 1957 you gained a place on the tour to England and you only got twenty-seven wickets on the whole tour. This must have been a very difficult time for you, wasn't it?

Hall: Well, I had only been bowling fast for a year and obviously I was very inexperienced and honestly I don't really think I should have made the trip, but the West Indian selectors, they thought that I had the potential and they decided to risk it and give me a chance, you see. The twenty-seven wickets I got – I never played in many games anyhow – but I think the experience has gone a long way in helping my career, you know.

Durden-Smith: Have you modelled yourself particularly on any one great fast bowler?

Hall: No, not really. I didn't have the time, you see, because all along I thought I would have the grade as a batsman and then suddenly there was this terrible switch and I became a fast bowler.

Durden-Smith: I remember seeing you bowl a marathon spell at Lord's in 1963, which, in fact, very nearly won the match for you. [*He bowled forty overs in the second innings of the Lord's Test.*] Do you have to keep very fit?

Hall: Oh, extremely fit, because, you see, you never know when the captain is going to ask you for an effort of say twenty overs in a day and you look very foolish if you can't because you are unfit. And another thing, it is a very lonely feeling out there in the middle when you have to bowl fast because you've got the ball, you've got thirty or forty thousand people looking at you, expecting the best you know, and the batsman, he's just there waiting for the loose ball and if you are unfit and you then bowl a lot of bad balls – it would be a very lonely life for you.

Durden-Smith: How do you keep fit then?

Hall: Well, I have often thought that it is only necessary to run and develop the right muscles. It is not necessary to get big arms because your arm is just your connecting link while you're bowling, you see. If you can have good legs and look after your feet, if you can have them free from blisters and things like that, if you can have the right boots . . . I am sure if all youngsters do this they'll find it's a lot easier if you're bowling fast.

Durden-Smith: After a day's play do you talk about the game or do you like to forget it?

Hall: Well, it depends on the situation. Sometimes, the boys will like to discuss what we have done wrong, you know, but if everything has gone right there is hardly anything else to say except to congratulate the fellows who've done quite well and sometimes I just drift away and forget the whole thing.

Durden-Smith: Well, now you've had three tours here. You've played for Accrington in the Lancashire League. What do you like about England most?

Hall: In the League for instance, I did enjoy living in Accrington and liked meeting people and going down and having a few drinks with the boys, you know, and things like that. It was a good feeling when I was fortunate enough to be on the winning side. We won the championship, I think it was '61 or '62 in Accrington and it was a great feeling, you know, to be champions because the people in these small towns look forward to League cricket and it's a great thrill if you can win it for them.

Durden-Smith: In Test cricket, in different parts of the world, the spectators obviously generate very different atmospheres. Have you found this?

Hall: Oh yes, most definitely. In the West Indies, the crowds are very knowledgeable and they obviously have studied the game and they know before a team comes, they know who are the best players, for instance, if a batsman is vulnerable outside the off-stump you would get someone in the crowd saying attack his off-stump. And they are very noisy, of course. And in England, I have found the crowds are very quiet, you know, very polite. They would probably applaud if you snick a ball through the slips which would never happen in the West Indies and, of course, in Australia they are wonderful crowds there too, especially in a place like Sydney, where you've got the famous Hill and you hear some of the greatest gags in the world. I can remember once playing against Ken Mackay, who's very famous for blocking the ball, a rather defensive batsman, and he was going through this thing for about an hour and then suddenly a guy in the crowd said, 'Well, Mackay, you'll never die of a stroke.'

Durden-Smith: You've got a great reputation as being a wit.

Hall: Well, I don't know. I would say that I've got a pretty good sense of humour but when I turned professional six years ago I thought, well, if I'm going to play this game nearly every day, because I found that it was like going to the office, you know, and if I wasn't going to enjoy it, well, I don't think there would be any sense in playing the game, you see. When I go to bat, of course, people seem to laugh. Sometimes I go to drive the ball and miss it completely and the bat goes and hits me straight in the rump or something like that, you know. But it is all good fun. I find that enjoying the game is the most important part of it and when I'm bowling I'm quite serious, but you have to be, you see, because if you are not serious when you bowl you'd probably find that the batsman would get on top of you.

Durden-Smith: What would your advice be to any young boy now who wants to be a fast bowler?

Hall: Well, I feel that all boys should remember that fast bowling is fifty per cent inspiration and fifty per cent perspiration and you must look after yourself. You should have a sense of humour, too, because believe me you need one. I think because I began bowling at a very late stage I was able to more or less put more into it. What I really mean is that if a boy begins to bowl when he is twelve and he flogs himself the wrong way, by the time he gets to twenty I think he could be a spent force. It's a lot of hard work and if you're not successful at the beginning, you must remember it is only the man who's going to go on and despite disappointment will really make the grade.

*   *   *

Frank Worrell was another West Indian cricketer elected to the office of Senator – this time in the Jamaican Parliament. Worrell was one of the most elegant and accomplished of batsmen, a left-arm bowler who commanded a variety of styles and a phlegmatic captain who always appeared to operate with statesmanlike control. The year after this interview with Rex Alston he was deservedly knighted for his services to cricket. Tragically, three years after that, Worrell died of leukaemia, which gives a poignancy to some of his words which was not apparent when uttered.

Frank Worrell

'People Today', Home Service, June 1963

Alston: Frank, everybody knows you as a great and a gifted cricketer, who's given a great deal of pleasure to lots of people all over the place, but we'd like to know a little bit more about the other Worrell, the Worrell that isn't always playing cricket. Now you were born in Barbados, is that right?

Worrell: Yes, I was born in Barbados, in the Parish of St Michael, and there I spent my first twenty-three years, apart from the odd excursion to the smaller islands and the odd cricket tour. I resided there until 1947 when I went up to Jamaica with the Barbados team and got to like Jamaica and stayed on.

Alston: Barbados has got a reputation of producing a lot of good cricketers. For instance, you and the other two Ws, Walcott and Weekes, all came from Barbados, am I right?

Worrell: Yes, Barbados seems to turn out batsmen in the main. I suppose the reason is that there is a very small island and a lot of the cricket is concentrated in roughly a radius of three miles.

Alston: Just round the town of Bridgetown.

Worrell: Round the town of Bridgetown, yes. And what normally happens is that any chap that wants to see one of the international players batting can walk or cycle just a matter of half a mile and in the course of an evening the youngsters can see no fewer than three matches. This is of great advantage to the youngsters because by a process of observation and emulation they can get the short cuts to the top as opposed to other large areas where if you're lucky you only see one match per Saturday.

Alston: A lot of people in England have the theory – I'm interested to know what you think about this – that West Indians, Indians, Pakistanis have a quicker eyesight, a quicker reaction than the white races. Do you think that's true?

Worrell: I don't think there's a lot of substance in it. I'd say that the people of West Indian, Asian descent seem to be looser-limbed, with a greater suggestion of agility than the people who've probably been brought up in this cold climate, but whether you relate agility with reflexes. . . ?

Alston: Now, do you have any recollection of problems connected with your colour and with meeting white people?

Worrell: Not in Barbados. I think we're more or less culturally homogeneous. You find the races went to the same churches, drank from the same communion cup, went to the same schools and we've played in the same teams and there's little or no suggestion of separation between the boys at school. On leaving school, you found the chaps of European descent gravitated towards the banks, whereas the only openings for the coloured boys were in the Civil Service or teaching, and then five or six years after that you find the chaps getting further and further apart. But basically I don't think there's any suggestion of hatred of the races. It just meant you found yourself in a different clique on leaving school and there it stayed.

Alston: You must have been looking ahead and thinking, 'Well, I'm not going to go on playing cricket till I'm sixty or seventy, how am I going to earn my living?' Now, did that suddenly come to you in the course of those early years?

Worrell: Not until after 1955 when I went to the West Indies to play against the Australians. I suddenly thought the best thing to do was to try and prepare myself for the future, so I came back and went to Manchester University where I studied for three years.

Alston: And what did you read?

Worrell: I read a degree in economics, actually, but I specialised in social anthropology and sociology. This was between 1956 and 1959.

Alston: Didn't you find it rather hard work after playing cricket for so many years to get down to books again?

Worrell: The first six months I found were very, very trying – the old brain was for ever strained. But I got over the first period and it just became routine . . .

Alston: Now have you a family, Frank?

Worrell: I've got a daughter thirteen years of age and she was born in Lancashire in 1949 and stayed there until 1959. Then she's been back in the West Indies and she's coming across and we're hoping to get her into school here sometime this year.

Alston: You want her to be educated in England rather than in the West Indies?

Worrell: Yes, I think I'd prefer this.

Alston: Why?

Worrell: Well, I attach a lot of importance to the finishing touches and our formal education at home is as good as you'd probably find over here, but then I find that the sort of social graces aren't as in evidence at home as I would love to see it. As a young lady I would like to see her educated here.

Alston: There's a bit more sophistication possibly being an older country?

Worrell: Yes.

Alston: That might have something to do with it. And now, when the question of marriage arises, which will inevitably happen, would you like her to marry an Englishman or an Australian or would you prefer her to marry a West Indian?

Worrell: Well, I don't think I'm particularly bothered about that as long as her husband or fiancé has got the same sort of interests as she's got. I mean, I think I could quite easily be happy whether you were Japanese, English, German, French or whatever. I find that in the West Indies I know several families where a young lady of European descent has married a chap of African descent and these things seem to be working quite well, and I think the world is going to become more and more multiracial and what we regard now as an exception, in fifteen to twenty years' time will probably be accepted by everybody.

Alston: Yes, I think the modern generation, the younger generation, is accepting it far more than my generation. It's a process of evolution, isn't it?

Worrell: Yes, I think so.

Alston: Coming back to cricket, Frank. How important is the team spirit of a side of a longish tour like this quite apart from what happens on the cricket field?

Worrell: Well, it is absolutely necessary on a six months' tour like this where you are playing six days a week because if there's any sort of division you find that these antagonisms will probably destroy the actual performances on the field.

Alston: Do you think that it's a good thing that once you've established yourself after the first months for the team to disperse a bit more so that they get a bit fresher?

Worrell: Yes, I've always been in favour of individuals who are resting, getting away from the game, because you seem to burn up just as much mental energy watching the game when you're not immediately involved than when you actually play the game. It was always best for chaps who were resting to get away from it all. Go to the sea or beach or river or what-have-you. I don't advocate chaps sitting around the place.

Alston: When you were appointed captain for Australia . . . what was it, two years ago? Had you the opportunity to put any particular views into practice as a team captain as a result of being on so many other tours? Did you do things which other captains hadn't done?

Worrell: The secret of our success was the fact that we gave the players the feeling that they're responsible individuals and left it more or less to their own devices to fit in, and it's amazing how marvellously the chaps accepted this sort of challenge.

Alston: Did you do a great deal of talking to the team or did you get it all over in the early stages and say, 'This is my philosophy, now go and do what I ask'?

Worrell: We had a pep talk at Perth . . . and occasionally during the course of the tour when things seemed to have been going wrong, we sort of gave them a little memory-jogger and everything went well. We had three serious talks in the course of the tour.

45

Alston:	That tied Test match now at Brisbane, what were your feelings about that? Now you were in the field, weren't you? You were in command. It was your decision as to who was to bowl the last two or three overs. It was your decision to place the field and so on. Were you nervous?
Worrell:	Not really. I was a bit worried, knowing West Indians as I do. I felt they might have cracked up under the strain, in the past they've always cracked up. On the field I was very much concerned about holding them together. I was walking around saying, 'Steady on boys. Steady on boys. Don't let it worry you.' You know, 'Bad luck boys, steady on boys,' and we just seemed to have come through.
Alston:	That last over, Wesley Hall bowled it, the fast bowler?
Worrell:	Yes, that's right.
Alston:	And six runs were wanted.
Worrell:	Yes.
Alston:	And three wickets to fall . . . It's a story-book thing, isn't it?
Worrell:	Yes.
Alston:	Did you bring Wesley Hall back for that over or had he been on before?
Worrell:	He'd bowled three or four overs before that with a new ball. We were very fortunate in that tied match in that the last chap was run out by Solomon who moved across from cover, picked this ball up, back to the stumps and he just turned around and threw it with one movement and hit the stump from about more or less a straight line.
Alston:	He had one stump to aim at?
Worrell:	He had no chance to aim, he just turned around and threw.
Alston:	And what were your feelings? You don't remember?
Worrell:	Well, things were a bit chaotic because we had a faction on the field feeling that, 'Well, we'd won by one run,' and another faction felt that we'd lost by one run, and I seemed to be the only one who was conscious of the fact that it was a tie.
Alston:	So your mathematics really helped you there?

Worrell: Yes, I had much more time to think than most people.

Alston: And when you were due to go, you had, I believe, almost a sort of state procession through Melbourne, isn't that right?

Worrell: Yes, it was a motorcade and what impressed us so much was the spontaneity of it because we'd accepted a function which was thrown by the Lord Mayor at the Town Hall. The Town Hall from our hotel was just a matter of forty yards which we'd intended walking, and then the evening before the reception John Priestley, a journalist attached to the Melbourne *Herald*, came and asked me whether we minded driving around the block. He said he'd arrange the open cars and I said, 'We see no objection to this.' John, in the evening paper, just put a little note to the effect that the rest of the team would be driving around this block and this article didn't have any prominence in the newspaper and much to our surprise the following morning half a million people were lining the streets. Traffic was at a standstill and as we were just easing our way through the crowds, the Australian people converged on the vehicles saying things like, 'Good on yer boys, you morally won, come back soon.' Well, tears came to my eyes every time I heard this because I realised I didn't have a chance in the world of going back to Australia as a player, and for this sort of thing to have happened at such short notice and the average Melbournite could have only read this thing on his way home in the evening paper and everything was so spontaneous, that our chaps were really sad, you know, at the thought of leaving the area.

Alston: A wonderful tribute it must have been, it must have been a great moment for you.

Worrell: Well, it was. It brought tears to my eyes.

Alston: Well done, Frank. Would you call yourself a nervous cricketer? When you go in to bat do you get butterflies?

Worrell: Not really. At one stage in my life I had a peculiar form of nervousness because I'd have a full night's sleep on the eve of a Test match, of any match, and I found that on arrival at the ground, any time our captain won the toss, suddenly I felt sleepy and I retired to the massage board and was fast asleep until I was awakened to go in to bat. On the occasions when I got out quite early on, when returning to the Pavilion there was never any suggestion of sleep, and on other occasions when you got the runs you came back and you're as right as rain. So I took this as a form of nervousness, because it wasn't as if I had been out all night, and for the past five or six years this doesn't happen.

Alston: I remember talking some years ago now to a well-known English player who played in a good many Test matches and we were talking about captaincy and I said, 'Well now, surely you were given instruction, weren't you? You know that you must push the play along because it was necessary to get a certain number of runs in time to win the match.' And he said, 'Oh no, no. All the time I've played I've never had any instructions from the captain that way.' The idea being presumably that if a fellow is a good enough player to play for England he should know how to play the game. Now, do you think that captains should give this advice? Say, 'Look here now, we've got to keep a run a minute going for four hours because we're going to win this game'?

Worrell: Yes, captains must do it because the players want the assurance. If you don't give the instructions to the boys they're going to feel they've got to attempt it on their own, and if they fail to get runs, they're likely to be dropped, saying, 'Oh well, he's taking a liberty.' But if he does it under instructions he feels then that he'll be given a second chance because he acted . . .

Alston: Yes, he's done what his captain asked him to do. Well, I was amazed when I heard this – to find that English captains didn't advise and instruct because I'm sure they should.

Worrell: This is absolutely necessary.

Alston: Now about yourself and away from cricket, Frank. What is your present job?

Worrell: Well, I'm Warden to a University Hostel – a hall of residence actually.

Alston: This is in Jamaica?

Worrell: This is in a Hall called Irving Hall where we've got 280 students and I'm supposed to be in loco parentis to the lot of them which is quite a pleasant job.

Alston: You're the Administrator really, are you?

Worrell: Yes, of this Hall of Residence, yes.

Alston:	You're responsible for discipline?
Worrell:	Discipline, moral welfare, general advice, looking after all their personal comforts.
Alston:	But what about the future? When you're aged fifty, what do you think you'll be doing?
Worrell:	I've got no idea. Actually I'm a fatalist. I keep on drifting in the breeze, so to speak. But it's quite conceivable that I will still have the job as a Warden.
Alston:	And finally. You've had a wonderful life so far. Mostly cricket, much travel. Have you got any regrets in the way that your life has gone?
Worrell:	None at all. I'd love to live it all over again.

*   *   *

Another legendary figure of West Indian cricket is Learie Constantine – menacing fast bowler, exuberant batsman and phenomenal fielder. And the legend is not confined to cricket. Constantine worked tirelessly in his efforts to educate people in pursuit of racial tolerance. He had, to quote his fellow Trinidadian, C. L. R. James, 'revolted against the revolting contrast between his first-class status as a cricketer and his third-class status as a man'. Constantine went into Law, wrote a book titled Colour Bar, *was elected to the Trinidad Legislature, appointed a High Commissioner, received a Knighthood and eventually a Life Peerage and was a Rector of St Andrew's University. Oh yes – he was also a Governor of the BBC.*

In 1953, Constantine gave three short talks on 'Cricketing Characters'. This was the third.

Spectators
Learie Constantine

General Overseas Service, July 1953

You people who watch *cricket* are just as important as the most famous players. More so, in fact. For if it weren't for your shillings, there wouldn't be any big cricket. Apart from that, the spectators often bring more personality and colour to the game than many players.

Most of us who have played at Lord's, or the Sydney Oval and places like that, have particular characters in the stands that we look out for every time. Like Yorkshire Annie, for instance, at Lord's. She's a grand institution and, speaking for myself, when I was playing at Lord's, if she wasn't there I felt the omission as if someone had taken away Father Time off the Pavilion.

So many of us look out for that impressive figure, always dressed in deep black. What's more, I always listened for her comments – you could hear them at the wickets quite well. She not only understood the finer points of cricket. She understood cricketers! And woe betide the player out on the middle who roused her wrath. All he wanted after that was an underground tunnel back to the Pavilion. A grand lady, bless her – even if, from about 800 yards away, she did once give us some pungent advice about how to hold a bat. You can always trust Yorkshire, can't you.

Away on the other side of the world, there's Yabba. How well I remember his scarlet face and ear-splitting yells when I played at the Sydney Oval. He sits there on 'the Hill', a huge, fat chap in a brown cap and, really, some of the advice he gives livens up the game for everyone concerned. Wally Hammond told me one very amusing tale about Yabba. That was in 1947 – Wally had just returned from his last tour of Australia. He was batting, he told me, in a Test at Sydney when England was in difficulties. Wally was playing carefully.

'Give him one in the ribs to wake him up!' yelled Yabba. And he really could yell. Wally was hot and tired, and didn't see anything funny in it just at that moment. He marked where the big, brown cap was, and waited for the loose ball to come along. In Australia you have to wait some time for those. But you know what Wally was like!

Well, the loose ball came, Wally jumped out at it, his bat whirled. It was a six, and the ball went like a bullet so close to Yabba that it made him move. As the bowler retired to begin his run for the next ball, Yabba's voice came across the grass like thunder – 'Give him one on the foot! He's too lively!'

What can you do with a spectator like that? Nothing satisfies him. They say Yabba sells rabbits from a barrow in the Sydney streets. That's where his name comes from, 'Luvely yabba – tasty, luvely yabba, come on, get your yabba.'

Then there is my own country, Trinidad. We have our mascots, too, Taffy of Trinidad and Flanagan of Barbados. They are familiar figures in all important matches in Barbados, Trinidad or British Guiana. Flanagan is an old groundsman of a club in Barbados. Brown-skinned, short, slight, shuffling and wonderfully dressed in an old blue serge suit and white gym shoes. Wherever the Barbadians went they took him to do nominal duties as baggage man. He has a sharp tongue and, being a Barbadian, a great knowledge of the Bible, from which he makes apt and joyful quotations. In his list of the world's greatest men, George Challenor would take the highest place.

Taffy, too, is small, but very dark and more stylishly dressed. His tongue is as sharp as Flanagan's. He, in turn, is an inseparable accompaniment of Trinidad teams wherever it plays. Through all public stands, members' pavilions, ladies' stands, players' dressing-rooms, they together roam, unchallenged, keeping up a continual interchange of witticism and chaff.

Then out home we have the 'tree-top supporters' club'. Some of the spectators who can't afford the gate money climb up surrounding trees overlooking the pitch and view the match from there. At critical moments in a Test, each tree has several men precariously balanced in it. Then, when something exciting happens at the wickets, these spectators are so eagerly cheering, clapping and shouting that a branch snaps, or someone loses his hold and down he goes, falling on the heads of those beneath. Yes, many of our people out home find that it pays to have a place nearest the Angels.

It was a spectator, a well-known one, who helped to put Len Hutton on the map as England's Number One batsman. The name was Syd Howard, the famous Yorkshire comedian. When Len Hutton was young, like other young men he wanted to smoke and drink and be a good mixer. But he found that cricket needed all he could give in physical fitness. The turning point came when Len was seventeen, when Sydney Howard said to him, 'You're going to be really great if you'll keep off smoking and drinking till you're twenty-one. Do it – and I'll give you a present to celebrate.'

So Len decided to try to qualify for that present. It's not easy you know, for a boy coming in to cricket to make that decision. I know, because I also made the same resolution and did not stop at twenty-one. Four years later, when Len was twenty-one, he'd forgotten all about the present. Then one day Syd Howard turned up in the dressing-room.

'Kept your promise, Len, lad?' he asked.

Len thought it over a bit. 'Yes, I have – and it's done my batting a world of good, too,' he said.

Syd pulled a gold watch out of his pocket and handed it to the startled Len. 'I told you you'd be really great if you stuck it out, lad,' he said. And that's how Len Hutton won his first gold watch. As for his cricket – well, what do you think?

Spectators – they are the very spirit of the game. In England, so grave and patient and well-informed. In Australia, so fiery and shrewd and bold. In India – oh yes, I have played cricket in that wonderful land – so intent, so joyous over a player's successes, so sympathetic when he doesn't do well. In New Zealand, so much like the English crowds, and in Ceylon so critical, yet so appreciative of their own players' success. I got the impression that they were always wanting the other side to win.

And my own people in the West Indies – of course, I'd rather play before them than anywhere else in the world. Perhaps they spoilt me, but I don't think so.

Of course, not everything that happens on the field is understood at once in the stands. There are a few little incidents that we keep to ourselves. At any rate at the time! And this happens especially in what are known as 'blood' matches.

You know what I mean. Traditionally there's always a bit of extra ginger when certain sides play certain other sides. For instance, Yorkshire versus Middlesex.

In this fixture in 1947 at Lord's, the wicket was pretty funny and the Tykes were holding on to the tail end of their innings with blood, toil and tears. But their last men were in and Jim Sims was bowling. You know how Jim bowls? Well, if you don't, I must tell you sometime.

Well, Jim was bowling. Fred Price was keeping wickets. The ball came down short of a length, and the Yorkshire batsman stepped back and tried to knock the cover off it with a hook stroke. The bat whizzed so that people could almost hear it from the Pavilion.

But you know how it is – that ball had some leg-break in it and, instead of middling it, there was an edge and away went the ball behind the wicket.

OwZAT? yelled Fred Price, leaping aside with the ball safe in his gloves. You know Fred is a grand scout. There is a tale that when he was born they found a twin set of lungs, and that soon afterwards he broke the glass in the bedroom window once by appealing in his sleep.

Anyhow, OWZAT? yelled Price, and the umpire put a hand to the place where one ear should be and raised a finger on the other hand to point to Heaven.

At that point, the spectators saw all the players standing round the wicket doubled up with laughter. Yes, including the batsman.

Now when a Yorkshireman, last man in a bulldog stand, laughs when he gets out – laughs mind you! there's some very funny business going on. I wanted to know what it was. Thousands of spectators wanted to know what it was. But there was no explanation. Just a lot of men laughing like lunatics out there on the most sacred piece of turf in all the world.

You can guess what I did. I went round to find out, and this is what had happened. Fred had made a big jump for that catch. Then, at his terrific appeal the umpire stepped aside a bit. In doing so he trod on something hard. And Fred Price growled at him, 'Get off my blasted teeth!'

Between the jump to square leg and the big appeal, they had jumped out and the umpire was standing on them. And they tell you the umpire is always right!

*   *   *

Learie Constantine first learned his cricket on a cocoa estate in Trinidad with a sun-dried orange for a ball, a bat made from a coconut tree and the kitchen crockery used to practise catches. Jamaica is as far distant from Trinidad as London is from Madrid and yet Neville Dawes, a Jamaican, would have had no difficulty in recognising that scene. It depicts, through the bare essentials, a few stitches in the tapestry of 'village cricket' in the Islands.

Dawes contributed this cricketing sketch to 'Caribbean Voices', a programme of verse and prose by West Indian writers broadcast in the BBC's Special Service for the West Indies.

Ball Ground
Neville Dawes

'Calling the Caribbean', April 1957

We walked and ran at scout's pace across the fields that Saturday morning to the ball ground which was two miles from the village. Even in the sunhot the dew was still on the grass. There must have been twelve of us boys hurrying that morning but only James Anguin, Teacher Anguin's fourteen-year-old son home on holiday from Kingston, would be playing for Orange Bottom's first XI against the team from Glad Stone, St Mary. James had batting gloves, white shining batting pads, a blazer, and cricket boots with nails. He was our prince that morning. We took it in turns to carry his new bat; and in our hurtling strides we used it to drive imaginary balls for sixes.

At John's Hall we overtook a group of women with large shut-pans on their heads: the pans smelled of corn pone. Whenever we heard the echo of an axe chopping wood we thought it was the sound of ball on bat, and that the match had started without us or James.

Orange Bottom ball ground is at the foot of a well of hills and all around it on the sloping grass the villagers sprawled for a gala day – all the schoolchildren, old men leaning on sticks, and a great many women. 'Dey doan come yet,' one of us said, as we crawled through the barbed wire.

The Orange Bottom team were assembled in the bell-tent set up and owned by the captain, Busha Grant. We peered at them through a large hole at the side of the tent – the fast bowlers, Nattie Campbell, the butcher, six foot three, and Alex Barrett, the shoemaker, very short and sturdy; the two stone-wallers, Ferdie Lawrence and Manfred Williams, the joker. Manfred was wearing red braces and hunting boots: he was very popular at concerts where he used to blacken his face and put a large white circle around his lips like a white comedian impersonating a negro. Busha Grant was cording up an old bat with glue and twine; Boysie Rickets, secretary of the team, was

53

polishing the match ball which had been recovered by Alex Barrett and reddened with annatto.

Behind the tent women were making up fire for the curry-goat and rice. The outfield had been cleared of animals, the pitch rolled, and the stumps placed. Our umpire, Clausie, was ready with his long white jacket and walking stick. But there was no sign of the Glad Stone team.

It was long past noon; the air was heavy with bees and butterflies and the smell of the sun on the grass. A fight started near the road where some women were selling tie-leaf and potato pone. We lobbed a tennis ball at James Anguin who was all dressed up in pads and gloves.

Suddenly the voices grew excited and in the distance we heard singing and the sound of a truck engine. Nothing can equal the thrill of the sound of a truck bringing cricketers singing on a Saturday afternoon.

'You hear the Bedford, man?' asked Jabez as we skipped about excitedly. First we saw handkerchiefs waving at us through the trees, and then, as the truck came nearer, the driver double-declutched with a flourish. Then we heard what they were singing.

> Glad Stone bway dem a' warriah, Oh!
> Glad Stone bway dem a' warriah . . .

It was the traditional self-confident challenge, the call to battle.

Orange Bottom, led out by Busha Grant in his sun-helmet, took the field. Busha set the field for Nattie Campbell – one wide slip, a very fine third man lost in the dip on the boundary, two back-stops behind the wicket-keeper (Nattie Campbell was fast, you see), and the rest of the team in indeterminate positions between point and square leg; but there were no fieldsmen near the wicket.

The game began with Nattie Campbell's long loping run-up to the Glad Stone opening batsmen: one of them wore green tropical trousers and brown-and-white leather shoes. We could not follow the ball descending from Nattie's high bowling arm but we saw the cloud of dust halfway down the wicket where the ball pitched. We notched the score on bamboo-joints with our penknives – there was no scoreboard: runs came steadily from byes and unintentional glances from the edges of their bats and from no-balls called frequently and with determination by our umpire, Clausie. We did not notch the no-balls although we knew they counted as runs. Whenever one of Nattie's 'bailers' hit a Glad Stone batsman on the hands, often splitting a finger, or one of Alex Barrett's 'shooters' nipped one of the batsmen on the toe we yelled with delight.

When the score reached 20, James Anguin ran fifteen yards across the long-on boundary to catch a skier with one hand. 'You *see* dat bway?' asked James's grandfather who was watching the game with dim half-seeing eyes under a huge umbrella. 'You *see* dat bway, sah?' he asked again, swaying with delight on a little camp-stool. We threw down our bamboo-joints, said,

'See James here!' and we ran fifteen yards to catch imaginary skiers in our outstretched right hands, reliving the wonder of the catch. We were James Anguin.

The fall of that wicket brightened up the Orange Bottom attack – Nattie Campbell and Alex Barrett bowled unchanged – more fingers were split by 'bailers', more toes nipped by 'shooters', more wickets fell. As the wickets fell, the Glad Stone batting became more rustic and wild: one wild, swinging fellow, who swung his bat with the left hand alone and with eyes apparently closed, carted three of Nattie's 'bailers' right to the square-leg boundary for six. We notched a sad 50 on our bamboo-joints.

When Orange Bottom started their innings the sun had dropped behind the hills and a cool breeze was blowing. We were afraid of Wilfred Clarke, the Glad Stone fast bowler.

He was a long man with a forehead that sloped backwards streamlined against the wind: on a day long past but forever fresh in village story he had clean-bowled the great George Headley for a duck at Palmer's Park. Today he had 'banned his head' with a large green-and-white handkerchief, and he bowled with fury. He devastated our batting, and we watched the funeral procession with our mouths open and our bamboo-joints and penknives idle.

Wilfred Clarke broke Busha Grant's middle stump, and a fairly straight pimento stick was cut to replace it. Our gloom was deep. But with the score at 10, Alex Barrett came in hitting.

He took a mighty sweep at the first ball bowled to him, missed it, and his bat flew high over mid-on's head. He ran down the pitch before the next ball was delivered and hit it clean for six into a banana walk. He hit three more sixes, was dropped four times, and fortified himself between overs with little wineglasses of rum. When he finally left, the score was 40 against Glad Stone's 73. Manfred Williams came in last and began his stonewalling and clowning. He would stop the ball dead in the blockhole, strut round behind the wicket-keeper, lean on his bat, cross his legs and wait for a fieldsman to come and pick up the ball. Then one of Wilfred Clarke's deliveries struck Manfred squarely on the pads.

'How is he, umpire?' asked the Glad Stone team. The Glad Stone umpire raised his finger decisively. Manfred did not move but prepared to receive the next ball.

'You gaan,' shouted the Glad Stone umpire, 'lbw.' Manfred turned to the wicket-keeper. 'What 'im say?' he asked quietly.

'Him say you gaan, my frien',' the wicket-keeper informed him. 'Legs before wicket.'

Manfred laughed. He looked up towards the field where Hezekiah Shand was burning bush: Hezekiah was Manfred's crony. 'Hezekiah!' Manfred shouted in a tone that was half-amused, half-outraged. 'Hezekiah, you no hear ya nuh? Dem say me legs. Fram me barn you ever hear me legs yet?'

'Which legs?' we heard Hezekiah answer. 'Is tief dat umpire tief.'

'But the umpire give you out already,' said one of the Glad Stone cricketers. 'Yu mus' be a sport, man.'

Manfred planted his feet firmly, gripped his bat in both hands and lifted it menacingly to his shoulders. He said, 'Nat a Jack man move me from here tiday. From I a play cricket hi never legs *yet*. Doan is leg stump dis?' he asked pointing to his block, 'den *how* I mus' legs?'

The logic of that satisfied us.

'Dat umpire is a tief.'

'Stay deh Manfred bway.'

'You doan out. Is tief dem tief.'

Manfred took up his batting stance again. Busha Grant started to go out to the wicket, but the villagers shouted at him, 'Busha, you better stay where you is.' The Glad Stone captain, perhaps sure of victory, ordered the bowler to continue the game. It was soon over and we had lost – Manfred was bowled without a shadow of doubt. But Orange Bottom was satisfied to lose the match. As Manfred made his way to the tent, somebody said, 'Tha's a serious Jamaican.'

We went behind the tent afterwards and got plates of hot-curry-goat and rice and mugs of cool sorrel. Then we played catchings and bowl-for-bat until the Glad Stone team was ready to leave. As their truck started up they began their farewell song.

> Wi bid you goodbye an' we gaan
> Wi bid you goodbye an' we gaan
> Wi glad fi meet
> An' we sarry fi part
> Wi bid you goodbye an' we gaan, Oh!
> Wi bid you goodbye an' we gaan . . .

Four of us hitched on to the back of the truck and fell off, bruising our hands, after a few yards. Then we ran behind the truck almost as far as the river.

*   *   *

Howard Marshall first joined the BBC in Savoy Hill days after a spell in journalism and a rocky run as a steward in a cargo boat. His was one of the first distinctive voices in cricket broadcasting. Here, Marshall is at the Oval, giving a summary of the day's play with ten minutes to go, in the third Test match between England and the West Indies in August 1933.

England *v.* West Indies, Third Test Match, 1933

Howard Marshall

England have had some ups and downs at the Oval here today. They won the toss, and at one period they lost 4 wickets for 68. Still, they have retrieved the situation now to a large extent, and the total at this moment is 309 for 9. I will just give you the individual scores:

Walters, c Merry, b Martindale	2
Bakewell, c Headley, b Sealey	107
Hammond, c Barrow, b Valentine	11
Wyatt, c Achong, b Martindale	15
Turnbull, b Martindale	4
Langridge, c Barrow, b da Costa	22
Ames, c Headley, b Martindale	37
Barnett, run out	52
Nicholls, b Achong	49
Marriott, NOT OUT	0
Clark, NOT OUT	8

I am speaking to you from a little box right alongside the scorers – I get a perfect view of the ground, and it is a good sight. It is a lovely summer afternoon with the sun shining and the players casting long shadows on the turf, and a big and enthusiastic crowd sitting round the ground. As a matter of fact, when I came over Vauxhall Bridge on my way here this morning and saw grey clouds stretching away into the distance I was a little uneasy about the weather. Still, the wind came from the north-east and the clouds were high, and the omens generally were propitious.

I always like the Oval – it is a friendly, informal sort of place. Incidentally, it is burnt pretty brown just now except for the patch of emerald green out there in the middle. As soon as I got here there was news going about.

I will break off now to say that Martindale has just sent Marriott's off-stump cartwheeling out of the ground, and the English innings has closed for 312.

Well, to go on with the story. I heard that the harassed selectors had completed the English team by bringing in Barnett; and then we heard that England had won the toss, and pretty soon the West Indies had taken the field and Mardindale had sent down the first ball of the match to Walters from the Pavilion end. Almost before we had settled in our seats, England had run into trouble. Martindale made the fifth ball of his first over run away and Walters just caught a touch of it and Merry at third slip held the catch at the second attempt. And that was one wicket down for 2 runs.

And then, with Griffith on at the other end, England had a stroke of luck, for Hammond played a somewhat casual-looking shot to a ball outside his off-stump, just touched it, and Headley got both hands to it but somehow he dropped it – and I never saw anyone look more miserable in my life. After that, Hammond and Bakewell had a careful look at the bowling – the wicket was pretty fast, by the way – and Martindale in his third over constantly tried bumping the ball – not leg theory, just pitching the ball at his feet and making it rise head high. But Bakewell popped a fine shot over slip's head. Martindale at this point had a fine leg, a deep fine leg and a mid-wicket, and Hammond placed an excellent shot – a late cut – which sent the ball racing over the baked turf to the boundary. The score then was 22, and Valentine (fast-medium) came on for Griffith, and da Costa (slow right-hand) for Martindale. Bakewell promptly slashed da Costa through the covers, but Hammond trying to turn Valentine to leg was beautifully caught at the wicket by Barrow standing up, so that Headley's mistake had not really proved very expensive, and England had lost two valuable wickets for 27.

Things were not going very well, and Martindale was brought on at the Pavilion end to greet Wyatt who started very confidently, when Grant soon made another change, bringing Achong on to bowl his slow left-handed spinners. As it happened, Grant made many changes before gaining any further success for the West Indies, for both Wyatt and Bakewell settled down to steady cricket, and, as a matter of fact, they were rather up against it – they had to retrieve a very bad start – and slowly but surely they began to get the upper hand. Bakewell particularly played well, and I think he vindicated himself thoroughly as an opening batsman for England, and for three-quarters of an hour the English innings proceeded calmly without incident.

The West Indies were on their toes, though, and Grant in the gully set them a fine example by some magnificent fielding. Still, it was not until ten minutes past one, after an hour and forty minutes, with the score at 62, that Martindale made Wyatt play a little early to a ball outside the off-stump and give an easy chance to Achong at extra cover. That was three down for 62, and England had their backs to the wall and ten minutes later they were in still worse trouble, for Turnbull, playing a sort of half-cocked, defensive stroke, was bowled neck and crop by Martindale, and the scoreboard read: 68 for 4.

James Langridge, the Sussex left-hander, had a pretty heavy responsibility then, when he survived a prodigious and deep-throated appeal for lbw by Griffith. It was about this time that we felt we could have done with Jardine and his solidarity [*he had scored a century in the previous Test, but was injured*] – this was just the sort of situation which would suit him admirably. Still, Langridge and Bakewell survived until the luncheon interval, when the score was 73 for 4. The West Indies had done extremely well, although it seemed now that England was definitely on top.

The game now was extremely interesting, and when Martindale and Griffith took up the West Indies attack again after lunch, there was a big and very keen crowd. Martindale continued to bowl extremely well; he is really a good bowler, and once he made Langridge edge one dangerously through the slips. Bakewell in the meanwhile went on batting admirably and at twenty minutes to three he reached his fifty by driving Griffith past mid-off to the boundary – a fine stroke.

As the 100 went up, Grant made a double change, and brought on Valentine and Achong, but the batsmen seemed quite happy. Bakewell was opening out a bit, using his feet to Achong and driving him on the full pitch, and runs came steadily – not fast, but fast enough considering the state of the game – but then, when Bakewell had thumped Valentine for a couple of fours in succession – one, a beauty through the covers – Grant brought Martindale and da Costa on, and in da Costa's first over the patient Langridge took a flick at one and was caught at the wicket. It was twenty past three then, and the partnership between Bakewell and Langridge had added 79 runs, and the English score was 147 for 5 – not very good on a plumb wicket.

Still, Ames is a pretty useful No. 7, and there was Barnett to follow, so that there was no question of the hutch being open yet. Then England had another escape, for Ames edged Martindale to first slip – a difficult chance, but a chance none the less – but first slip let it go through his fingers. Ames was not upset though, and in Martindale's next over he crashed two bouncers outside the off-stump through the covers to the boundary. All this while Bakewell had been approaching his 100, and at a quarter to four he reached it. Everyone cheered, and drinks went out to the players. As it happened, Bakewell did not last much longer, for when the batsmen were apparently rooted on top and Grant had put on Headley and Sealy, Bakewell tried to drive Sealy – a medium right-hander, by the way – but Headley leapt in the slips and caught the ball in his extended right hand, a superb catch, and an appropriate end to a very fine innings. Bakewell had played extremely well for four hours.

The total then was 194 with six wickets down, and Barnett came in to join Ames, who was getting very lively. It was not long, however, before Ames played a nasty one from Martindale and was caught by Headley in the slips; and the score was 208 with seven wickets down.

The West Indies had every reason to be pleased with themselves, and then came one of those changes which makes cricket the most incalculable of games. Nicholls, the Essex left-hander, joined Barnett and gradually the balance swung. Before that, we had really felt that the West Indies were constantly dangerous, but now they suddenly became harmless. The bowling lost its sting; Nicholls and Barnett looked supremely confident, both playing some grand off-side forcing strokes; and the runs mounted up, and we felt that we were at the beginning instead of very nearly the end.

Grant brought all his guns to bear – Martindale, Griffith, Headley, Sealy, da Costa – but that was no use, Barnett and Nicholls went remorselessly on, till they carried the score to 302 for 8, a partnership of 94, when Nicholls was bowled by Achong.

Well, that was pretty near the end, because Barnett cut Martindale hard to Grant in the gully soon afterwards, started to run but, before he could turn, Grant had thrown his wicket down and he was out. A fine piece of fielding.

And then, after that, as you heard, the last wicket fell very quickly and Marriott was bowled neck and crop by Martindale, and the England innings closed – I will just repeat the score again – for 312.

Three days later, at the end of the match, Marshall drew some conclusions on that summer's Test series.

Impressions of Series
Howard Marshall

Marshall: I expect you have heard that the third and final Test match between England and the West Indies very quickly came to an end this morning, and the England team won by an innings and seventeen runs, a rather unexpectedly easy victory. England have thus won two out of the three matches this summer and one was drawn.

Still, I think it would be a mistake to consider this tour purely in the terms of wins and losses. Personally, I think it is far more important to realise that we have had with us a team of enthusiastic and popular cricketers. If you wish to be enthusiastic about it, you can remember when Headley and Barrow entirely mastered the England bowling and the West Indies had scored 333 for 6 when stumps were drawn, and you can recall that excellent last-wicket stand at Lord's and the wonderful performance of Constantine against the MCC, and plenty of equally good performances which have shown us the qualities of these West Indian players. What many of us will chiefly remember, though, will be the spirit in which our visitors have played their matches. They have reminded us, and I think we needed to be reminded in England, that cricket is not altogether a cold-blooded sort of mock warfare but that it is still a game to be enjoyed, and that there is still an element of adventure about it.

Nothing, for instance, would ever persuade Roach that it was not his job, as one of the opening batsmen, to attack every ball sent down to him, and those who saw him hooking and cutting the fast balls sent down to him at the Oval yesterday will surely pray that he never steadies up and allows sound defensive technique to dim his natural brilliance.

And here I think we may fairly say that, though in Headley they have a first-rate batsman, the West Indies have not yet acquired that experience and solidity which would make them consistently better opponents for Australia and England, and I for one hope that fact does not worry them unduly. They have made fine progress and above all they are happy cricketers, and so long as they so obviously enjoy playing the game we shall enjoy watching them and playing against them on our grounds.

Now this evening I have brought Mr Grant up to the studio with me. Mr Grant, as you know, is captain of the West Indies team, and an excellent captain he is, and he is going to speak to you now and give you a few impressions of the tour. Here he is – Mr Grant.

G. C. Grant: I gladly accept this opportunity of thanking you for the welcome you have given us, the members of the West Indies cricket team. Everywhere we have played we have been given a great reception, a reception which has been a constant source of joy and encouragement. We have been fortunate in having a good summer. On many occasions the brilliant sunshine has reminded us of our homes in the tropics. Assisted by the fine weather, we have had quite a successful tour and the results have exceeded expectations.

Well though we have done in our county fixtures, we

have, I am sorry to say, again disappointed ourselves in the Tests. Our bowling and fielding have, I venture to think, always been up to Test standard, but only at Manchester in the second Test did some of our batsmen give of their best. For our defeat at Lord's and again today at the Oval, we have no excuse to offer. On both occasions the better side won. We congratulate the English XI on its successes, and we trust that one of these days not many years hence we will be in the happy position of wishing our opponents better luck next time.

It has been a great pleasure to play cricket in this country. The press and the public have done all in their power to help us. I will not say we have always agreed with the comments of correspondents and spectators, but I do say we have greatly appreciated their support.

Yet another month of cricket lies ahead of us. I trust that in the remaining matches your support will continue and be deserved, so that when we leave these shores you will say, 'Come again,' while we in our turn will reply, 'Gladly we will.'

*   *   *

Few have given such service to the game in varying capacities as 'Plum Warner'. In 1939, the former Middlesex and England captain and recent Chairman of the Selectors was invited to talk about West Indian cricket and cricketers, as a 'trailer' to the summer's visitors.

West Indian Cricket and Cricketers
'Plum' Warner

Saturday Talk on Sport, May 1939

My first recollections of cricket are of playing in my nightshirt on a marble gallery in Trinidad at half past six in the morning. I was bowled to by a boy by the name of Killibree which, in the patois of Trinidad, means humming-bird. Armed with my little bat, I sometimes broke the windows of the rooms looking on to the gallery and I got quite used to my father's remark, 'There's that wretched boy again!' It was always countered by Killibree assuring him that, 'Mr Pelham he make a good batsman, sir, when he grow big, sir.'

Now this summer we welcome once again a team from the West Indies. I suppose we can say that cricket began in those lovely islands (in a more or less organised form) when Lillywhite, the famous Sussex bowler, was engaged to coach in Trinidad in the sixties; but in this country we knew little or nothing of West Indian cricket until Mr R. S. Lucas's team visited the West Indies during the winter of 1894-5. Since then, many teams have gone out to the West Indies and this is the sixth visit of a West Indian team to England. The first was in 1900 under the captaincy of my brother, Archer. I remember I had the pleasure of playing for them at Leicester. The qualifications in regard to first-class cricket were not so rigid in those days and, after all, I was West Indian born.

Conditions in the West Indies are almost ideal for cricket. The weather is certainly hot but seldom oppressively so. The wickets in fine weather are extremely good, although immediately after rain they are practically unplayable because the ball not only takes any amount of spin but jumps head high. The four great centres are Trinidad, Barbados, Jamaica and Demerara, and in all these places the wickets are of grass except in Trinidad, where they are compelled to use a matting wicket because of the ravages of the mole cricket which eats grass in great gulps. These matting wickets play extremely well and far more truly than the matting wickets which many of us have experience of in former days. Today, South Africa has grass wickets of a type which causes the batsmen to lie awake at night.

One of the difficulties of organisation in the West Indies is the fact that Jamaica is a thousand miles from Trinidad, but in spite of this handicap which keeps Jamaica out of the inter-colonial Tournament, played annually between the other three centres, the standard of cricket in Jamaica is high. They have benefited much by the visits of teams got together by Lord Tennyson, Sir Julien Cahn and, on one occasion, by a Yorkshire XI.

Now what may we all expect of this West Indian team, which is captained by Mr R. S. Grant, a brother of G. C. Grant who led the last side to this country in 1933? First of all, I am sure we can look forward to seeing a very lively side, who will play the game in the delightfully happy and enthusiastic manner which has always appealed to our public. But brought up amongst perpetual sunshine, amidst the glamour and warmth of their beautiful islands, set like a string of pearls in a glittering sea, you should not judge this team on their form during the chilly days of May. They should be given time to become acclimatised.

I am told by one who has a particularly close knowledge of their form that this is the best West Indies side that has ever come to England, in the sense that it is a better-balanced side than any before it. Their fielding is bound to arouse enthusiasm, with the example of Constantine – the greatest fieldsman that I have ever seen – to inspire them; and the fact that there are only two men in the team over thirty suggests that many a probable four will be converted into a single; and their throwing is both hard and of long range.

Besides being a great fieldsman, Constantine is also the type of batsman who a few years ago could – and no doubt today still can – win a match for his side in half an hour. He is a genius and makes extraordinary strokes. While he is at the wicket something exciting is fairly certain to happen, and I shall always remember a hit of his in the match between the West Indies and Middlesex at Lord's, in June 1928. G. O. Allen was bowling from the Pavilion end and sent down what was apparently a fast good-length ball just outside the off-stump. Constantine flashed his bat at it and the next minute the ball was flying over extra cover's head on its way to the top seats of the grandstand. It was a most amazing stroke and he followed it later in the match by another one off J. W. Hearne. Constantine played back at the ball and hit it so hard that although it may be said to have been technically a catch to the bowler, the ball arrived in the Pavilion, after striking the railings in front of it, scattering the members in all directions. That stroke was an unfortunate one for Hearne, for it ended his career for the rest of that season, one of his fingers being badly damaged.

It may well be said that the side is full of personalities and their zest and energy in the field will delight us all. There should be few dull moments. The team, as usual, have several fast bowlers. Martindale, a man of fine physique, is probably as good a fast bowler as there is in the world today and he is really fast. Constantine is not as fast as he used to be but he may be expected to acquire considerable pace during the first few overs at the start of a match, and he and Martindale will probably test the very best of our opening batsmen. They tell me that Constantine has developed a clever slow ball as a contrast to his more steady delivery. Johnson is a fast-medium left-hander with a nice easy action who makes great pace off the ground, but he is of rather slight physique and will have to be very carefully used. Hylton, with tremendously broad shoulders, is fast medium – he can also bowl leg-breaks, and Williams, if not as fast as Martindale, can keep an end going for long spells. Clark is a googly bowler, rather faster than usual with his type, and can keep a length. Cameron, like his captain a recent Cambridge blue, is another of the same method, though much slower through the air, and J. B. Stollmeyer is also a googly bowler. The side would appear, then, to have a good variety of attack and the chief interest will probably centre in the fast bowlers who really do 'let her go' and who bowl with great zest and energy.

Barrow, who made 100 in the Test match at Manchester in 1933, is the wicket-keeper again, and it is a great asset to a side when the wicket-keeper is also a good batsman. Weekes, the reserve wicket-keeper, is said to be a fine left-handed batsman who hits the ball exceedingly hard with very little effort, and may well play as a batsman.

The batting will centre round Headley, one of the best batsmen in the world today with a tremendous record behind him. He has been called the 'Bradman of the West Indies', and with some reason. He is of medium height but very strongly built and possesses most supple wrists and is as quick on his feet as a Pavlova. I am told that latterly he has taken to playing a great deal off his back foot (he is a right-handed batsman), and it may be that accurate bowling supported by a well-placed field may limit the rate of his scoring in comparison with that of past years.

The brothers Stollmeyer – the younger of them is only seventeen – are already of established reputation in the West Indies, and Gomez has plenty of strokes. Sealy is described as the prettiest batsman in the West Indies and Bailey is the holder of the highest score ever made in inter-colonial cricket in the West Indies (268).

The captain, Grant, is a capital all-round cricketer. He bowls off-spinners round the wicket, is a more than useful batsman and an extraordinarily good field anywhere near the wicket. I have vivid recollections of his splendid fielding in the University match of 1933. He was also a great goalkeeper in his Cambridge days, who went very near to an international cap. Mr Grant is a man of very attractive personality and I'm quite certain that he will get the best out of his team. With him comes Mr G. M. Kilroy as Manager for the second time. He knows all the ropes of Managerial and we are delighted to see him again.

English cricket today is very much alive and is certainly on the up-grade, but no Selection Committee will be so rash as to underrate my countrymen (I'm going to call them that), and in any event people who are fond of cricket may be certain that the West Indies will play the game in a manner that will appeal to them.

Now I want you to forgive me if I close this talk with a personal experience. Soon after I had come home from Oxford, Lord Hawke gave me a place in his team to the West Indies and, in the first match of the tour, in Trinidad, I was lucky enough to make a big score. As I wended my way back to the Pavilion, a man who had bowled to me as a little boy came out from the crowd and, backing in front of me with tears in his eyes, said, 'This is a great day for me, Mr Pelham. I bowl to you when you so high, Mr Pelham, and I now see my little boy make 100. I go home and tell my wife tonight, sir, and she die of joy, sir!' To such men as this I owe much, and any good fortune which I had at cricket – and I had a lot – is largely due to them.

*   *   *

MAINLY AUSTRALIA

At the height of the Second World War, 'Plum' Warner joined Arthur Mason in a studio to contribute to the series 'Giants of Sport'. The theme of the discussion reflected happier times as they exchanged reminiscences of Victor Trumper.

Australia's Greatest Batsman
'Plum' Warner and Arthur Mason

Forces, May 1942

Mason: When 'Dave' Nourse, the famous South African cricketer, retired from the game, he was asked, 'Who do you think was the greatest batsman you ever saw?', and he replied, 'Oh, Victor Trumper, without any doubt.' An opinion worth having, that; and the opinion, too, of every Australian cricket-lover when Trumper was in the heyday of his brilliant career, nearly forty years ago. It is an opinion, moreover, that time has not changed. In his day Trumper was unrivalled.

His batting career began when, as a boy, he was one of a side of Sydney colts who played against the England XI then visiting Australia. And a few years later, in 1899, he was included – at the last minute admittedly, but still included – in the Australian touring side. A wise last-minute decision by the selectors, for in that year's Lord's Test match, young Trumper, at the age of twenty, celebrated his first appearance at headquarters with a glorious innings of 135 not out. It has been written about that innings, 'Before he had batted half an hour it was obvious that a new star of unsurpassed brilliance had joined the Southern Cross.' Sir Pelham Warner can vouch for the truth of it, too.

Warner: Yes, it was the first time I had seen him bat. What struck me was, first, his complete naturalness of play; batting seemed a part of himself. Secondly, his general figure and face with his fair hair and boyish look made a strong appeal. He was about five foot eleven, slimly and gracefully built, quick as lightning on his feet and with lovely wrists. His late cutting was a sheer delight; he forced any ball the least short of a

length wide of mid-on, and every now and again he 'gave
the bowler the rush' as they said, and was down the pitch
with the speed of thought. The England bowlers were
Jessop, at that time very fast for a few overs from round the
wicket, Mead of Essex, Rhodes, F. S. Jackson and C. L.
Townsend, a slow bowler with a break both ways. He
treated them all alike. There's a photograph of him at
Lord's jumping out to drive. See that, and you will have an
idea of the great Victor Trumper going in all his glory.

Mason: In that season, too, he made his highest score in England –
300 not out, against Sussex. Darling, captain of the
Australians, who was at the wickets with him for some
time, was afterwards asked by M. A. Noble, 'Well, what do
you think of the boy?' Darling, himself one of the greatest
left-handers in cricket history, throwing up his hands, said,
'And I thought I could bat!'

In this country, Trumper was often seen at his best, but
never more impressively than in the season of 1902, one of
the wettest of English summers. It was no cricket season for
an Australian batsman fresh from his own sun-swept
wickets. Game after game was played on pitches almost
ruined by rain but, when other batsmen could do little more
than make a poor best of a bad job, Trumper gave a series
of the most brilliant batting displays. In that wet summer,
his aggregate was astonishing: 2570 runs, including eleven
centuries, two of them in one match, against Essex, and
one of them a century before lunch in the famous
Manchester Test match won by Australia, amid
tremendous excitement, by three runs. And at that time
England had an array of bowlers not now to be seen –
Lockwood, Barnes, Hirst, J. T. Hearne, Wass, Trott,
Braund, Rhodes. But none of them troubled him any more
than did the wickets, wet or dry. He came to England again
with the 1905 Australian side, but meanwhile he had been
doing great things in Australia.

Warner: In March 1903, I was in Australia with Lord Hawke's team.
In the match against New South Wales, Trumper made 37
in the second innings – a small score, I know, but one I shall
never forget. He and R. A. Duff, a fine forcing batsman,
short in height but of a nuggety frame, were a great first-
wicket pair, the pride and joy of the Australian crowds. As
they came out to bat you could hear the hum round the
ground, 'Here they come, Trumper and Duff,' just as in

later years they used to say, 'Here they come, Hobbs and Rhodes.'

In this match, I remember Trumper and Duff scored 72 runs in twenty-seven minutes. And the huge crowd roared as their powerful strokes found the boundary. It was a desperate situation for any captain. I kept changing the bowling, without effect. Finally, I put Bosanquet on instead of Hargreaves, of Warwickshire. This was too much for a man in the crowd, who yelled, as New South Wales spectators can yell, 'What are you doing, Warner, you ruddy fool? Can't you see the scoreboard? Hargreaves is the only bowler who hasn't been hit to Hades.' I went to my place with my tail between my legs, and Bosanquet lopped up to the crease in his leisurely way. His first ball was of good length, just outside the off-stump, and Trumper moved across to cut it late. But the ball was a googly and down went Trumper's off-stump. My friend in the crowd was broadminded about it. 'Beg pardon, captain,' he shouted, 'I was the ruddy fool, not you.' That, incidentally, was the first googly bowled on the Sydney ground. From that day to this, it has always been called the Bosey ball out there. It's never 'So-and-so is a googly bowler,' but 'So-and-so bowls the Bosey.'

Mason: It was wonderful cricket that Trumper was playing in those days, from 1903 onwards. In fact, his innings of 185 not out in that same year was described by Dick Lilley, England's wicket-keeper of many years, as positively the best innings he ever saw, an opinion which was by no means Lilley's alone.

Warner: I share it for one. It was a famous match altogether. R. E. Foster beat all records with his great 287, and England had a huge lead of 292 on the first innings. In the second innings, the Australians' batting order was altered overnight, and Trumper, instead of opening, came in at the fall of the third wicket. The star of Australia seemed to be setting when a lithe and graceful figure appeared on the field to a yell of appreciation, of admiration and of hope. What an innings it was: such ease, such grace, such style, such power! Our bowlers were helpless against him; all except Rhodes, who, with a strong outpost line – a long on, a long off and a deep extra cover – kept him fairly quiet. Never did a slow left-handed bowler bowl more finely on a perfect wicket than Rhodes on this occasion. He kept the side together, and sent down forty overs and two balls for 94 runs and five wickets. We won eventually by five wickets, but Australia ran us hard, and her gallant uphill fight on this occasion was a monument of determination. An Australian XI is most dangerous when you think you have got them beaten.

Mason: And it wasn't only England that suffered under Trumper's lash. The South Africans, too, had a taste of his brilliance in 1910. Against them, Trumper made 661 runs in nine innings (two not out). The great South African all-rounder, G. A. Faulkner, told against himself this Trumper story. He had the idea that 'before Victor looks round', as he put it, a fast yorker on the leg stump, first ball, might out him. And he duly delivered his first ball to Trumper, a fast yorker on the leg stump. 'But', said Faulkner, 'all that happened was that Victor slid his front leg forward, flicked his bat across from the direction of point, and the ball sped between his legs to the square-leg boundary.'

And outside Test matches, there were the Australian inter-state games, in which he was always the sheet-anchor of the New South Wales side. In a New South Wales *v.* Victoria match, with the Sydney wicket a quagmirish gift for the bowlers, he hit 101 runs in fifty-seven minutes, the rest of the side making 38 between them. On a Melbourne glue-pot wicket, he hit 74 by the simple process of smiting nearly every ball on the full – the other ten batsmen making 48 between them. Playing for Paddington, his district side, he gave, one afternoon, an astonishing display, hitting 335 not out in two hours forty minutes. Nothing that day could stop him. As C. B. Fry has said, his only defence was attack, and a Test match innings, as well as any other, often found him attacking the first ball of the match, and as likely as not with a master-stroke to the boundary.

Warner: There's one question about Trumper that nobody who saw him can help raising, even though it will always remain unanswered. Was he as good as Bradman? On figures, no, but in spite of Bradman's wonderful performances, you will find it difficult to meet an Australian of Trumper's time who will admit that Trumper has ever had a superior. And don't forget that, apart from his batting, he was a superb fielder, a really great deep field, with a hard low and accurate return, and a dead-sure catch. Bradman is a great fielder too. So was Macartney. And Macartney's admirers also ask, 'What did Trumper do that Charlie Macartney couldn't?' We could go on trying to draw comparisons, but one fact remains – the old-timers in Australia still view Victor Trumper as the greatest of all Australian batsmen.

Mason: Of course Trumper's batting was not wholly a matter of long innings and big scores, though he played many a long innings and made many a big score. There was an innings of his of a mere 80-odd, played at Lord's against MCC. Five England bowlers were in that side, but I can still see MacLaren clapping his hands to far-off fieldsmen in the hope that they would go where they might stop Trumper's dazzling shots. The stamp of genius was upon his batting, with a natural elegance of movement towards any and every type of shot. The bat in his hand flashed like a sword, with incredible swiftness and power. I can still see, for one example, and across many years, a square-cut off a rising ball in a Test match on Sydney Cricket Ground: Trumper on his toes and perfectly balanced, his bat high above his head, the whirling downward stroke, and the seemingly simultaneous smack of the ball against the boundary fence.

The normal armoury of a batsman's scoring shots was only the beginning of his equipment. The thing that crumpled up his opposing bowlers was the variety of his attack on them. Perhaps in the seasons from 1911 onwards he had lost a little of his fire. Yet in the southern summer of 1914, he was still able to play a grand innings of 253 against New Zealand, in that country. On 28 June 1915, he died.

Warner: I remember coming out of the War Office about six o'clock that evening. We were then in the throes of another Great War, but instead of the usual war news, the posters of the evening papers carried, 'Death of Victor Trumper. Death of a great cricketer.' As Major H. S. Altham put it in his splendid book, 'In the midst of the breathless business of making war, England paused for a few moments to pay tribute to a glorious cricketer.' A few months later, I received a letter from Clem Hill, in which he said, 'Poor Victor has gone. If there was ever a better batsman, I never saw him.' And he added, 'He had the funeral of an emperor; the streets of Sydney were lined five and six deep.'

Thus passed the most popular of all Australian cricketers. He was universally loved, and no wonder. For quite apart from his cricketing genius, he was a most delightful man. Modest to a degree and with a great charm of manner, he had a smile that many will remember as long as, or longer than, his scores.

*   *   *

A comparison with Bradman is inevitable in any discussion on 'Australia's Greatest Batsman'. Brian Johnston interviewed 'The Don' for the 'Where are they now?' spot in 'Sports Report' in February 1966. Extracts from this interview are given below.

Don Bradman

Johnston: What is it that makes people talk about cricket and write about it so much?

Bradman: Oh dear, this is a difficult subject. We could spend hours by the fireside talking about that. Why is it Sir Robert Menzies thinks that this is the greatest game in the world. It enriches the intellect – it enables you to develop your mind. I think it's something like great music, a symphony which has developed over a long period of time. It's different from any other game, it's fascinating, there's so many angles to it, so many tactics that can be employed, so many beautiful features that you can look for, so many surprises. It's all rather indefinite to pin-point, but it has a character about it I'm sure that no other game has ever had.

Johnston: Do you think it's improved since you've played it?

Bradman: Well, I think cricket is always improving. I think all games are always improving in some way or other. The tactics may change and people may not like them. Let me take tennis. You have this serve/volley game which a number of people say today is not as attractive as the old base-line game was, but without any doubt at all the modern tennis player would easily defeat the old-time tennis player because his tactics are more successful. I think cricket tactics have changed too. But I have no patience with people who say that the modern cricketer is no good. Individually, I think he is still a wonderful cricketer but he has to fit himself into the tactics that are employed today.

Johnston: Don, you made 300 in a day of the Test matches in the thirties. What would you back yourself today, if you had all your faculties, you know?

Bradman: Well now, Brian, that's rather rude, isn't it?

Johnston: (laugh) No, I mean physical faculties. If you were back aged twenty-five.

Bradma: Ah. Well, I can recall very vividly back in the 1930s in a Test match at Adelaide, the opposition decided that they were going to restrict my run scoring rate and as a result they placed a very defensive field and I found it pretty difficult to get more than one, or two. Fours were at a premium and it's testing my memory a little bit you know, but I think that in a full day's play I was able to get somewhere in the region of 200 runs. Now, no man on this earth could ever get 300 runs in a day if the opposition set out to contain him, to place a defensive field, bowl negatively and so on. This is the crux of the whole matter. It depends what the opposition does all the time. Things haven't changed in the sense that if you were up against spin bowlers with a reasonably placed field you would score just the same today as you could ever score – anybody could. But you can't do it if you're batting against four men on the boundary and the bowler's taking five minutes to bowl an over. It just cannot be done and it never could be done.

Johnston: Now you say you can be contained but I think that one of your great attributes was that you found the gaps between the field. How were you able to do this?

Bradman: Well, I suppose this has been exaggerated over the years, you know. In another fifty years' time you'd be surprised how good I was.

Johnston: Don, coming to the present day now. We have Doug Walters aged nineteen coming straight in and making 100 in his first Test. Now you made 100 in your first series against England – you were about the same age; he says he hasn't been coached very much, you weren't either, were you?

Bradman: No, I never had any coaching at all. None whatever. If I had, I think some of my most productive shots would have been cut out in the first twelve months. And if you look back on the game òf cricket, Brian, I can't think of any really great cricketer, and I mean really great cricketer, who was coached. I don't think you can make a great cricketer by coaching. You can make a mediocre cricketer into a good cricketer, you make a good cricketer better, but I'm talking about a great cricketer, a genius. I think he's got something which is individual. Take O'Reilly. I'm sure if he'd gone to a coach in his young days, they would have changed his grip and you would have never heard of him.

Johnston: Doug Walters has got one thing on you. He bowls a lot and takes wickets in Test matches. Did you ever get a wicket in a Test match?

Bradman: Ah well, you see, he bowled a lot more overs than I did. I don't think they ever recognised my worth, Brian. And of course, when I became captain – well, I couldn't bowl, could I?

*   *   *

The Sports Report team captured a number of fascinating interviews for the 'Where are they now?' series, mostly with fondly remembered footballers and cricketers. In December 1965, Brian Moore persuaded a personality with a famous voice but unknown face, who had practised his art from the so-called 'dead' side of the microphone, to recall the pioneering days of broadcast cricket.

Howard Marshall, whose BBC career began as an announcer, had played a crucial part in the development of Outside Broadcast commentary by successfully combining hard news with human impression. His employment for the Corporation seemed full of 'ins and outs'. After leaving to work for the Daily Telegraph, *Marshall rejoined the staff in 1943 as a Special War Correspondent before becoming Director of War Reporting. 1945 saw him disembarking from the 'battleship' in Portland Place once more to accept a job as Director of Public Relations with the Ministry of Food. Subsequently, he went into business although he still made broadcasts on special occasions.*

Howard Marshall

Moore: What exactly was the formula for cricket broadcasting in your day?

Marshall: Well, it was much easier in the early days in one sense, which was that we waited for the things to happen and then rang up Broadcasting House and said Bradman's going to make 100 and we ought to come over or whatever it might be. Then they'd cut us into the programme. But, of course, whenever we did that, Bradman got out or took two hours to make 100 or whatever it was and it was very difficult to get him right on the knob for the big moment.

Moore: And you'd cut in on any programme?

Marshall: Any programme except Children's Hour which was sacrosanct. You couldn't touch that.

Moore: Who was the greatest batsman you've seen, would you think?

Marshall: I think I must say Don Bradman. The man you expected more than any other to make 100 every time he went in. Which he so often did.

Moore: What about the best bowler you've seen?

Marshall: There again I think it goes to an Australian. Among so many candidates I think O'Reilly. I remember getting into trouble, for when O'Reilly was bowling well I suddenly broke into song, and said, 'If you're the O'Reilly they speak of so highly, Gor blimey, O'Reilly, you are bowling well.' Which was in the days when they were rather more sensitive about difficult words than they are today.

Moore: Did you get any letters as a result of this?

Marshall: Oh, lots, yes. Saying that children had been listening and it was most improper to say Gor blimey!

Moore: When you were doing cricket commentaries, Mr Marshall, you had no scorer, you had no statistician to help fill your ears with facts and figures?

Marshall: Back in the early days that was perfectly true and very difficult it was until the late and very much lamented

Arthur Wrigley came to join me at Manchester in 1934. Until then we had to work it out in pencil, have several people running round to the score-box for confirmation and so on and so forth. It was very difficult indeed. And in those days, too, we were sometimes square on to the wicket. We didn't watch it from behind the stumps so we couldn't really tell what the bowler was doing, which was another very great difficulty. I remember doing a match in which Hedley Verity scuttled out the Australians twice in a day at Lord's from the Tavern, so we couldn't see what Verity was doing. Obviously the Australians couldn't either, so it didn't matter so much.

Moore: Which cricket memory do you treasure most?

Marshall: Well, there are so many they come crowding in, but I think I must say the great Hutton record when he beat Bradman's record, at the Oval. I remember we were sitting on a blazing hot day on the tin roof of the Oval stand as he was gradually approaching the record and Bradman crowding him all he could to try and set up a catch and Hutton getting paler and paler and paler and more ghost-like. Then the final triumph and the roar of the applause. Wonderful day, wonderful occasion.

Len Hutton's record-breaking innings in 1938 was remembered again in March 1970 when D. Mason interviewed L. O.'B. Fleetwood-Smith who, of course, had good reason never to forget. He had been wheeling away with left-arm wrist spin from a distance of twenty-two yards for much of the two and a half days and had conceded nearly 300 runs for one wicket.

L. O.'B. Fleetwood-Smith

Fleetwood-Smith: . . . You woke up in the night time and your arm was still going around.

Mason: Tell me what was Hutton's innings like?

Fleetwood-Smith:	A marvellous exhibition of concentration, durability and stubbornness and proved the fact that he was so fit that he was still running short, sharp singles when he was over 300.
Mason:	Was it without blemish?
Fleetwood-Smith:	Without blemish, except one occasion when in the forties and getting towards 50 and I happened to spin one. I think the only one for the whole match and Hutton thought he was bowled and Barnett thought it had bowled him and he forgot to stump him and Len went back and he said, 'I'm not coming out again today,' and he didn't. I remember I said to him, 'Len, we'll break the monotony, I'll give you a couple of full tosses on the leg side and you hit 'em for four, liven it up, give us something to do like.' 'No,' he said, 'they might be trappin' that.' So he didn't do anything.

In 1952, after Hutton, as the first professional captain of the England team, had led his side to victory in the series against India, Howard Marshall presented this personal portrait for the BBC's General Overseas Service.

Len Hutton
Howard Marshall

When Len Hutton was chosen as England's captain against India, the sports writers made a lot of fuss about a professional leading England and the break with the tradition of having an amateur captain. In fact no one was surprised, and very few can have given the lost tradition more than a wistful thought.

Hutton was the obvious, the inevitable choice. He has been moving steadily towards this eminence ever since he was born thirty-six years ago at Pudsey in Yorkshire. There is, indeed, a quality of inevitability about Hutton – about his character, and the expression of that character in his batting. Hutton lives and works to a slowly conceived but unalterable plan. He builds his life, and his art – for batting of his quality is an art – steadily and quietly, stone by stone.

I was having a drink at Paddington station not long ago, and alongside me was a man taking a sandwich and a cup of tea: Len Hutton it was, with his wide jaw, his well-spaced blue eyes, his rather large, rather battered boxer's nose, his deliberate movements – and he looked up and saw me and smiled, a broad smile, showing strong teeth, a smile which brought out deep wrinkles round his eyes, the wrinkles of a man who laughs often – or perhaps of a man who spends many hours concentrating on the flight of a ball in bright sunshine.

We talked of this and that, cricketing talk, ordinary talk, for Hutton is not a man who gives much away in conversation. He talks hard sense, and deflects leading questions as if he were deflecting the spin, and but for that smile you might think him a shade dour, a shade dull and unforthcoming.

But the smile was there, warm and welcoming and kindly, the smile of a man sure of himself, and at peace in his own chosen world. It has been said that he is unemotional, calculating, and that cricket is a business to him. Well, so it is, to be sure, and when you are born and bred in Yorkshire you do not talk much about playing cricket for fun.

You can imagine the young Hutton – the stripling Hutton, for he was a rangy sort of colt when he was young – playing at the age of fourteen for the local club of Pudsey St Lawrence, and loving every moment of it, and round about then going one famous day to Leeds, the day when Bradman made 304 runs and struck despair into our hearts. And sitting in the great crowd there, young Hutton must have thought deeply – his mind projected into a world where cricket was not just a light-hearted game but a career, a way of life, a matter for concentrated attention. Not a thing to love: a thing to study, to master, as that little wiry, quicksilver genius Bradman had mastered it.

And so Hutton began to read all the books, applying himself to the business in hand as another man would apply himself to trigonometry, and certainly his professors, great Yorkshire players like George Hirst and Herbert Sutcliffe, were not surprised when Hutton scored his first century in a county match for Yorkshire at the age of eighteen – and no other player had ever been as precocious as that.

But perhaps precocious is not the right word: this was merely the inevitable pattern of his life taking shape. And it took shape in spite of setbacks – he was out for nought in the first innings he ever played for Yorkshire. He was out for nought and one in the first match he played for England – against New Zealand, that was.

Gradually, though, it dawned upon the connoisseurs that here was something more, much more, than another stolid Yorkshire opening batsman – here was potentially a master player. He might be a little constricted, perhaps, a little miserly in the spending of his powers. Here was none of the fiery gallantry of the young Hammond, for example, forcing glorious and daring runs from unwilling bowlers. No! This was a logician, taking runs, whenever the bowler faltered, by applying the basic principles.

There could be no doubt that both temperament and technique were there, and Hutton steadily took root in the England side until there came that day in 1938 when England and Australia met at the Oval in the experimental timeless Test. Hutton was then only twenty-two, and he looked rather worn and fragile, as if the strain of big cricket were telling upon him. Indeed, he had missed a season through illness in 1935, and so when Wally Hammond, captaining England, sent Hutton in to open the England innings on that blazing August day, and said, 'Now, Len, you stay there for ever,' he must have had some doubt in his mind about Hutton's power of endurance. Certainly he could never have guessed what was to come – an innings of 364 – the highest-ever in Test cricket, and it lasted for thirteen hours, twenty minutes: thirteen hours, twenty minutes of the fiercest concentration in sweltering heat against an Australian attack spearpointed by the great Bill O'Reilly.

I was privileged to describe almost every ball of that innings over the air. Even for a commentator it was something of an endurance test; what it must have been for Hutton out there in that broiling heat I cannot imagine. Hutton's feat in that great innings was a triumph not only of technique but of character and concentration.

Well, whatever happened to Hutton subsequently, nothing could take away the glory of that tremendous performance from him. And almost the next thing of importance that did happen to him was an accident in a gymnasium, when he was a PT instructor early in the war, an accident which caused him to have forty-six stitches put in his left arm – and that arm is now two inches shorter than the other.

An accident like that might easily have closed the cricketing career of lesser men, and we wondered how it would affect his batting. Hutton studied the problem calmly, and discovered that a light and unusually short-handled bat was the answer. It is true that after the war, when he resumed his full responsibilities for Yorkshire and England, there had to be some adjustments of technique – some recovery of full confidence. After such an injury anyone might be expected to shape a little warily against, say, the rasping bumpers of Keith Miller and Lindwall.

He was indeed left out of the England side in the third Test of 1948, and there were those who felt that he might never recover his full powers. Hutton shrugged his shoulders, and remarked that it was all in the game, and went steadily on reorganising his methods and regaining his confidence. Today, without doubt, he is recognised wherever cricket is played as the best, the most technically accomplished batsman in the world.

There is in his batsmanship none of the elemental violence of a Keith Miller, and yet he will hit a four off the back foot with such perfectly applied power that the fielding side have scarcely moved before a small boy is throwing the ball back from the boundary. He does not seize bowling by the scruff of the neck. He analyses it, and then destroys it by logic and reason. His methods are those of the ju-jitsu expert rather than the all-in wrestler. He catches his opponent off-balance, as it were, and sends him toppling down by his own momentum.

A great batsman, indeed, of the classical school, and now the first professional to captain England, and the proprietor of a flourishing sports outfitters' shop in Bradford. And I am not sure that the Bradford shop is not the clue to it all – the evidence of the planned life, the rock-steady background to achievement.

Hutton still lives in Pudsey with his wife and two sons. When, not long ago, he shared in a record-breaking partnership in South Africa, he rang up his wife in the evening, and his wife, on being asked what he had said about his new record, replied, 'Oh, he didn't say anything about that. He just said he was well, but rather homesick.'

Well, that for me ties up with his smile and his friendliness. I do not myself subscribe to the picture of a dour and unemotional Hutton. And I do not think we have yet seen the end of the development of his character. In Yorkshire they speak of Hutton affectionately as 'Our Len'. It may be that one day we shall all speak of him with similar possessive affection, as already we think of him with pride.

*   *   *

Before the unparalleled events at the Oval in 1938, the merits or not of timeless Tests had been exercising many cricketing minds. The first three Tests in the series that year had produced a stalemate, with draws at Trent Bridge and Lord's and a washout at Old Trafford. So in July a round-table discussion was aired with former Australian wicket-keeper 'Bertie' Oldfield, the Hampshire Secretary Alastair MacLeod, two one-time captains of England Arthur Gilligan and 'Archie' MacLaren, and an anonymous spectator giving their views. Howard Marshall was in the chair.

'This Test Match Business'

Marshall: What we are all of us really concerned about are these successions of draws which seem to take all the point out of Test matches. People come thousands of miles across the ocean to play cricket in this country – and these abortive and quite profitless draws are the result. We must all have strong opinions about those and I'm going to ask the people round the table here one after another to give us their views. And first of all, Mr Oldfield.

Oldfield: I am fully convinced that the present system of deciding the Ashes is anything but satisfactory. Personally, I don't think four days is sufficient in which to complete a match, particularly when we have two sides more or less evenly matched. Of course if rain interferes the game might be over in two days. But I think what would be interesting would be a reflection on the series of Test matches played between England and Australia in England since the war; and I think you will find that 1921 was the only time that the Ashes were decided before the final and last Test match. Of course, I think a great deal of that can be traced to the fact that Australia was an infinitely better team than England on that occasion – England was suffering from a lot of casualties during the war and she wasn't at her strongest. But since Test matches have been extended to four days (they were then three days), since 1920 to 1930, these matches have ended in a draw until the last Test match at the Oval, and I think the only way out of the trouble is to play these Test matches to a finish as they are in Australia. As far as I can find out, every Test match since 1877 has been played out in Australia. And it remains a puzzle to me, and I think most Australians, when we come to England, to find Test matches limited either to three days or, as at present, four days. I would say limit them with a proviso. As we just recently had an experience, incessant rain might make a complete washout – to six days in order that the counties' fixtures and programme can be arranged accordingly.

Marshall: Well, now what about a county's fixtures, Mr MacLeod?

MacLeod: From the county point of view, one has got to look at it from a financial point of view; and from that point I agree with a six-day Test match – four of them – and the last one played out to a finish; provided, too, that it is started on a Wednesday so that the counties are not upset more than is necessary; because it's very hard on a county – take a county like Gloucestershire, who have Barnett, perhaps, and Hammond away and even Sinfield, waiting to play in a Test match – to go on and carry out their ordinary county fixtures without these stars. It's very difficult for a county to carry on in that way because people will not come and watch them if their best players are not playing. That's merely from a financial point of view; but from my own personal point of view I should like to see the Test matches go back to three days. I think four days are no good at all, and neither one thing nor another; but in a three days' match, provided that the wickets are made natural again and not doped, you will get the batsmen playing – they'll have to play with skill and not just pat the ball when they feel like it – the bowlers will have a better chance of getting the batsmen out. I think that, provided these wickets are made natural, you would get a finish in three days.

Marshall: What has Mr Arthur Gililgan got to say about that?

Gilligan: Well now, I'm absolutely dead set in my mind about these Tests. I want to see six-day matches with a Saturday start. All the people I've spoken to lately agree with the view that these four-day matches are absolute washouts. A man I was talking to today told me that he had sold his tickets on the last day because he wasn't going to watch a drawn match. 'But', I said, 'supposing we'd had six days, what would have happened?' He said, 'Oh, I should have been there right up to the death; anything with excitement and a definite result I should have been there to see.'

Marshall: Now Mr MacLaren, what have you got to say about it?

MacLaren: I'm sorry to say I hold an opposite view to our friend Arthur, and I feel very much that the bowler has been very badly treated ever since the groundsman has taken to doping the wicket. That robs the bowler – I was going to say of fifty per cent of his skill. There is no life in the wicket – it's as dead as dead can be; the batsman has only got to keep his straight bat, the ball comes off slowly; if it turns it's just as easy to play a slow-turning ball as a straight one. I'd like to see a return to the natural wicket and shorter Test matches – the natural wickets where it forces the batsman to play a more lively game; I'd like to see these players today, especially on the Australian side, batting on the Lord's wicket as I knew it. It was always full of fire. I say the Australians because they play in their own country, naturally, a safer game than we do over here. I don't object to four days, but what I do object to is a very big change being made from four to six days when the bowlers have not yet been tested properly; the present-day bowlers have not had their wicket to bowl upon, and the batsmen are on top undoubtedly. But I don't put it down to the batting being any better than it used to be.

Marshall: That raises another point. What does the spectator go to see? Does he go to see really good batting; does he go to see wickets being taken? Well, we have got a spectator here, and I'm going to ask him what he thinks.

Spectator: I feel difficulty in giving my point of view with all these distinguished cricketers here; but the spectator has got a very definite point of view. Without him, Test matches would not exist, nor would county matches; and he goes to see, I think, good cricket, interesting cricket, and, if possible, exciting cricket. And he really does want to go and see a finish: there I agree with Gilligan. Just one thing, I think, rather worries us, and that is: if we are going to have these timeless Test matches – six-day Test matches – as Oldfield suggests, is that going to make the batting very slow?

Marshall: What do you think about that, Oldfield?

Oldfield: I don't see how it can possibly make the batting any slower at all. In Australia the matches played there are always interesting, and the wickets are always good; but if the wickets here in England are going to be made of the ordinary natural soil, you'll find that these Test matches won't last probably more than four or five days. In that case, I think, the public will be more satisfied to walk away from the ground feeling that England has had a good win – marvellous batting by Wally Hammond and perfect bowling by (shall we say?) O'Reilly – and, on the other hand, you will find them walking away when the match ends in a draw completely disgusted and disappointed.

Marshall: Well, this question of wickets does seem to me extraordinarily important, and Mr MacLaren has got a very long experience of wickets – perhaps he's got something to say about that.

MacLaren: The wickets today are totally different from what they were in the days when I played. The Oval wicket was, of course, always a good wicket; but I'm talking of the Oval wicket that hasn't been doped. I never remember playing on a doped wicket in my life. We always finished our Test matches in three days, partly because the game was played at a very much faster pace. You had, on the good batting wickets, the opening batsmen on both sides not playing the good-length ball but driving the good-length ball. There was no blind-length ball to the first four or five batsmen on either side.

Gilligan: But, Archie, doesn't that point to the standard of batting being better now? Don't you think the standard of batting is better if the match was finished in three days in your time, and it now takes four days to . . .

MacLaren: No, I do not!

Gilligan: You think they were better players?

MacLaren: On the other hand, when we first started we had to knock the ball out of the ground for six to begin with.

Oldfield: Yes, but you haven't got to go back to the pre-war Test matches to have them finished in three days. In 1921, at Nottingham, Armstrong's team beat England in two days. But then, I think, you'll agree the reason of that was not so much the wicket but the fact that Australia was infinitely superior. And then I think that if you get back to the matter of wickets, you will probably find these Test matches will finish in three days and four days, just the same as they did in 1921.

I think so far the main objection that I've heard about these Test matches being played to a finish in England was the strain placed on the players. Well, of course, I can't quite follow that. The strain of cricket in Australia is greater than that in England. Now take the Test matches played in Australia and let's only take last year when Gubby Allen brought a team to Australia. After very many failures in the early Sheffield Shield matches against slow bowling, England came out and won the two Test matches in Brisbane and Sydney – and what a blow to our prestige, because we had our good slow bowlers in. That was because the Englishmen adapted themselves to the bowling and the conditions and they won through. Here's the point that I want to bring up: the interest in the public never lagged in Australia because those Test matches were played to a finish. Now, you take conditions here; there are five matches to be played and there's only one out of the five that the authorities have agreed to be played to a finish. In fact, do you know where we stand after the fourth Test match is played?

Gilligan: The whole thing is this: you say there's too much reliance placed on the last match; really you can have four drawn games and then the last match may be won with the toss of the coin with wet weather about. You can say England won the toss and bats for two days; and it rains during the weekend and Australia have to go in and bat on a sticky wicket and are outed, or if you like to have it your way,

Australia wins the toss and England are outed twice. I mean, isn't too much being placed on that last Test?

Oldfield: I think far too much is being placed on the elements. We can't legislate for the weather.

Gilligan: Well, Archie, having been to Australia and played Test matches there, I think you agree that Test matches should be played to a finish here.

MacLaren: Up to a point only, because I feel certain that the batting today is not as brisk as it used to be.

Marshall: We must get down to causes; if we say that it's all deteriorated, why is it? One side is saying we must have time-limitless Test matches and we must accept modern conditions and modern wickets, and we must extend the matches; the other side says there is something wrong, but doesn't say why it's wrong, and what would be the effect if that were put right.

Gilligan: Don't you think that in 1958 they'll be decrying their cricket then and saying the bowling is not as good as it was twenty years ago? Now we're all saying, in 1938, the bowling's rotten, the fielding's rotten, and the batting's not so good. Time eliminates everything. You forget bad bowling sins. You take the great bowlers of the past: they've had their bad spells the same as the present-day bowlers.

Marshall: Well, let me sum up very briefly. We've got rather a balance of power here. We have got Mr Oldfield very definitely in favour of six-day Test matches; with his experience of Australian conditions and realising the greater strain in Australia, he thinks there would be less strain here and we could play them quite happily to a finish and get a result – and that's what he's out for. There's Mr Gilligan says exactly the same thing; and he says that everything should be sacrificed to Test matches – County cricket and everything – they are the main interest. And then there's Mr MacLaren who says that four days should be enough – wickets should be made natural, as the present low standard has arisen partly from this effect of wickets, and that timeless Tests mean slow batting and dreary cricket. There's a County Secretary who says that from the financial point of view he thinks that these timeless Tests will of course be valuable, provided they start on Wednesdays – but that personally he would like to see natural wickets back again and Test matches reduced to three days. The spectator says he would like definitely to have a finish – he'd rather have five days instead of four – spectators would rather see runs than bowling; he doesn't like county matches used as practices by Test teams, and in fact he's all out for some real cricket which gives him value for his money. But what we're all quite decided upon is that we want a finish in these Test matches, and we hope the authorities will give the matter some sort of attention.

As a postscript to that discussion, it is revealing to read 'The Spoken Word' by Hugh Gray in the Listener *for 1 September 1938.*

I never thought I should hear complaints about a broadcast of a Test match. I never dreamt I should be bored by one myself. But there we are, the unexpected happened with the last Test. For dreary hour after hour it went on . . . that is if you bothered to listen. 'O'Reilly is going up to bowl. He's turned now. He's starting to run. He's running. He's bowled. A good length. Leyland is taking no risks. He plays it carefully back to the bowler. No run.' In other words timeless Tests have raised not only a cricket problem but a broadcasting problem too. I doubt if any commentator in the world could have stood the strain and it is not Howard Marshall's fault that I don't want to hear that low-pitched sonority of his again for a long time.

*   *   *

The benefit of hindsight is only useful if we are willing to learn from history. The predictions of Neville Cardus, based on a recent visit to Australia and uttered before the 1938 season had really got under way, can therefore be illuminating for those who will assess next season's tourists.

Cricket in Australia
Neville Cardus

Northern Programme, May 1938
It is well known that in Australia every little boy is either a potential Bradman or a potential O'Reilly. The population of the country is less than London's, yet Australia goes on year after year producing cricketers as good

as our best – not to say greater. I decided last winter to visit Australia for health reasons – and also to take a few notes. I had seen Australia during the visit of an English team; I had seen the entire nation organised for Test matches – all work abandoned for the day. But I wanted to see how Australia prepared for war – I mean for a Test match season, so I went back last December to observe matters in an ordinary Australian cricket season. I was in the country two months at the height of the summer. I stayed in Sydney and Melbourne, two of the chief centres of cricket in Australia. And in those two months I did not see a single first-class match for the simple reason that not a single first-class match was played in the whole of Australia during that time.

If I were to write a history of cricket in Australia I should imitate the famous history of snakes in Ireland – 'There is no cricket in Australia.' Here is a paradox. Australia is crazy about cricket; the nation has a natural genius for cricket. But more first-class matches are played in England in a week than in Australia in a long season which stretches from October to April. There are only four first-class teams in Australia – New South Wales, Victoria, South Australia and Queensland. An Australian first-class season consists of only a dozen games. Australia has to pick a Test match team from less than fifty players – for Queensland is seldom in the running as a nursery of international cricketers. There are no professional first-class players in Australia – Bradman's earnings out of first-class cricket in an Australian season are nothing exactly – yet he draws thousands to the inter-state matches.

In England our first-class cricket is organised elaborately. We play every day from May to September. Some two hundred or three hundred men devote their lives to cricket, making a trade or craft of it. And at our schools the game is taught by professional coaches. There is next to no coaching in Australia. Another curious fact is that there is no mid-week cricket in Australia, and little or no net practice – because it is dark in Australia on summer evenings at seven o'clock. Australia's genius in cricket, her consistent mastery and power to challenge the best of ours, is based entirely on Saturday afternoon cricket. Bradman and O'Reilly, in an ordinary Australian season, are Saturday afternoon cricketers, exactly as Horace Blenkinsop is a Saturday afternoon cricketer for Teddington; or Bill Muggridge is a Saturday afternoon cricketer for Toad-in-the-Hollow.

The secret is an efficient tradition, a lovely climate, and a passion for the technique such as we rarely find amongst club players in England. Australians take to the game much as Viennese and Hungarian children take to the violin. The smallest boy in Australia knows, or seems to know, how to handle a bat. I have never yet met a grown Australian who at some time or other has not played fairly good cricket.

The team now visiting us is, like all Australian cricket teams, the cream of the cream. There is no skim-milk in Australian first-class company. Two or three men have been left at home who, I am certain, would walk into any

English county – for instance, Ebeling, who is a superb bowler with the new ball – and Rigg, one of the soundest and prettiest batsmen I have seen for years. It is an error to say that the present Australian team is merely a case of Bradman and ten others. Without Bradman, the present team would probably go near winning a rubber against an English team that was without Hammond. Eight of the Australians are new to us, and I would like to say something about them tonight – Bradman, McCabe and the other familiar names have received plenty of advertisement . . . I expect much from Hassett on good wickets – and I don't mean merely runs but pretty runs, stylish batsmanship. It is a tendency of the present age that most discussions of cricketers and athletes in general begin and end with reference to their abilities to bring about results; we see them merely as cogs in machines designed to win – win – win. But a national game is not only a competitive affair – if results were everything, well, why not play all our rubbers at tiddly-winks, or with brickbats at forty paces? Cricket, especially, depends on an attractive and stylish technique. No player has ever made a lasting reputation in the game unless he has contributed charm and personality as well as made vast runs and taken endless wickets.

Now Hassett in good form is a batsman who would delight us if we were sitting where we could not see the scoreboard – or even if we did not know the way a cricket match is won and lost. He uses his feet daintily, and his bat is quick and fluent, with a strength which never becomes excessive or vulgarly violent. Nearly all Australian batsmen are stroke-players; the perfect wickets of Australia encourage players to hit the ball cleanly and with relish. Even the poorest schoolboy can learn to bat on a smooth pitch in Australia. The concrete wickets there are admirable, and they should be municipally supported or endowed in this country. I don't know how the idea got about that Australians are usually slow batsmen. Probably because Collins once batted all day at Old Trafford for forty or thereabouts. But Collins on that occasion was saving the game – and, in any case, perhaps he thought something of the kind was expected of him at Old Trafford. Only three times in the history of Test matches between England and Australia has a batsman scored a century before lunch on the first day – and each time this bold and brilliant deed has been done by an Australian – Victor Trumper, Macartney and Bradman. When I was in Australia a few weeks ago, I heard quite a lot of doubt expressed about Fingleton's claim to a place in the team. The objection against him was that he often scored slowly and did not use his strokes. In England, I am sorry to say, we often discourage a young batsman because of his strokes. 'Ah,' he is told, 'you might get out; you must not drive or cut until you've been in several hours.' I don't think that Gimblett of Somerset would have been neglected for so long in Test cricket if he had been an Australian.

One of the first things I noticed in ordinary club matches in Australia was the popularity of the hook amongst batsmen. At the first sight of a short ball, the youngest baby strikes the attitude necessary for the performance of the hook. Badcock is brilliant with this dramatic hit. He is, I think, the most dangerous and the most personal of the newcomers. In Australia, he has played innings almost as good as anything done by Bradman, for audacity and power of stroke-play. Against Allen's team he was unfortunate to get caught on bad wickets at Brisbane and Sydney – he was dropped for the games at Melbourne and Adelaide. Then he was brought back for the decisive rubber game at Melbourne. And though he was playing not only for Australia in a critical engagement, but was playing also for his English tour – a terrific honour for an Australian – he went in and cut and hooked the English bowlers right and left and played one of the most brilliant innings I have ever seen in a Test match. Badcock is not much more than a boy yet. He may have to adjust his methods to slower English turf – though, as a matter of fact, Badcock learned his cricket in Tasmania, where the weather and the wickets are almost English in their variability. He is certain to score a lot of runs here – and he will be popular, for he is a most lovable boy, a Patsy Hendren in the making.

Fingleton is Woodfull's successor. He has more than Woodfull's strokes and all of Woodfull's patience and barn-door defence. Like Woodfull, he uses a short, almost imperceptible, lift-up of the bat – he seems to be expecting shooters every ball. But he can hit, by a sudden last-minute push or thrust. His footwork is even pretty – if you saw a film showing Fingleton's feet only you might easily think a great and free stroke-player was at the wicket. Like most Australians, he plays every ball as though it were his first ball – I mean that his concentration is enormous. Australians do not play cricket every day as a rule – and so their minds do not tire easily. Bradman watches the ball as keenly when he is 200 as he does when he is receiving his first ball. And if Bradman hits five fours from five loose balls after he has made 200 he will play the sixth as vigilantly as if it were his first – if it is a good ball. That is Bradman's secret, that and his ability to get close to the best ball. The whole secret of batting is to get over the ball – Bradman even seems to get behind it. His bat has cat's whiskers. He is perhaps a greater player today than ever he was. He can score 100 an hour *with restraint*. He scored 100 in sixty-five minutes at Worcester the other day, and none of us guessed he was travelling half as fast as all that.

I am sorry about the accident to Barnes – he is a daring and dashing batsman – a typical young Sydney man. [*Barnes fractured a wrist-bone playing deck games on his journey to England.*]

The bowling of the team will depend heavily on O'Reilly and Fleetwood-Smith. McCormick has already made himself famous by his orgy of no-balls, the other day. This was an unhappy experience for a fast bowler. No more terrible fate could befall a fast bowler than a mess-up in his run to the wicket. I believe that McCormick had some difficulty with his run in Australia quite recently. He takes a long run, and critics have said it was unnecessarily long and likely to wear him out in a day-by-day English season. I hope McCormick will go on bowling in his own way, no matter how long his run. At his best he is very fast for spells of half an hour or so – he can achieve a pace as fast as any I have seen recently. He has left Bradman standing and knocked the great man's leg stump flying. And he is one of the most charming cricketers I have ever met . . . I should not be at all surprised if Waite did not some day take a few startling and quick wickets in a Test match while the ball is new – he can swing from leg with a most disconcerting speed and zip from the ground. Ward is in a different class – he is potentially a great spin bowler. He can turn the ball prodigiously from leg and he has an action nearly as low as Grimmett's. Also, he understands the value of flight. But I doubt if Bradman will call upon Fleetwood-Smith *and* Ward in the same Test match. Two leg and googly bowlers are a luxury and likely to get in one another's way. White is a more than useful left-hander or embryo Verity.

The responsibility resting in O'Reilly is rather tremendous. Grimmett will be missed by him surely. But O'Reilly is a great worker. Remember how, at Old Trafford in 1934, he bowled all day in heat as terrible in its humidity as Brisbane's. I find O'Reilly a most interesting bowler to watch. His technique includes every ball of a great medium-paced bowler – the quick spinner from leg stump to off, the usual off-break – the usual variations of speed and length. But also he commands the googly which is rare in a bowler of his style – a style noted for its accuracy and normality. The googly belongs to the freak bowler – but O'Reilly follows in the traditional line of length bowlers. I have seen O'Reilly keeping Bradman quiet and bitterly on the defence for an hour or so – without a man in the outfield. O'Reilly has a temperament which is whipped up by the occasion. I have known him bowl with utter lack of hope and purpose – a mere toiler under the sun. Suddenly he has taken a wicket and then, you saw the man's tail stand up, and the whole of his being kindle to hostility. I fancy that O'Reilly will reserve himself for the big matches – and rightly so. He is as important to the Australian team as Bradman himself – perhaps even more so.

I should like to say a word about Barnett. Most of us were surprised when Oldfield was passed over. Well, Oldfield is still a great wicket-keeper. And as the Australians are always realists, we can conclude that Barnett would not have been given his chance if he had not put forward clinching qualifications. Barnett, like Oldfield, is a quiet gentlemanly wicket-keeper – his appeals are requests to the umpire, not challenges and intimidations. He does his work with a swift, ruthless politeness. The whole team, indeed, is quiet and gentlemanly – and determined to give us a thoroughly delightful defeat in the rubber, if they get half a chance.

*   *   *

Three weeks after the dissertation by Cardus on Cricket in Australia, Frank Gerald gave a fifteen-minute talk for 'I Was There' on 'The First Team from Australia, 1868'. Gerald was something of a character and Radio Times *printed a potted biography:*

That fine old sportsman Frank Gerald, author of A Millionaire in Memories *must be one of the oldest actors still in active service, for he made his first professional appearance in 1868. He saw fourteen Grand Nationals in succession, rode over the Grand National course when he was sixteen and was tipped a 50-1 winner by Nat Gould at the Chester races.*

There is little that he has not done in his adventurous life. In 1879 he played Association Football for Wales against Scotland on the Wrexham racecourse, and three years later in Auckland played for New Zealand at rugby. He has acted in as many as fourteen Shakespearian roles in one week for the salary of £1 and once took part in a show at the bottom of a silver mine. In 1882, at Timaru, he had a friendly bout with Jem Mace and put the gloves on in real earnest with a boy whose name – Bob Fitzsimmons – was to become famous.

Broadcaster Moray McLaren described the human side:

This is a pertinacious old fellow, who is well in his eighties but is an extraordinarily lively old boy with a clear blue eye and firm speech and looks very like Thomas Hardy. He has travelled all over the world and has now settled down to the task of being a professional octogenarian.

The First Team from Australia
Frank Gerald

National Programme, May 1938

Nine days ago when the Australians were playing Surrey at the Oval and I was watching the match, I got lost in thought and found myself dreaming of other matches I had seen on that same ground. It was a very different Oval that was pictured in my mind, as I sat there not noticing the interval, and very different players that took the field. We had driven on to the ground in a wagonette and pair, through a wooden gate, where the Hobbs gateway now stands, and a post and rail fence ran round the ground. My memory had carried me back just seventy years! Seventy years marked out by great matches I have seen, great players I have known, famous partnerships I remember, big scores I have watched grow bigger and bigger. Indeed, the way back is so plain because either here at home or out in Australia, I have seen almost every Test team. I may have missed two: I know Majuba Hill kept me in South Africa in 1881. But what made me stay in my seat and miss my lunch was the strange coincidence, that seventy years ago Australians were doing exactly the same thing – playing Surrey at the Oval, and I a boy of thirteen, a young cricket enthusiast, was watching them. And what makes the occasion more memorable still is that this was the first match played in England by a team of cricketers from Australia. The match was played on Monday and Tuesday 25 and 26 May 1868. And now it is 1938, and, the Good Lord be thanked, I am still 'watching'!

As far back as 1856, 1862 and 1864, the great professional cricketers of their time sent teams to Australia. With the 1856 team a Surrey groundsman, Charles Lawrence, went. Lawrence did not return with the team, but tried his luck at the goldfields; luck did not come his way, so he tried his hand at cricket again, and in conjunction with a Mr Cousins, also a cricketer, got together a number of Aborigines, knockabouts and hangers-on round the 'diggings' and up-country camps. Cousins and Lawrence found these 'blacks' apt pupils: the Australian Aborigine will learn games, and play games, all day and every day – but work? Well, that is a different matter.

An uncle of mine, who had been out in the Ballarat Rush, took a great interest in this team of Aborigines, and drove a party of us over from Worcester Park to see the match at the Oval. Lawrence lost the toss and led his team of little black fellows on the ground. A crowd of ten thousand gave them a great welcome. The visitors barely understood this and were rather scared, but when their captain explained they joined in and cheered and clapped themselves. This was part of the game and they started! The Australian Aborigine doesn't grow up, he is always a child: he loves play, he will play any game, however childish, all day long. They chased each other round the ground, twisting and turning and dodging until their captain blew his whistle, and then those black boys were soon lying panting on the ground around him. Talk about 'brighter cricket' – their cricket was never dull, there wasn't a dull moment in it!

Then the names these black fellows answered to were as quaint as the players themselves, and read funnily on the score-sheets and in the newspapers; here are some of them: Charley Dumas, Squeeter, Tiger, Mullagh, Red Cap, King Cole, Rover, Bullicky, Dick-a-Dick, Twopenny! The Surrey team included Mr Baggaly, who made sixty-eight, top score. He was stumped by Bullicky – a good keeper of the wicket, who scorned gloves and pads. Other members of the XI were Messrs Boultbee, Calvert, Miller and J. D. Walker whose 'lobs' left the blacks 'guessing'.

The Surrey batsmen appeared and the game started. Those black boys became so many ebony statuettes, studded about the ground in the queerest attitudes, silent as the grave until a ball was bowled – then pandemonium broke out; those silent statues one and all sprang suddenly to life, and not until the bowler had the ball again did they lapse back into silence.

I think our visitors from Australia showed up better in the field than at either batting or bowling. They seldom missed a catch; they didn't use pads or gloves and they played barefooted. They could throw the ball any distance, and with wonderful accuracy – dead on to the wicket every time. Their outfielding was a feature. Probably the Australian Aborigine is the fastest runner in the world – remember Harry Samuels, an Aborigine, beat our famous World Champion sprinter, Harry Hutchins, on the Sir Joseph Banks running grounds at Sydney about 1884–5, and I hardly think Clem Hill or even Don Bradman himself could cover the distance to save a boundary Dick-a-Dick could.

Their running between the wickets was a sight to see and *hear*. They tore up and down the pitch, screaming their native backchat at one another, while the rest of them, gathered round the scoring tent, broke into a wild corroboree. The match lasted two days and ended in a victory for Surrey by an innings: 222 against 83 and 132.

Financially, the venture was a great success: crowds came to see these little black fellows play cricket. Their tour lasted from May until October. In all they played forty-seven matches against many counties and most of the big cities and districts. They lost their opening match, but they beat Middlesex on the old Islington ground. In addition to the Oval match, I saw them win against Manchester and district at Longsight and against Liverpool and district on the Bootle ground.

On this latter ground, on the third day, they ran races – sprints and hurdles, and gave an exhibition of native games, including throwing the boomerang: this drew an enormous crowd, and, as it turned out, the public got plenty of excitement for their money. When the time for the boomerang throwing arrived, the ground was cleared, not even an official or a groundsman was allowed inside the rails. All round the field of play every inch of space was occupied, there wasn't a vacant seat on the stands, and even the roof was packed. The band stopped playing and from the Pavilion a solitary and curious figure strode out alone. To the very centre of the ground he came, and there he squatted and looked around while the crowd cheered. From head to foot he was wrapped in his blanket, and only his big head of bushy black hair, whiskers and beard, and his big flat feet could be seen. Then the blanket fell to the ground, the little man, erect upon his feet, threw back his head, as if sniffing the air – the boomerang in his hand – the next instant, without an effort on the thrower's part, the boomerang went whirling into the air! It rose high over the crowds, it circled far above the dense throng on the stands and, after completing its voyage round the field of play, came back to earth only a few yards from where its thrower stood motionless. The crowd roared themselves hoarse with cheering. An encore throw was promptly given and even a third was asked for. The third time is not always the lucky time. The Bootle cricket ground was not far from the river and was rather exposed; it was late in the afternoon, and the wind was rising. The boomerang rose into the air, but when it was whirling over the stand a sudden gust of wind stopped it in its flight; for a moment, like a gull battling against a gale, it hung there, and then swooped down and buried itself among the terrified crowd on the roof! A panic was narrowly averted but, strange to say, little harm was done. Those were the days of the bustle and the chignon; the boomerang struck a lady on the head; luckily she was wearing an 'outsize' in chignons and that saved her – even a hideous fashion has its uses!

Such were the pioneers of cricket from Australia, and perhaps there was a certain amount of poetic justice in the fact that these pioneers were the natives of the soil. In the case of New Zealand it was the same: a team of Maori footballers, many of whom played barefooted, were our first sportsmen-invaders.

Time passed, a short nine years, and cricket history had been made; there was a different tale to tell. On the Melbourne ground in 1877, Australia beat All England (Lillywhite's team) by 45 runs. This victory may be taken as the start of what is now known as Test cricket, and the next year, 1878, D. H. Gregory's XI, under the guidance of genial Jack Conway, came home to meet England on even terms. In their first match they were badly beaten at Nottingham, but a few days later, Australia gained her first victory in England by decisively beating the MCC at Lord's. This victory set the seal of success upon the tour, and the prestige of Australia was established. The first 'Test' played in England at the Oval, on 6, 7 and 8 September 1880, was won by England, but two years later on the same ground Australia won a breathless victory by 7 runs!

And so, through the ages, the grand game has been lost and won. Fortune has swayed this way and that, but the scales have been evenly balanced, and the net result to date gives Australia but a slight lead. And the hours that I have spent watching it, and the memories of it that I have gathered and treasured, are among the happiest of my life.

And now, another season has started, the Australians are here again and excitement is in the air! The sequence of matches between us, though slightly varied, has never been broken; the interest aroused has increased a hundredfold; it is a bond of sport and friendship that binds us together, and as an international sporting event it is unrivalled and unchallenged. So let me wish success to the great game and to those who play it. I hope to see this season's Tests, they may be my last – well, I have had a good innings. I have seen cricket, and on and off the field I have tried to play it!

*　　　*　　　*

'Percy' Fender, the inspirational ex-Surrey captain and England player and co-holder of the fastest first-class century (by the clock) in cricket history, became a recognisable 'cricket voice' of the late 1930s. His summaries at the end of the Ten o'clock News showed the same effervescent flair and style that had been displayed so frequently on the field. Fender recorded his opinion of events in the third Test match between Australia and England in January 1937 at Melbourne for the National and Regional programmes. Australia had an advantage of 124 runs on the first innings (England being skittled out for 76) and by the end of the fourth day were on their way to a massive second innings total.

Australia v. England, Third Test Match, 1937
Percy Fender

No, no, no. I can't bear any more questions tonight. I don't know how many Australia are going to make and I don't know how many Bradman is going to make. I – well, I've got a headache frankly. I don't know whether that headache is due to the cricket or some other cause, but anyway, I've got one.

Today's performance has been a wonderful one. Bradman and Fingleton put up a magnificent performance in consolidating the position which Australia had earned for themselves overnight. There is no question about it. It is almost, if not quite, an unassailable one. I rather think that Australia will go on batting right through. That is their way, you know, in cricket in Australia. They don't take any chances if they can help it and in this situation there is no possible reason why they should take any chances because, after all, if rain comes at any time they can always declare now with absolute safety. It is just the same sort of position as Chapman had in Brisbane in 1929 when he batted again instead of making the Australians follow on and eventually left them 742 to win.

I rather feel that they will just go on and probably try and run up a record total, a record win if they can, and in fact deal with any records that are available.

Now the wicket of course – I am very surprised at the way in which the wicket played yesterday. From all accounts it played extremely well and I didn't anticipate that that would be the case. One cannot therefore say very much about the future, and if there is a good wicket for England to bat on, that will be something for them and they should take advantage of it, I hope. England has had three consolations today really: Ames's wicket-keeping – all accounts of his work have been very, very good indeed: Verity's bowling

– forty-five English overs for seventy-five runs is a very big performance, especially when a man like Bradman is batting the other end – a very fine performance; and the fielding, they have stuck to it very, very well indeed. One hears praise of the English fielding during yesterday all the way through – and it must have been a very heart-breaking job for them.

Allen's big job now is to make the best of a bad job and keep his fellows going, as I am sure he will do; keep their spirits up and place them in as good a position as he can to make the best of a situation; and the best they can make of it now, really, is that they shall have as much batting practice as ever is possible against the Australian bowlers, and particularly Fleetwood-Smith.

Wednesday 6 January (fifth day)

Did I hear you say 'certain defeat'? I think I'd like to put the word 'almost' in between 'will' and 'certain', because you know nothing about cricket is certain until the last ball has been bowled and, if I may say so, no one knows this better than the Australians. That is why they batted through, as I expected that they would, and that was why, for instance, in the second Test at Sydney, I was one of those who suggested that Allen should have batted again rather than take the chance of seeing Australia make enough runs in their second innings to leave England some to get. You must never take a chance playing cricket in Australia if you have a certainty in front of you.

Now today's play illustrates to my mind the one drawback of Australian cricket. To all intents and purposes the result was a foregone conclusion and that so early that really and truly there is very little comment that one can make on the play itself. You know the thrills of the game in Australia are not apparent to everybody in this country. They talk about the boredom of 180 runs scored in a day and so on, but I can assure you – I have watched it and I have played it out there – I can assure you that the thrill of a day's cricket in Australia is at least as great as that which we get from any single day's cricket in this country, and I am not forgetting the thrill of trying to get runs against time, or trying to get the last fellow out against time. In this connection there is no question of time, so there is no question of our fellows trying to put up a stout, hearty defence and get away with it towards the end. That, to my mind, is the one big drawback of Australian cricket.

Well, as for the rest, we can only regret that our batsmen have not taken a little bit better advantage of the opportunity offered to have a little practice, and match practice in the middle at that, against the Australian bowlers. But we have got the fourth and fifth Test matches to look forward to.

Australia had won by 365 runs, Bradman had made 270 in the second innings and the match had attracted over 350,000 spectators, a record for any cricket match. Fender conducted the post-mortem in an optimistic frame of mind.

Thursday 7 January

Well, I am afraid as to the future I don't pretend in any way to be a prophet. Really and truly we can only look at the future today in the light of recent experience. Now I spoke the other day of three consolations which were quite visible to the English side in their then probable defeat, and I think that England's second innings have provided us with a fourth, because Leyland's innings was one which must be outstanding in the circumstances.

Of course some of us can remember that Leyland made his first 100 in a Test match against Australia in Australia on this same ground at Melbourne in the fifth Test in 1929 for Chapman's side, and doubtless he has got a friendly feeling for that ground. I only hope he will make a good many more 100s on that ground for us.

Personally, in this not very terrible defeat, I see nothing whatsoever that should disturb us. One thing stands out and that is that neither side has a sufficient superiority of cricket power to beat its opposite number when its opposite number has the benefit of the conditions; that is to say that, if rain comes in, neither side has the ability to face it and win through in spite of it. I must say it would be a most attractive affair if we could in this series see one match at least played out under conditions which were constant all the way through. There doesn't seem to be a great deal between the two sides and it would be a pity – one can't help saying it – no matter who wins, it would be a pity if this rubber should be decided really on rain and practically nothing else, because, as I say, I don't think either side can, if the luck in the rain sense goes against it, I don't think either side can win through.

Now I rather feel that perhaps Allen may make two, possibly three changes for the Adelaide match, and I don't think at Adelaide Australia will be able to go into the field without a fast bowler, so that we shall have a different set of men to look at and deal with; and providing the weather conditions remain constant and the wicket is the same all the way through, I feel, as I did before this match started, that it is just a shade at present in favour of England.

Unfortunately for English cricket-lovers, Fender's confidence was misplaced. Australia won both the fourth and fifth Tests comprehensively, with Bradman scoring a double century and century in consecutive innings.

*   *   *

Three months earlier, on 12 October 1936, Fender had broadcast more poignant news.

B. J. T. Bosanquet – An Appreciation
Percy Fender

Bernard James Tindal Bosanquet passed over today; and a short while ago – actually, to be exact, only last Saturday week – I was playing golf in his company.

'Bose' was the first man to bowl that type of ball which in Australia is still called the 'Bosey' and in this country is called the 'googly' – a ball which turns from the off, although delivered with a leg-break action. He, in his day, called from the newspapers the same type of headlines as did a more recent controversy: they said of his bowling that it was spoiling the spectacle of cricket because no batsman could be expected to make those grand cover strokes which are the glory of the game if they could not tell which way the ball was going to turn.

'Bose' was also a hitter – a good hitter on occasion; but his name will really be more connected with his bowling. He played for Middlesex more or less regularly from 1900 to 1908, and on certain other occasions for England in Australia in 1903, and in England in 1905 he contributed largely to the winning of the Test matches by England. He was one of the very few hitters to score 200 in one innings and two separate 100s more than once in a match.

'Bose' has left his indelible mark on the greatest of all games that this country knows. What greater thing can any *cricketer* wish?

*   *   *

The first time any cricket commentator went from England to report from the front, as it were, was when 'Jim' Swanton took the boat to South Africa for the winter tour by Wally Hammond's MCC side in 1938-9. Incidentally, it was also the first time cricket had been broadcast on a regular basis in South Africa. When reminded of this tour recently, Swanton commented, 'This was my first visit before the asperities and inhumanities of apartheid had begun to bite – at least so far as a young visitor was concerned. Later, of course, the atmosphere was quite different.'

With the MCC in South Africa

E. W. Swanton

When I joined the MCC they had played six first-class matches, against most of the South African provinces, and they were waiting for the first Test, which began at Johannesburg on Christmas Eve. Actually just about a third of the tour was over but of course the most momentous part lay ahead of us.

Those first days of mine were really very hectic. Over Christmas we had the first Test. Then the morning after it was over both teams got into the train and swirled away in the dust down to the Cape. And the second Test (over the New Year) began the day after we arrived. The night that was finished off we went again, this time to Port Elizabeth. There are two ways to get to Port Elizabeth. One is through what they call the Garden Route across the rich Cape farming country away to the East Coast. The second way, the railway takes you right up into the Karroo again (that's the semi-desert stretching away towards Griqualand and the Free State), before you bear sharp right. That way you describe two sides of a triangle – and that, of course, was the way we had to go because the direct trains didn't fit in. As far as I remember we could have gone by the Garden Route if the match had ended on the third afternoon. But we never had very high hopes of that and, in point of fact, by then I don't believe the first South African wicket had fallen in their first innings.

I remember our Port Elizabeth visit pretty well and I'm going just to sketch that visit very briefly because it gives a fair cross-section of the tour. To start with, of course, the Mayor was at Port Elizabeth station. But he was a very considerate Mayor; he realised it was 7.30 in the morning and that we'd been thirty-six hours in the train and, God bless him, he just shook hands with Wally Hammond and the managers and reminded us we'd be meeting again at lunch. Well, we went off to our hotel and had a bath and breakfast, and when we'd done that there were plenty of very kind people anxious to take us to play golf. Luckily for me, I knew how good the Humewood links were – as a matter of fact I had heard from the designer – an Englishman who has made some very excellent courses in this country – all about how he had constructed this magnificent course out of bush five or six feet high, plunging about on horseback armed with a bell with which he used to tell his assistants where he was. Humewood reminds you of Sandwich – or Deal – and it has what I rather think is a very unusual distinction; you can see the sea from every single hole. In my opinion it's one of the world's courses, and I personally spent every minute I could on it.

In due course we had our mayoral lunch, and a lot of Scotch jokes from the Scots mayor. It was one of the things I noticed – that if a man had been born in Scotland, no matter if he had been fifty years in South Africa, he spoke with a Scots accent – in fact some of them must have become broader and broader as they went on.

Talking of mayors, by the way, there was one who put up a very good turn. He very kindly gave a big cocktail party in honour of the team. He got on to his hind legs and said how happy he was to welcome the MCC team and particularly their distinguished Captain Mr . . . ('What was your name again?') . . . Mr Hammond!

After the Port Elizabeth mayor had finished, the obvious thing to do seemed to be to bathe. All round the coast you get the most excellent surf-bathing and Port Elizabeth was just as good as anywhere else. When we'd finished bathing, my particular host asked me whether I'd like to have a look at the cricket ground. Of course I said yes, and when we got there some time after tea we found Len Hutton having some net practice, and he had bowling to him the oddest collection I have ever seen on a cricket field. Old men in braces, young boys in shorts, Indians and some Malays, including one rather elderly one with what I took to be a very doubtful action who (after they had been going well over an hour) claimed the shilling that Len had put on his stumps. Somehow or other he had managed to 'Play on'. Genius is said to consist of an infinite capacity for taking pains – I remembered that the great W. G. Grace always used to begin strenuous practice somewhere round the middle of March. Len Hutton made 200 the following day.

Over the weekend we had a dance, more golf at Humewood, a very gay Sunday evening supper party with a lot of rowing gentlemen in scarlet coats from a place called Swartkops, and then we went by road, through Grahamstown (where I was lucky just to take a brief view of St Andrew's where so many famous Oxford and Springbok rugger players have come from), to our next port of call, East London.

It was not a terribly strenuous tour. There was always just the one match every weekend and, according to how far off the next match was, one had leisure to enjoy the sort of hospitality I have described at Port Elizabeth. The heat wasn't really tiresome either. The hottest day I remember was at Victoria Falls, where it was ninety-nine in the shade, but we were not up there for cricket. There was one real scorcher at Pietermaritzburg, but at Durban (where it can be stifling) we were lucky and there was always a bit of wind in the final Test to make our visit easier.

The MCC played eighteen matches altogether: they won nine of them including the only Test that was completed, and drew nine. Not only weren't they beaten, but there were only two occasions when things looked really awkward for them. In the fourth Test at Johannesburg I think they probably would have lost if the third day's play had not been rained-off and of course we all thought they were a beaten side when South Africa set them 696 to win in the fifth Test at Durban.

I'm not sure that on those easy pitches the MCC always *batted* as excitingly as they might have done, but they certainly were a great draw everywhere (so that the SACA made a profit which will be very useful to them in developing the game there), and their fielding alone was worth going a long way to see. But you needn't be with an English team long on tour to realise how much more important than anything else is the reaction they cause off the field. And here the MCC really came out with flying colours. There were men like Bryan Valentine, who outside cricket hours would play anyone at any conceivable game they liked – he's a scratch golfer, well up in the tournament class at lawn tennis and squash – Norman Yardley and Hugh Bartlett, two young Cambridge captains of wide accomplishments outside their cricket – who've left an enormous number of friends behind them. As for Wally Hammond, the captain: in the personal control of his team off the field as well as on it, if I may say so, he did splendidly. While in the background all the time was the manager – Flight Lieutenant A. J. Holmes – keeping things running smoothly and winning for the MCC a general reputation for courtesy as well as for good sportsmanship. I'm sure everyone in the team will look back on those six months as among the happiest they have ever spent, and one really did feel, wherever one went, that the team was genuinely popular.

The average South African is keener about rugby football than about cricket: almost anyone you meet will talk about the technique of rugger as eagerly as he'll discuss politics. Cricket is not his national game. Yet I'm sure that as a result of this tour, cricket has gained a lot of ground. Take my own case. I went out to do twenty broadcasts for the South African Broadcasting Corporation. By the end I'd done over two hundred – so that some of my rather ruder friends out there said they couldn't switch on their wirelesses during the Tests without hearing how Verity had bowled another maiden to Bruce Mitchell – or that Paul Gibb had let another one from Gordon go by! In fact I really, as you might say, threw such a lot of mud (perhaps this isn't a very happy metaphor but you'll understand what I mean), that some of it *must* have stuck.

I was very struck by the exceptional fairness of the crowds. When, in the last Test, England was scoring even more slowly than South Africa had done there wasn't a sign of barracking. I remember one incident which convinced me of the South African essential good sportsmanship. Hutton and Gibb came in during England's second innings at 5.55 p.m. in a poorish light. After one ball Hutton appealed against the light and from the crowd beneath my box there was a general cry of 'Uphold it – Uphold it', which the umpire proceeded to do.

The grounds themselves are most attractive. Johannesburg has a magnificent cricket ground with probably the best playing surface in the world, and Newlands, with the Table Mountain in the background, is simply lovely. Durban is pretty, too, with a charm about it which carried us through ten days as well as can be expected. If the last Test match had been played in some settings I can think of we should all have turned a little bit mental before the end of it.

There are days on this tour I shall never forget. There was one Sunday at a place called Maccauvlei where we had a golf match between the MCC and a team collected by our host Mr Victor Kent, who's chairman of the enormous Wanderers' Club at Johannesburg. We went about forty miles out of Jo'burg by car, just across the Vaal river into the Orange Free State, and on the banks of the river we found this country club that more than lived up to its very attractive name.

There was a night at the Durban Country Club (talking of country clubs), when Lord Nuffield announced his gift of £10,000 to South African cricket – and incidentally I remember showed himself a very nimble performer of the Lambeth Walk. Another thing I remember about that evening was Wally Hammond's anxiety, because there were all sorts of wild ideas floating round as to how the money was to be used, and he, being the one neutral party on the committee, became the chief arbiter. They decided in the end, if you remember, to have a sort of junior Currie Cup for schoolboys – a great fortnight in the Christmas holidays when all the best young players should meet – at Durban, or Johannesburg, or Cape Town as the case might be. And I think most people thought that that was quite the best solution that could have been found.

Then there was the trip to the Falls – a quite unforgettable experience – and an afternoon when we went up the Zambezi in a launch to a place called Kandahar Island, and saw on the way great crocodiles slipping into the water as they heard us approach, and when we got to the island the monkeys were so tame that they came and ate out of our hands. Personally I found that a rather more pleasing experience than when the baboons came just as close to us, no doubt with the most amiable intentions, in the Rain Forest back at the Falls themselves.

Lastly, you cannot forget the Cape with its glorious flowers, and those fine Dutch farmhouses, with the great mountain as a backcloth. It was a great trip. And as to the kindness which we met everywhere, I have tried to convey an impression of it – but you must go to South Africa yourself really to know its charm. They say that if you want to return to South Africa you must throw a tickey (that's a South African threepenny bit) into Table Bay as you leave.

I threw my tickey in all right.

*　　　*　　　*

GRACE REMEMBERED

A. C. MacLaren, a classic batsman in the traditional mould, was a sound, somewhat authoritarian skipper of Lancashire and England. An aloofness of manner could not have helped when it came to dealing in the business world after his cricket days had finished, and he was constantly in search of financial stability. 'Archie' made several forays into journalism and broadcasting and his talk on the Australian Test matches of 1930 is the second earliest cricket talk extant on the archive files. In 1935 for 'I Knew a Man' he recalled with affection memories of his predecessor as captain of England.

W. G. Grace
A. C. MacLaren

October 1935

My first introduction to W. G. Grace took place in the Old Trafford Pavilion, and I well remember watching the great man tying his MCC sash round his waist, as I gazed in admiration at what appeared to me to be a very genial Father Christmas with a black beard. He was of massive proportions, and was more suited to the role of Father Christmas than of a great cricketer. The whole place was alive with merriment, as was always the case when W. G. was present. He put out an enormous paw, saying, "Ow are you, little man?' and then continued his chaff surounded by Lancashire members and one or two players.

So inspired was I by this great man's presence, that when my father said, 'Now, my boy, you have seen the captain of England,' I informed my mother that same day that I also would be captain of England when I grew up. It was an extraordinary coincidence that he should have wired to me at the end of his Test cricket career to take his place as captain.

I had played under W. G. on the previous visit of the Australians, and my affection for this dear old man was such that it inspired my own cricket ability. For I could not have wished to serve under a more encouraging, sympathetic, and appreciative captain. There was always the feeling on my part of complete security whenever I had the good fortune to be one of his team. The delight expressed by him on every occasion, at anything out of the ordinary on the part of the fieldsmen, acted as an incentive to every man to produce his best. Indeed, I will go further – the winning atmosphere his presence created seemed to make everyone produce *more* than his best.

For some reason a certain few held the opinion that W. G. was not as good a captain as would be expected. This was not my view. In all the matches I played with or against him I can think of no occasion on which adverse criticism would have been justified. He invited most generously valued opinion. I ought to make it clear to my listeners that I was too young ever to have seen the champion at the zenith of his career – in those years when one *can* only be at one's best – for he was distinctly an old man for a Test cricketer when I first played under him.

This, however, did not prevent him from being top scorer in one of the three Test matches in which I played under his captaincy, and again in the Gentlemen *v*. Players match at Lord's on his fiftieth birthday against the cream of English bowling, on a difficult wicket – a really wonderful performance.

We all know that as a batsman his methods were of the soundest: he had every stroke on the board at his command, while his concentration was most marked. An outstanding feature was the accuracy with which he placed the ball between the fieldsmen, particularly in the cutting strokes through the slips. One can truthfully say that on all wickets and against every type of bowling he remained supreme. I once asked him which bowler he liked least of all. He paused for a moment, then rapped out, 'Archie, I love 'em all.'

People have asked if W. G. ever appeared to be nervous, and on my referring this question to him he replied, 'Well, I always feel better after my luncheon.' Certainly his play gave no indication that he was ever nervous. He demonstrated to all of us that wet wickets and hard wickets all came alike to him.

Which reminds me of an amusing incident that took place before my playing days, when Yorkshire were playing Gloucestershire. W. G., whilst batting, was handed a telegram which in those days was always brought out to the player on the field. Tom Emmett, the left-hand bowler – a rare Yorkshire character – appeared to be interested. W. G. called out to him, 'I've got my diploma, Tom.' Shortly after W. G. slipped and sat on the muddy wicket to hear Tom call out as he picked himself up, 'Ah see thou'st got diploma all right, Doctor.'

W. G. was always held up as a true model of physical fitness, and my mother was the first to tell me that he neither drank nor smoked; but it was not long before I had good reason to doubt the accuracy of my mother's statement, for I now frequently had the opportunity of seeing for myself. Certainly he was most careful of his diet, but on one occasion after a long innings, when, as often, he was the guest of the evening, one of his team, noticing he had gone beyond his two glasses of champagne, remarked to him, 'I thought you said, W. G., you never had more than two glasses of wine at dinner?' 'Ted,' replied W. G., 'I said I could drink any *given* quantity.'

The very soundness of his successes left no room for any lack of confidence in himself at any time, even when age was overtaking him. This he showed in his reply to my expression of sorrow at an unusually early return to the Pavilion after opening the innings against Australia: 'There's a second innings yet, Archie.' Another saying never to be forgotten by cricketers, and which should still give all food for thought, came from him. 'The beauty of this game lies in the knowledge that there is always something to be learnt, every day you play it.' And this from the champion of champions.

I can't remember ever seeing W. G. hit by the ball, let alone hurt, and I might also add that he never missed a match through ill-health. A. N. Hornby, my first captain, a great one and a fine international player, told me of an occasion when, owing to lack of accommodation, he shared a bedroom with W. G. As he opened the door in the morning W. G. woke up and said, 'Where are you off to, Monkey?' 'I am just going to have my cold bath.' 'Oo,' said W. G., ''ow you do make me shudder.'

His dominating personality on the cricket field is well illustrated by an incident which I witnessed in a match between Lancashire and Gloucestershire. He was particularly quick to notice if any of the opponents thought the umpire was generously giving him the benefit of the doubt in an lbw decision. In this match I was fielding first slip, and an appeal from Mold, who had hit the old man on the leg, was disallowed. I asked Mold quietly at the end of the over his opinion of the umpire's decision – to receive an irritable reply, 'It would have sent the middle peg flying.' W. G. happened to overhear this remark and he called out, 'What's that you say – what's that you say, why you have been *throwing* at me this last half-hour.' But afterwards in his calmer moments he apologised to Mold for what he had said.

Only once did W. G. put the boxing gloves on with me. On a soft wicket, after hooking the slow bowler Charlie Townsend to the outfield, stationed at mid-wicket, I slipped and knocked my leg stump almost flat with my left foot in starting to run at the completion of my stroke. W. G. immediately shouted, ''E's out, 'e's out, toss 'er up! toss 'er up! 'E's out, 'e's out!' So, as I was in the middle of my run, I joined in the chorus, calling out to the umpire, 'I'm not out, I'm not out.' Nice behaviour on the part of two international bats! When I got to the other end, W. G., instead of appealing to the umpire, walked towards me with lowered head, like an infuriated bull, and said, 'Ain't you going out, Archie?' 'Not until the umpire gives me out,' I replied slowly and emphatically. Then he turned to the umpire and said, 'Well, 'ow was it?' 'Not out,' said the umpire. Then the band began to play with a vengeance, and, as I made 70 more runs after this happening, W. G. had a howl for every run made, which I received in silence.

I am not going to attempt to give all his records (it is enough to know he established all records as a batsman, and many as a bowler), but I should like to mention one or two of his best performances in some of the games in which I appeared as a member of his side or against him. If anybody has any doubt in his mind as to the best years of his life, surely the performances of

W. G. from 1870 to 1876 are most convincing. In every one of these years he made a century in the Gentlemen *v.* Players match; on three occasions he made two separate centuries in this annual match. And on two occasions he made over 200 in one innings. I emphasise this period because he was only twenty-two in 1870. It must not be overlooked that in spite of all this century-making W. G. got through a tremendous amount of bowling, never failing to obtain from 1874–8 his hundred wickets for the season, with his wily slow deliveries. Innumerable catches were made at deep square leg by his brother Fred, whom the old man was always feeding with his leg-breaks.

Of all my cricket mementos I prize most of all the medal given to me and to all who played in the Gentlemen *v.* Players match at Lord's on W. G.'s fiftieth birthday in 1898. The difficulty of the wicket was shown by this incident. I don't think in the whole of my career I would be hit on the hand by a bowler more than three times in a season. Yet in this match, in the ten minutes' batting I had before the luncheon interval, I was hit on the fingers three times by Lockwood, the Surrey and England fast bowler, with balls that appeared to rise straight up from the pitch and yet were well enough up to force forward play.

In this match, one of the greatest in which I ever played, F. S. Jackson, Prince Ranji and one or two more of the regulars were playing on this difficult wicket. We were in our best form and put up the score of some 250 runs – an excellent score in the circumstances. But it was W. G. who got the highest score. That feat has always remained in my memory. It was probably the best performance of any batsman I ever saw – taking into consideration the state of the wicket and the age of the man, to say nothing of the fact that he was playing against a very fine side, including the best professional English bowlers, who opened our attack in Test cricket.

At dinner that night, when we had drunk the dear old man's health, his reply, as always, was brief. 'Thank you, boys. If the professionals had had to bat today on that wicket – well, I don't think they would have done better than we did.' Then he sat down, to get up again, and add, 'I'm a doer, not a talker,' to a chorus of 'Hear, Hear,' and 'Well spoken, old man.'

This performance of the old warrior has caused me to put him for all time on a pedestal by himself. When I am asked who was the best in any department of the game I start my reply with the words 'always excepting W. G. . . .' A world-famous international in his prime told me he doubted whether W. G. was quite the player he was ever made out to be. I replied, 'Wait till you are fifty, when you won't look so pretty at the wicket, and then get top score in the biggest match of the year on a bowler's wicket.'

We who never saw W. G. in his prime can only guess how great he must have been in his younger days. Where he excelled in his old age for a cricketer was in his knowledge of the limitations imposed upon him only by increasing years. He never attempted to do with the bat what his age prohibited, but rightly preferred to *wait* for his now fewer opportunities for scoring in front of the wicket than to *make* them as he used to do in his earlier days. He retained in a marvellous manner almost to the last those occasional taps through the slips off the shorter pitched ball outside the off-stump, always most cleverly placed to beat the fieldsman; as well as dealing in the telling manner, which was probably one of the strongest features of his batting in his palmy days, with any ball on his legs.

He was rarely, if ever, at fault in throwing a 'cross' bat at the ball of driving length on the off-side. He would send it humming to the on-side boundary over short mid-on's head – rather than play the more orthodox stroke, through the covers. In the December of his cricketing life, when he used to captain London County, it was not too easy to get as many of the counties to play against him as he wished, owing to their already well-filled programme.

On one occasion, however, Lancashire, during my captaincy, came to the rescue, gladly giving up their three days' holiday in the middle of the season to give him a game. So along came W. G. and his merry men, among them W. L. Murdoch, the famous Australian captain and batsman and a former opponent of W. G. It was out of the question not to put our full strength against any side at the head of which was the old man himself, to say nothing of Billy Murdoch, who in Australia was held in the same reverence as our own champion in this country. I have the most vivid recollections of this game.

The old man won the toss from me on a perfect wicket, and out stepped these two stalwarts to provide a batting treat, which at that period of their lives was beyond all expectations. They both topped the century. It was remarkable that the effectiveness of their cutting allowed no weakening of the slip positions, thereby making their driving more telling when the bowler required that extra field on the off, who could not be spared. Here was a spectacle provided by two past masters of batting, whose repertoire of strokes was little less than it had been in their heyday.

The conditions were perfectly suited to these two old men. Sunshine in a cloudless sky, warmth in the air and a perfect pitch beneath them. What more could they want? I am sure that no two cricketers ever enjoyed themselves more, or could have been more completely satisfied with their exhibition of batting – ever to remain a delight to those who had the fortune to witness it.

As I am speaking now, I can see W. G. and Billy Murdoch standing at the top of the steps of the Pavilion as they were leaving the ground at four o'clock on the last day, just as we were dismissing the end batsmen – waving and calling to us, 'Goodbye, Archie' – 'Goodbye, Billy' – 'Goodbye, W. G.'

*   *   *

Even today, there are still perhaps a handful of old-timers who can remember seeing W.G. bat. Writer and broadcaster David Foot spoke to one of them, retired schoolmaster Tom Barrow, for the West of England Home Service in October 1965.

Tom Barrow on Grace

Barrow: When he was batting, he always, before the ball was being bowled to him, used to smooth his beard with his left hand.

Foot: Do you recall any landmarks in this fantastic career of his?

Barrow: Yes, when he got his hundred 100s our flunkey came out in what we should now call evening dress with a tray and glasses and a bottle of champagne, and the players gathered round and they drank his health in champagne.

Foot: Didn't your brother once bowl him out?

Barrow: Yes, he bowled him out when he was about thirteen years of age. We went up to the county ground and W.G. was in the nets practising and he had a single wicket and let us boys bowl at him. My brother had a rubber ball and he came behind Murch and bowled and old W.G. was surprised to find a rubber ball bowled at him and my brother bowled him out middle stump.

Foot: What was his reaction?

Barrow: Old W.G. was so annoyed, he turned to Murch, he said, 'Murch, take them off the ground,' and my brother was taken off the ground at Ashley and when he got to the entrance he turned to him and he said, 'All right, my son, mind you come back again when your man's gone back to the Pavilion.'

Foot: Well, Mr Barrow, W.G.'s been dead now fifty years. Looking back how would you sum him up?

Barrow: I would sum him up as a great man, a man who was loved but who had a lot of enemies, because they did not understand the man. They did not understand his kindly spirit.

W. G. Grace would appear to have been more vulnerable than his batting record suggests. That is, if one takes the title of journalist Michael Green's talk, for the Home Service in July 1963, too literally. Mind you, Grandad didn't do quite as well as Tom Barrow's brother.

My Grandfather Nearly Bowled W.G.

Michael Green

All my life I've suffered under the handicap that my grandfather nearly bowled W. G. Grace. Grandfather was something of a legendary character to me; he lived in Bristol all his life, and was a keen local cricketer. The story, as told to me as a child by numerous aunts and uncles, was that grandfather was one day at the county ground in Bristol when W. G. Grace appeared at the nets and wanted someone to bowl to him. Apparently there was no one there to bowl, so the doctor called my grandfather over and said 'Will, can you give me a bowl?' 'All right, Doctor,' said my grandfather, 'I'll bowl you one of them new twisty 'uns.'

Well, W. G. Grace took guard and my grandfather ran up and delivered to the doctor a twisty 'un, which shattered his stumps. To Dr Grace's surprise my grandfather rushed down the wicket, seized the ball, and ran off the field shouting, 'I bowled the doctor, I bowled the doctor, I just bowled W. G. Grace.' The story goes that he went home, placed the ball in a box which he sealed and wrote on the top of it 'Ball with which I bowled W. G. Grace.' That ball was carefully preserved over a great many years and eventually it came into my possession.

You can see, then, the moment of shattering disillusion which came at the age of fourteen, when I was in the habit of playing on a local recreation ground in Leicester with the very ball with which my grandfather had bowled W. G. Grace. Well, I lost it, and I came home in tears, and my mother asked me why I was crying. I said, 'Mother, I've lost the ball with which grandfather bowled W. G. Grace,' and she said, 'Don't worry, we've got another of them upstairs.'

I made further enquiries after this and discovered that the actual truth of it was that grandfather did not actually bowl W. G. Grace; the fact of the matter, which was reluctantly confided to me, was that grandfather saw W. G. Grace bowled in the nets and managed to get hold of the balls after the net practice was over. But as far as I was concerned, grandfather did bowl W. G. Grace, and I've spent the rest of my life trying to live up to that.

This would be a great burden even for a good cricketer, but for me it's been almost impossible. The main reason why it's impossible is that unfortunately I'm not much good at cricket. I am, as far as I know, the only bowler in the history of cricket who has landed an off-break vertically on the square leg umpire's head. My attempts to bowl fast are even worse, and the last time I tried to do so, my first ball was so short that I hit my own foot and had to be carried off seriously injured. I'm the sort of player who always bats number eleven, and when the opposition see me come in number eleven and swish wildly at thin air, they think 'he must be a fast bowler, because he's obviously not played for his batting,' so they spend the rest of the game while we're fielding looking at me in the field and wondering when they're going to put this fast bowler on. Of course I never do go on, but I always think that my moral value as a potential fast bowler is probably far greater than my actual value if I ever did really bowl.

But I have had one or two experiences in cricket that even grandfather didn't have. For instance, I played cricket in Corfu. One doesn't associate the Adriatic with cricket, but Corfu was in British occupation until just over a hundred years ago, and one of the relics the British left behind is cricket. The Corfuites, or Corfuians, or whatever they call themselves, are extremely keen on cricket, and each year they welcome a number of British guest teams for an annual cricket week. It was in Corfu, playing in the centre of the town on the town square on a surface composed of short white stones, that I had the unique experience of being given 'out' by a Greek orthodox priest with a beard. When I got out I asked the scorer what was the name of the bowler and he replied 'Prometheus'. Not only that, but it turned out that the chap who caught me was Archimedes. I always reckon it was worth going a thousand miles to be got out by people with names like that.

I've also had the interesting experience of playing cricket in Yugoslavia; at least, it's part of Yugoslavia now, but when I was playing there just after the war it was in military occupation and was disputed territory between the Italians and the Yugoslavs. I was playing for my regiment, and I can't say I liked army cricket; for one thing the batting order seemed to be arranged strictly in order of rank, so that you opened with the major and finished with some private or trooper from the cookhouse, and the bowling was arranged in the same way.

There aren't many cricket grounds in Yugoslavia, as you can imagine, and we were playing on top of a large plateau overlooking the Adriatic. I was fielding just by the cliff, and behind me there was a gentle slope of about twenty yards and then a sheer 200-foot drop into the sea. I suppose it was inevitable that someone should hit a ball over the cliff. It rolled over the gentle slope and lost itself a few yards down, just in front of a bush. Being anxious to try and get a stripe, I crawled over the edge of the cliff and slithered carefully down to the bush and picked up the ball, and as I did so there was a minor avalanche of stones and rough earth and I found myself hanging on to the bush with my feet dangling over 200 feet of thin air.

I waited a few minutes and nothing happened, so I started to shout. I shouted 'Help', then I shouted 'Help' again, and then I shouted 'Help' again. It at last dawned on me that no one was paying the slightest attention. I suppose it's an example of exactly how useless I am on the cricket field that no one had noticed a complete square leg had vanished over the precipice and had not returned. Presumably the umpires had produced another ball and they were continuing to play. I don't know how long I should have been there – I couldn't have held on much longer – when to my great relief another ball appeared over the edge of the precipice and sailed into the sea. And sure enough, a few seconds later a soldier shoved his face over the cliff and looked after it.

I called up to him for help and he made signs that he would go and fetch an officer as the only man who could deal with a situation like this. He returned with Lieutenant Bird, who stuck his head over the cliff and said, 'Hey you, what are you doing down there hanging on to that bush?' I explained that I was hanging on to the bush because if I let go I would slide down the slope and fall over the edge of the precipice into the sea. So he said, 'Stop mucking about and come here with that ball.' I explained that I didn't want to muck about and the greatest desire I had in life was to come here with that ball, but I didn't honestly see how I was going to do it. He shook his head as if I had committed some unmentionable crime and vanished.

Half an hour later – at least, it seemed like half an hour, but it might only have been a few seconds – they returned with a long stretch of cable which is used for towing broken-down tanks. This was lowered over the precipice to me, I managed to grasp it in one hand, and with a tremendous heave they pulled me up the slope, myself helping by half-crawling. Instead of the welcome that I expected to receive on arriving at the top of the cliff, the first words that Lieutenant Bird said were, 'Where's the ball?' It was then that I realised that I hadn't brought it up with me. I seemed to be on guard duty rather a lot after that.

Most of my cricket, of course, has been played in England, and here I am glad to say that I have emulated my grandfather – I have played most of my cricket for offices and works. It is traditional, of course, that the basis of good cricket in England is the village cricket green, but personally I don't hold with this view. So much village cricket these days has been ruined by the commuters and the smart businessmen who've taken over the local team, so the poor old butcher and the baker can't get in any more, and even if they did get in they'd be expected to wear whites which they haven't got.

There's an awful lot of fun in office cricket that you never get in village cricket. I remember the time when we started to form an office cricket club and we approached the managing director. 'Sir,' we said, 'you have been appointed president of the office cricket club,' and we held out our hands. He looked up, he said, 'How much do you want?' We hummed and hawed a bit, and we settled for £3, which he paid over. Having spent his £3 on pads and a bat, about four weeks later we were surprised when he called us in and said 'By the way, where's the £3 I lent to the office cricket team?' It was this team that, when darkness threatened a vital fixture, produced a white ball which enabled us to snatch a last-minute victory as the moon rose over Morden.

But perhaps I've been rather hard on village cricket. I've had a lot of fun playing for and against villages. I always remember playing a side in Buckinghamshire which had a lot of young public schoolboys who used to turn out for them in the holidays. These lads had a habit of writing in large letters on the back of their bats their greatest scores, so that our wicket-keeper would see something like '58 not out, v. Harrow', or '76 v. Rugby'. This rather upset us, so when I went in to bat, I wrote in large letters on the back of my bat, '2 not out v. Rickmansworth Water Company,' '1 v. North London Gas Works,' and when they bowled me third ball, I wasted an awful lot of time by taking out a ballpoint pen and solemnly writing '0 v. Gerrard's Cross' on the back of the bat.

Although, unlike grandfather, I can't claim contact with anyone as illustrious as W. G., I have played against an England fast bowler, admittedly only in a charity match. The bowler in question was famous for three things – his ability to bowl fast, his hot temper, and his prejudice against the press – and consequently I spent a sleepless night before the game trying to think of what to do if I had to face up to him: not, you understand, how to score runs off him but how to avoid being hurt. Well, the next day, the fast bowler took himself off after a short spell in which he did little damage, apart from breaking someone's bat with the sheer force of his delivery, and I had hopes that I wouldn't have to face him. Unfortunately the batsman in front of me was a well-known cricket writer and when he went to the wicket the fast bowler made a special request to come back as he had some old scores to settle with the press.

The cricket writer lasted three balls. Every one was aimed straight at his stomach on the full toss and the third one found its mark, whereupon the wretched journalist was carried moaning feebly from the pitch and I was sent in to bat. I had hopes that my own connection with the press would not be known, so I slunk to the wicket as humbly as possible, only to hear the bowler say loudly to the umpire, 'Ah, here comes another of them professional liars.' I smiled at him in a lunatic grin, hoping to ingratiate myself, and was rewarded with one of the most vicious expressions I have ever seen in my life. I was still trying to think of some way of escape as he ran up to bowl, and then suddenly I had inspiration. As his arm came over I leaped to one side and while the ball whistled past where my navel would have been I called for a run and started off up the pitch. I ought to have been stumped by about five yards but the stupid wicket-keeper was standing so far back that instead we ran a bye to tremendous applause all round the ground. This, of course, only made my predicament worse, while the effect on the fast bowler was indescribable. In fact he distinctly said a very rude word to me when I arrived at his end.

During the following over, which was from a slow bowler, I made positively maniacal attempts to get myself out, lashing out in all directions, but of course when you try to get out it's the last thing you can do; the ball becomes magnetised and the bat just won't avoid it. I'd never scored so many runs for years. At the end of the over I carefully ran two when, to my horror, there was an overthrow so I was back facing the England bowler again. It was then that I saw my captain waving from the Pavilion. Taking it as a signal of declaration, I immediately walked rapidly off the field, feeling as if I had just been reprieved from execution. When I got to the Pavilion the captain looked daggers at me and said, sternly, 'What did you do that for?' I told him that he had signalled for us to declare, I had distinctly seen him wave. 'I was not waving,' he snarled, 'I was shaking my fist at you in disgust.'

I thought I had achieved some sort of cricket fame when quite a well-known club asked me to speak at their annual dinner along with one or two unimportant nobodies such as the county captain and some geezer from the MCC. I took special care over my appearance for the evening and decided to wear my Ealing third XI tie, which is so designed that it could be mistaken for Middlesex by someone who didn't know any better. I entered the reception and paused modestly at the door, waiting for the gasp of admiration and the inevitable whispers of 'Look, that's Michael Green, the chap in the Middlesex tie'. Nobody took any notice of me, and, as I was blocking the doorway, the waiter asked me to move and I was forced to stand inside and moon around by myself, trying to make one glass of sherry go a long way. Never mind, I thought, they'll get round to the fact soon that I'm the guest of honour. Nobody ever did, not even when I sat next to the president at dinner. After a couple of desultory remarks about the menu he completely avoided me and talked all the time to the chap on his left, some miserable professional cricketer who'd only played in about six Test matches. However, the time came when he had to introduce my speech, and as I shuffled my notes and rehearsed my opening joke, the president at last spoke. 'Tell me,' he said, putting his face close to mine and blowing port fumes all over the table, 'exactly who are you?'

By this time I was utterly fed up. 'I am the grandson of a man who nearly bowled W. G. Grace,' I replied firmly. I think grandfather would have approved of that.

*   *   *

above, *Cricket at Lord's, 1858. The dog seems the most interested spectator or perhaps it is acting as deep square-leg;* below, *Cricket at Lord's, 1887. The Victorian edifice casts a forbidding air over play.*

113

'Stumps Drawn'. An eminent cast of 211 assembled for Messrs Dickinson and Foster's painting (above) of Lord's on a Gentlemen v. Players day around 1894. Not all the personae named in the key plate (below) fitted into the photograph frame of the picture; however, the Earls of Londesborough and Darnley, Lord Charles Russell, the Hon. Ivo Bligh, Samuel Hoare MP, a clutch of Copland Crawfords, several Studds, a Bromley Davenport, A. C. MacLaren, A. G. Steel, C. J. Kortright, John Shuter and W. H. Iremonger were some of the many who did. Oh, yes, so did W. G.

THE MATCH BETWEEN THE ALL-ENGLAND ELEVEN AND TWENTY-TWO OF THE NEW SOUTH WALES CRICKETERS, PLAYED IN THE DOMAIN AT SYDNEY.—SEE NEXT PAGE.

England v. *New South Wales at the Domain in Sydney.*

The Scoring Table

Coming out

Going in

General view of the Match

A Parsee Cricketer

above, *'Ranji' in another world*

opposite above, *Cricket in India under the Raj;* opposite below, *Parsee ladies dutifully watching their menfolk play cricket, c. 1910–20.*

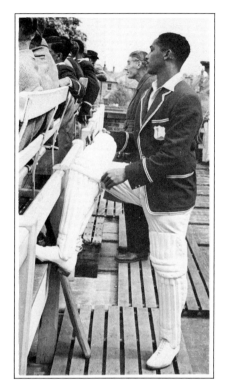

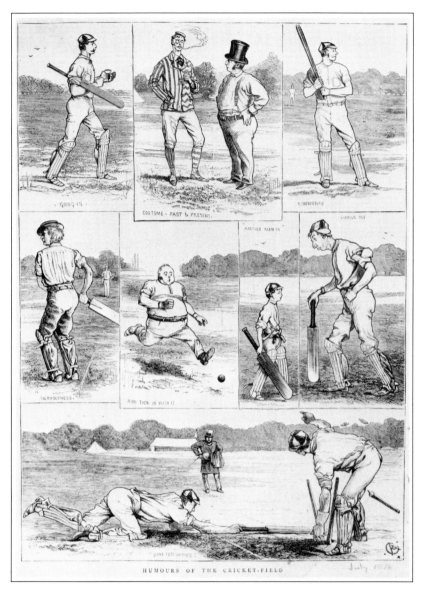

above, 'Humours of the Cricket-Field': some Victorian poses

opposite above left, *Frank Worrell waiting to bat against Cambridge University at Fenner's in 1950;* opposite above right, *Wesley Hall airborne;* opposite below, *Clive Lloyd talking to Neil Allen in 1979.*

above, *'A Nice Afternoon's Cricket'. You can't play without a ball;* left, *Cricket in St Vincent – another lost ball.*

FOREIGN BODIES

Who better to describe 'Cricket in the Seven Seas' than Lt Commander Tommy Woodrooffe, who occupies a fond first place in the recollections of all broadcasters as they relish in retrospect disasters real and imagined. Woodrooffe stepped on to posterity's podium on that day in 1937 when he went on board HMS Nelson *to describe for the nation the Illumination of the Fleet at the Royal Naval Review at Spithead:*

'The whole Fleet's lit up – and when I say lit up I mean lit up – by fairy-lamps – the whole Fleet's outlined – it's lit up – [long pause] – I'm sorry, I was just telling some people to shut up talking . . . It's gone, it's gone! The Fleet's disappeared – it's gone – and no magician could have waved his wand with more acumen – ' Woodrooffe, who had arrived at the ship much earlier in the day, had had a joyous reunion with a number of 'old mates' and they had not stinted themselves in refreshing inner parts. He had been allocated a swivel-chair for the broadcast and at this point in the commentary had been too 'tired and emotional' to realise that the chair had involuntarily turned ninety degrees. The Fleet continued to illuminate but poor Tommy did not. The broadcast was terminated abruptly.

Cricket in the Seven Seas
Tommy Woodrooffe

June 1939

You may think it a bit funny to talk of cricket and the South Seas in the same breath – the two don't seem to go together somehow – but I've played it there on an island right off the trade routes, and some 10,000 miles from Lord's, a place with the pleasant name of Nuku'alofa [*the capital of Tonga*]. I was in a sloop in those days, and we went there in the ordinary course of our duty. After dodging coral reefs, we landed and were met by our opposing captain and the sickly, sweet smell of copra. We soon reached the cricket field which was also used for football. It was the parade ground too for the royal guards and also the local market. You can imagine the outfield, and the wicket consisted of coconut matting, locally made, pegged down over the coarse grass. Coconut palms, swaying gently in the breeze, fringed three sides of the field and through them you could get glimpses of the deep blue Pacific. On the fourth side were the Houses of Parliament – a long, low shed with a tin roof. In the course of the match several balls landed on this roof and I wondered if the legislators would be disturbed. But I was told that Parliament wasn't sitting – it was watching the game.

Our opponents were a mixed lot; half of them traders and missionaries, who'd sunk their differences for the afternoon, and the other half natives, barefooted and ferocious-looking, who were being taught the rudiments of the game with the elements of Christianity.

Shortly after the start, Her Majesty the Queen arrived in state and with due ceremony both teams were presented. She drove up in an old Singer. She took up nearly the whole of the back seat, while her husband, the Prince Consort, no less majestic, acted as chauffeur. She graciously watched the match from the shade of the Houses of Parliament, surrounded by her Court.

The natives had eyes like hawks and, if their style was unorthodox, any ball they connected with travelled. There were no boundaries; but off the field itself there was no need for a fieldsman to exert himself. The whole village had turned out to watch and was only too eager to help a visitor – any hit to the palm trees was pursued by yelling hordes of delighted locals who fought strenuously for the honour of handing the ball back – and meanwhile the batsmen ran five.

As soon as the game was over – and I'm glad to say the sailors won – both teams at the command of Her Majesty were entertained to a feast. This took place on the field – in fact we all squatted down on the wicket itself – and deft-handed village beauties laid out the food before us. All the afternoon sucking pigs had been roasting on the boundary and now these were served on leaves with yams and breadfruit, and all kinds of tropical fruit. The sun was setting, turning the sea to deepest purple, and the sky to a dark green. About a hundred women and girls accompanied the feast with haunting songs – songs which had charmed Captain Cook, nearly two hundred years before – and as the moon came over the trees we walked silently and slowly back to our boats, escorted by our hosts.

Then there was another game and in very different surroundings. Nearly a thousand miles up the Yangtze river – right in the heart of China – was a little treaty port, whose English population was about thirty all told. There, the visit of a gunboat is always an event and among the other festivities they arranged a cricket match for us.

A suitable space for a field was found a little way outside the Chinese city and gangs of coolies were set to work levelling it off a bit and putting up a pavilion and shelter for the ladies. Not much could be done in the way of levelling as the Chinese have a habit of burying their dead anywhere and everywhere and little mounds are dotted about every few yards, but eventually a clear space was found for the wicket, though the bowler wasn't allowed much of a run.

As the ground was some way from the river-bank, we were met by a fleet of chairs, each carried by two coolies, and we set off feeling very lordly. We passed out of the neat, well-kept concession into the turmoil of the Chinese city. We went along smelly narrow streets, so narrow that two chairs could only just pass. They were thronged with street-sellers, beggars, workmen and merchants. We went past streets of shops selling repulsive-looking foodstuffs; past others where carpenters, potters and workers in silver plied their trade; and on through the teeming crowd, to emerge at last through the gates in the city wall into the fresher air of the countryside beyond. On top of the wall, which was about thirty feet thick, some young Chinese gentlemen were taking their afternoon's recreation and exercise. They were strolling along, carrying a singing bird in a cage and sedately enjoying its music.

After two reluctant spectators had been roped in as umpires, the game began. The graves interfered seriously with the fielding and anyone who tried for a high catch took a toss. A footpath led along one edge of the field and an endless stream of coolies passed by carrying goods to and from the city, but none stopped to watch what to them must have been a unique sight. I suppose they looked upon it as just another manifestation of the lunacy of the foreign devils. By tea-time both sides had batted twice, so honour was considered satisfied and we could get down to serious business in the Pavilion.

That was in China – and now back to a small place on the coast of West Africa. Our gunboat had been soundly trounced by the local white team, so we took on the natives, much to their joy. We played on the ground of the village school – a ground everyone was proud of. It had only lately been reclaimed from the jungle and boasted a lovely new Pavilion, the gift of a benevolent government.

Our opponents were all old boys of the school and though their fathers may have lived in primitive ignorance, and most probably did eat their enemies on the sly, the sons were all enlightened Christians.

When we turned up at the ground we found them in a great state. The beautiful new Pavilion was a splintered ruin. The field looked as if it had been hit by a hurricane. We soon learned that a marauding elephant had passed that way the night before. His route took him through the Pavilion and he'd obviously been out to inspect the wicket. He must have disapproved of it, because he'd evidently stamped on it. Moreover he was reported to be not far away at the moment.

In spite of these discouragements, we began the game. There was a marked reluctance on the part of deep field to retrieve any balls from the jungle, but the game continued without incident until there was an ominous crackling in the undergrowth behind third man. I've never seen the players clear a field more quickly. Both teams peered round the corner of the ruined Pavilion in a terrified silence. Then there was a roar of laughter as a small donkey broke his way out of the thick growth and trotted on to the field with a triumphant bray.

The cricket after that was not good. The players, white and black, were jumpy and inclined to keep the eye on the jungle and not on the ball. In fact there was a general sigh of relief when stumps were drawn and the game was safely over.

There's a lot of what I call civilised cricket in the Mediterranean – at Gibraltar or Malta or in Egypt – but it's also played in the most unexpected places. The first game of cricket ever played in the Mediterranean was, I believe, at Antioch in about 1670. The frigate *Assistance* was probably after Turkish pirates or something – at any rate her chaplain has recorded that he landed at Antioch with some of the ship's company and played at cricket a little way out of the town. He might have written that entry in his diary yesterday – instead of 270 years ago.

I remember once arriving at a small island off the Greek coast. As soon as we'd dropped anchor two doubtful-looking gentlemen came on board among the usual horde of fruit-sellers, washerwomen and bumboatmen. They rather amazingly asked to see our cricket captain and explained that they were respectively the captain and secretary of the local club, and challenged the ship to a game. They added as a sort of reference that cricket was their national pastime.

We felt as if we'd stumbled upon some curious relic of the past – like explorers who'd come unexpectedly on a long-lost tribe still living in a state of civilisation. How had cricket taken root here of all places? Did marooned sailors of some ancient shipwreck sow the first seeds or did the sporting chaplain of the *Assistance* land here too? We expected to see spoon bats and two sticks for a wicket and scoring by notches.

Anyhow, our team arrived the next afternoon in the middle of the small town, where there was the usual square of sunbaked earth, surrounded by cafés and all the principal buildings. But in the middle of this square there was a pitch of new matting and three shining yellow stumps at each end.

The hosts refused to toss. It was only right that their visitors – and such distinguished ones – should bat first. They insisted and as the afternoon was hot, our captain agreed quite cheerfully with visions of declaring at tea-time. But if he'd been familiar with his Classics he'd have been warned against trusting Greeks who bring gifts. The ship was all out for under twenty. A bad score even for them. The ball did amazing things. It shot, it bumped, it turned at incredible angles – it did everything but burst.

Between the innings both teams went into one of the surrounding cafés and when the local side went out to bat the wicket played well and true. We spent a warm couple of hours chasing the ball under tables and chairs, and disturbing portly citizens and their wives at their refreshment.

We returned on board, puzzled and annoyed, until one of the team who hadn't gone into the café between the innings mentioned that as he was strolling about he noticed that the party sweeping down the wicket had rolled back the matting and had also swept away what seemed to him to be a lot of small pebbles from each end. The mystery was solved; so we warned the next ship which was going to visit the place to be on the look-out. A match was arranged and in due course the same polite argument as to who should bat first took place. The visiting skipper insisted on tossing – and with his own coin. Luckily he won and he put the locals in, wondering how they'd deal with the situation. But they were quite unperturbed. They smiled a little sheepishly, then, in front of him and his side, rolled back the matting and swept away a choice lot of pebbles. The game then proceeded quite as if nothing had happened.

We discovered afterwards that these simple islanders had learnt their cricket from ships which were based there at different times during the war.

The interest taken in the game all over the world is tremendous and one sometimes comes across evidence of this in the most unexpected circumstances. Just after Chapman's side had won the third Test and the Ashes in Australia, a cruiser was sent out during a gale from the coast of New Zealand. They had instructions to look for a steam trawler that was reported to have run out of coal and to be drifting helplessly before the gale towards the South Pole.

By luck she was found. She *had* run out of coal. Her only provisions were rotting fish and she was on the last of her fresh water. She was in danger of foundering and she had on board about twenty men. Supplies were floated over to her and, as it was too rough to take her in tow, the cruiser stood by her all night until the weather should moderate.

I had the middle watch that night and at about 2 a.m. we saw her laboriously spelling out a message by a hand lantern. We watched the flashes anxiously, but the signal wasn't for help or to say that she was sinking. Instead it read, 'Please give us result of last Test.' We gave them the full scores, very slowly – owing to the heavy seas we were often out of sight of one another – and for the next hour or so storm and gale and the danger of the sea were forgotten. We were talking cricket.

*   *   *

Philip Snow, brother of C. P. and E. E., sometime captain of Leicestershire 2nds, was Administrator in Fiji and the Western Pacific from 1938 to 1952. He has been Chairman of the Associate Member Countries of the International Cricket Conference since 1982. Snow founded the Fiji Cricket Association and led the national side on a tour of New Zealand in 1948. He has written a highly informative and amusing book on Cricket in Fiji. *This script was for the series 'Travel and Adventure'.*

Cricket in the South Seas
Philip Snow

Home Service, November 1951

It is all quite different in the South Pacific. It is also (or perhaps therefore) refreshing. Cricket, particularly in Fiji, is played with distinction in a double meaning of the word. The Fiji representative team is distinguished by overseas standards through recent victories over the first-class New Zealand Provinces of Wellington and Auckland which included their Test players. Apart from their playing skill, of which the cricket world is but gradually learning, the Fiji cricketers look distinct. They take the field, at home and overseas, barefooted and it's odd how seldom, while batting in this way, the ball hits them on the toes. If it does, a cheerful smile radiates quite spontaneously. To people who kick footballs barefoot and who tread ceremonially on white-hot stones, the impact of a small leather ball at speed is no noteworthy affair.

But going on from the feet. Their bare legs are brown (no Fijians are anything like black); their calves are said to be the best developed in the world. They wear cream-coloured skirts (called *sulus*) which occasionally reveal brief undershorts because they're split up one side to the waist to allow for movement. The torso is long and lean, as is fitting in a race averaging a muscular six feet. Long powerful arms with large hands and tapering fingers harmonise with generally fine-drawn faces, the noses broad-based and frequently aquiline, mouths crowded with regular teeth, their whiteness accentuated by their brown surround, the whole surmounted by huge haloes of most carefully kept, crinkly hair. Modern fashion is, among men, unfortunately for shorter hair and severe partings, but I'm glad to say the handsome Fiji Police Force has always insisted, contrary to the leanings of almost every Force the world over, on hair being grown to the maximum.

Fijians bat and bowl briskly and field in the same spirit; all departments of the game are treated with an efficiency which a brisk approach does not always achieve. A good many Fijians have never really departed from the firm South Seas idea that cricket is a game intended only for the fastest bowlers and hardest hitters. That a player should bowl slow, Fijians and their fellow South Seas inhabitants consider, is due never to his own choice but to lack of physical development which prevents him from bowling faster.

In cricket tours beyond the coral and mangrove beaches of their islands, Fijians have made a remarkable impression. As long ago as 1895, a mixed European and native team toured New Zealand. They were not able to cope with the main Provinces, which did not spare the visitors by omitting their international players, but they were too good for the minor Provinces. In 1908, a team from the single Island of Mbau, no larger than St Michael's Mount – there are about 350 islands in the Fijian group by the way – Mbau achieved the colossal impertinence of a tour of Australia. It was entirely native except for one European and was again too strong for all except the principal State sides. Forty years later yet another team left Fiji. This time a mixed team found its way in 1948 to New Zealand where it established Fiji on the cricket map by gaining victories over the first-class Provinces of Wellington and Auckland. It lost to the other two main Provinces, Canterbury and Otago, only by margins of 30 and 40 runs.

Now the ceremonial South Seas drink is *kava* (it played a part on this tour); it is always prepared and presented with dead solemn ritual. On this tour it was always made before our matches began and occasionally brought out to the centre of the ground when Fiji was fielding, replacing the conventional lemon drink. At Dunedin, an Otago batsman, who was set, was persuaded to try the new drink. As he was swallowing the *kava* it was explained to him that it upsets the clearness of eye and balance a little. He was out to the first ball on resumption – a ruse that W. G. Grace might have appreciated.

A pleasant characteristic of Fijian cricket is a custom of the captain of the fielding side calling to his men, 'Captain, gentlemen' (or, if he is a Fijian, '*Na Kavetani*') – his men all then clap as the opposing captain walks in to bat. Cricket is the only game in Fiji in which all the races take part, so this custom is a specially happy one. We found the New Zealanders liked it a lot too, in 1948.

In the earliest days of European administration of the Pacific Islands when the intricacies of the game were being grasped by the natives, it became the tendency to play on every day of the week, the sides consisting of as many active men as could be mustered. It is known that in an early match a Tongan XI was composed of three hundred. Fielders used to sit unsuspected on tree branches or recline watchfully behind hibiscus bushes. The necessity, impressed upon them, to spend their time in a less eccentric manner was responsible for the disappearance of contests of this nature. A true account of one of the last of these should be found space for. Two villages in the remote and beautiful Lau Archipelago, half-way between the Fiji and Tonga Groups, played each other at the turn of the century with all their available man and boy power. Yandrana village batted first, fifty-odd of

127

them; they managed to score one run against the fifty-odd fielders sprinkled over the village green like so many bristles in a brush. A few of the fielders were lurking in the overhanging trees and on the slanting roofs of the thatched houses. I expect that run was a rushed, frantic one. When the Wathiwathi LIII or LV, or whatever the number was, batted, they found that runs came no more easily. They also secured one run, undoubtedly another desperate, dramatic one. Two runs were all that were scored in a whole day's play.

In the little-visited Lau Group, what most forcibly impresses one at the present day is the 1870-ish character of the institutions of the game. The Lauan chiefs in their splendid isolation were credited, before the Cession of the Fiji Archipelago to the British Government in 1874, with a tremendous half-supernatural power, often benevolently exercised. This power, the Fijians thought, rendered their states immune from defeat at cricket when this game was introduced to them after the Cession. The village of Lakemba for instance could not be beaten because it was the home of the *paramount* chief, who is endowed, naturally, with '*mana*' (miraculous efficacy). The high chief did not have to *play* to confer immunity from defeat; his existence anywhere about was sufficient. I once encountered the *mana* direct. The present-day paramount chief a few years ago hit me for the biggest six I have ever seen (and I have seen many at close hand – off my bowling). It was honestly, if only for a moment, lost in the sky. His team's win was never in doubt at any stage: no one could remember when, in fact, the team had last lost. Although the descendants of high chiefs have surrendered some of their atmosphere of divine right in the passage of time and through contact with more democratic society, they still cling firmly to many of their rights. One of them is the right to bat first. This they exercise, often with some skill for the chiefs were for long the only exponents of the game. And, after batting, the chiefs often exercise another right, that of disdaining to field or bowl or take any further part in the game.

Fijian umpires consider themselves undressed for their occupation if they do not carry a bat as the outward sign of their status. They adopt a more conversational attitude towards the batsmen in the serious moments of the game than their European counterparts. When they are giving guard, they invariably say to the batsmen something like this, 'Middle and leg. One to come. Now hit this ball into the ocean.'

South Seas batsmen tend to accept the fact of their being out with more surprise than most players of the game. When the wicket has been broken or a catch taken they look undisguisedly miserable at the moment of dismissal and start to walk as if in a trance away from the wicket, regardless of direction. They then invariably turn back to the wicket where they look dubiously at the stumps or the fieldsman who has committed the offence. Finally, and reluctantly, the irrevocability of it all makes itself felt and they walk with trailing bat and trailing feet to the Pavilion that means obscurity after limelight. The whole process upon dismissal takes up to seven minutes which in a clockless environment matters not at all.

When a fielder has made a catch, his custom is to throw the ball up in the air to an enormous distance in his immediate reflex of excitement. Viliame Mataika, in one of Fiji's matches against Auckland in 1948, delighted the crowd with a throw from first slip (where he took a hot catch) to outside the boundary and over where long off might have been standing.

From the time of the return of the Mbau Island team from Australia in 1908, cricket was scarcely played in the province of Thakaundrove for another thirty years. What happened was this: just after the Australian tour, the captain, Ratu Kandavulevu, paramount chief of Mbau and highest chief in Fiji, took the Mbauan team to Thakaundrove to play what corresponds closely to a festival match, so great ceremonial accompanied every part of this visit; etiquette was at its highest. The feasting finished at last, the cricket began. Ratu Lala, Tui Thakau, the highest chief of Thakaundrove and of great standing throughout Fiji, though not so omnipotent as Ratu Kandavulevu, went in to bat first. This was not due so much to his possessing the greatest ability among his side at the game, which he did not, but to his being of the highest rank. He received a trial ball, as everyone opening an innings does in Fiji whenever Fijians are playing together. The next ball he was out – a diplomatic gaffe of fatal consequence. For Ratu Lala pulled up the shattered stumps and called away his followers from the ground. Not only that, but he prohibited the miserable game from being played again in his domains, and this prohibition lasted for very many years. So there it was: the earliest abandonment in cricketing history of a game that has once begun. Here is the score:

Thakaundrove v. Mbau at Somosomo, Taveuni, 1908

THAKAUNDROVE

FIRST INNINGS

The Tui Thakau b Samu	0
Joni Tomasi Koka not out	0
Extras	0
Total, for one wicket	0

Bowling	O.	M.	R.	W.
Samu	0.1	0	0	1

Match abandoned on account of high dudgeon of High Chief.

Brighter Cricket
Neville Webber

Neville Webber, a New Zealander, recently watched a game of cricket in Samoa and described it in *Radio Newsreel*. 'Games', he explained, 'are nearly always played between villages, and the night before the match there is always a great feast followed by dancing and singing.

'As to the cricket itself, there are no such things as MCC rules. Teams vary from twenty-five players to 200 and more, and often include women and children; for a match is a real village occasion. Strict overs of six or eight balls are unknown: the bowler just keeps on bowling as long as the ball is returned to his end. Spin bowling and such devious devices as off-wicket bowling are despised. The idea is to bowl at the wickets just as fast and accurately as possible. The fielders are led by a combination of captain and clown who keeps proceedings at a merry pitch by doing such unexpected and uncricket-like things as turning a couple of cartwheels – which all his team must emulate.

'The batsman wears neither pads, gloves, nor boots. He must make a definite strike at every ball. It is a strict, though unwritten, rule that blocking is not cricket. To make the runs, the fleetest youths in the village are employed to race up and down a parallel pitch. The moment a man is out the next batsman leaps to the crease, for if he is not there within a couple of seconds the bowler may bowl his wicket over. The game may go on for a day, two days, or a week. And then, when it is all over, more feasting, dancing, and singing. "Your New Zealand cricket," repeated one of my Samoan friends, "ah, it is too slow for us. Such a sad game. It is because of these MCC rules, I fear."'

*　　　　*　　　　*

In October 1952 the Rev. F. Percival Ward gave a talk on Pitcairn Island, which was uninhabited until 1790 when settled by the mutineers from the Bounty. *From Ward's talk, which was recorded in Australia for later broadcast in England, is extracted the section on cricket.*

Cricket on Pitcairn Island
Rev. F. Percival Ward

Home Service, March 1953

For many years the people of Pitcairn Island have been fond of playing ball. Now, with a proper bat and a good ball, they love a game of cricket. It's not exactly a regular XI, for every available man is included so long as the sides are about even. What matter if there are twenty or thirty men on each side and what if the field is overgrown with grass and lantana, there are plenty of men to do the fielding and as they are all potential Jessops those fielders have something to do. The main science is to lift the ball with all the strength possible and send it flying over the heads of all the men into the undergrowth.

All the village goes out up the hill; they take their lunch and baskets of oranges and pineapples or mangoes and make a real picnic of it. They sit around on the long grass or under the trees interested in making their souvenirs or closely watching the game. Now and again some very witty barracking causes the whole countryside to rock with laughter and when they succeed in putting a batsman out, the opposing side will shout long and loud, 'DEAD, Dead's a HATCHET.'

If the game should be played in the valley under the banyans, the people have a natural amphitheatre where they can sit and watch. There in the centre of the village one of the big banyan trees was removed to make room for a good cricket pitch, but that doesn't stop the ball being sent flying into the banyan trees that still stand all too close in on two sides. Up the long roots, which hang thickly from the branches, those fieldsmen scamper like monkeys to the accompaniment of great shouts of barracking and laughter.

Having watched the men at their games for a day or perhaps two days, the women sometimes select sides for their turn. With great enthusiasm they continue the game, some of them being exceptionally good with the bat. Where the women sat making their baskets while the men played, the latter now take their positions as onlookers busy all the time on their woodwork, but taking a keen interest in all that is going on and shouting their encouragement or disapproval.

Though cricket may be played all the year round there is really a season for it and there is a season for flying kites. Of course, a steady north wind is a necessary condition for the kites. Fitted with what is called a 'singing engine', a paper that vibrates, the kites make music in the air, a huge buzz and with a number singing at the same time it's a remarkable noise. I counted eighteen kites up one day.

André Drucker gave several talks on English life and institutions as they appeared to the foreigner. In this talk he turned his attention to cricket.

Cricket Through Foreign Eyes
André Drucker

Midland Home Service, June 1954

As can only be expected from a country which is inhabited by the English, England is full of strange legends, queer customs, funny games. Perhaps the most perplexing one is that Summer Ritual which is called cricket. I know that many stories have been told about it. But mine is quite different and it may well be that Englishmen as well as foreigners could profit from hearing me thinking aloud.

There is a time in the year when Englishmen by common consent put the clock on an hour and by this simple expediency declare it to be Summer. Of course you understand that this doesn't change the English Weather into Summer Weather. Nothing will. It is being done because cricket is being regarded as a Summer Ritual Game and so for its benefit Summer has to be declared.

But even this ingenious promotion doesn't alter the fact that cricket is a game which is really quite unsuited to the English climate and that's what makes it so wonderfully English. If it were suited it wouldn't be half as much fun. The English love doing things which are – well, let's say, not quite normal; which startle foreigners who are so terribly rational and the more they can get foreigners startled about themselves, the more they enjoy being English.

They are perhaps the only people in the world who really enjoy what they are and wouldn't like to be anybody else – unlike all the other people in the world who think it's either their duty to be what they are or just bad luck and wouldn't mind swopping it for something else.

Where was I? Oh yes. Cricket.

England's green lawns and playing fields are the envy of the world. The English can grow grass as nobody else can and that makes them think that cricket is just the thing for it – which it is. But when they want to play it they find that grass is not enough and that they actually need a fine warm day with no wind and no rain. As this happens ever so rarely they have to postpone their ritual ever so often. That makes it the more precious to them so they will talk about nothing else but about the 'condition of the pitch', dry wickets, wet wickets, sticky wickets, wicked wickets. Even *not* playing it adds to the fun and helps to make it more English.

Cricket is the only game which the English have all to themselves. Nobody else can play it. That makes it so infuriating to the poor foreigners who always want to understand everything. So, they tell the English that it doesn't matter really because cricket isn't a game anyway but a ceremonial cult, an institution where both sides try to win but don't play to win. If it is a game at all, so they argue, then it is only fit for lunatics, which is not to be wondered at as all Englishmen are mad anyway. To which the English reply – all foreigners are crackpots, so what could they possibly know about *us*, let alone cricket?

And they are absolutely right. Only an Englishman can *really* understand cricket. To everyone else it is a ball-game, played with wooden bats by handsome men in white flannels. They are seen running a few yards for reasons known best only to themselves or seen immobilised in a crouching attitude as though suffering from stomach ulcers or seen swinging a bat one minute and next minute walking away to the Pavilion without apologies or explanations. Not even the most fervent cricketphobe can deny that they make a perfect picture on the spectacular green lawns, surrounded by people who are lazily licking ice-cream or reading sports papers or dozing in deckchairs with not a care in the world. Some are watching.

There isn't a foreigner worth his native salt who hasn't pondered over the character-building qualities of cricket which have made the English what they are. They all have given up pondering.

Then there are, of course, those terms which are so utterly alien to the aliens. You can't please an Englishman more than admitting complete perplexity over terms like bowling maidens over or somebody having a square leg or somebody being a silly mid-on.

It has been said that nothing happens in cricket. Well, nothing happens in those games either about which foreigners usually work themselves into a frenzy – tennis, football, hockey and the rest. They all work on the same silly principle of hitting a ball.

No. To me the bewildering aspect of cricket is not the *game*. It is the *English* when in the grip of cricket. It is a strange and enchanting phenomenon, a legend which could begin like this:

Once upon a Summertime the English play what they call Test matches at home. It is so called because it is the most testing time for the whole nation. It is played for the possession of the legendary Ashes, England's Holy Grail. Only the Crown Jewels surpass it in value. When the Test is under way, a strange, vibrating psychosis envelops the whole of the English Isles, jumps the oceans and affects every Englishman abroad wherever he may be.

At this time, the air in this green and tranquil land is loaded with high tension. Men and women walk about with nerves and sinews taut. In their eyes is an eerie flickering light, as in a tiger's. When things go not too well for the gallant boys of England, the country seems to drop into a stupor. No laughter rings out from one end of the isle to the other. Upper lips are worn stiffly. National Health teeth are grinding. Groups meet in the streets in front of cricket bulletins and analyse in hushed tones the tragic events. England, with no runs and all wickets fallen, is the nearest to Böcklin's Island of the Dead.

How different when things go well or are in the balance! The island hums like a gigantic beehive. The pubs run dry, poets and philosophers are carried away in sublime thoughts, statesmen and editors surpass each other in nobility of language, the working man puts his sturdy shoulders to the wheels with joyful vigour. The whole nation is smiling. There is a gaiety and abandon which knocks Vienna and Paris into an umpire's hat. Never are England's girls more beautiful, her men more boyish.

The outside world is stunned by these happenings. They have been led to believe that the English take their pleasures seriously. What nonsense! The English are the world's most hilarious watchers – when the home side wins.

The infection is general. What for instance did a crisis-ridden world expect to hear from the Australian Prime Minister after a vitally important State visit to South Africa in that memorable Test summer of 1953? When he was facing a battery of cameras, microphones and newspapermen, the eyes and ears of the globe literally on his lips, would we not have expected him to say,

'Gentlemen, the unity of the United Nations is the bridge which will cement peace and unmask the aggressors,' or words to that effect?

But no. His world-shaking utterance ran as follows,

'Gentlemen, there could be no greater farce than have five cricket tests drawn.'

Then he added with authority,

'Gentlemen, the last Test should be played out.'

A minute later the cables which link the continents quivered with this solemn news. Foreign diplomats, the peoples of the world sat up, panic-stricken. What was that he said? The LAST TEST?! Good Lord, is it as bad as all that?

Of course they had no clue to what he was talking about.

There is that steadfast old lady, the British House of Commons, behaving peculiarly in that mad season. The main parties which under the unwritten laws of the Constitution are paid to oppose each other bitterly, even on points they have in common, suddenly unite in a patriotic desire to drop any controversial business which would require the presence of their members in the House. But for a few rheumatic politicians who can't stand fresh air anyway, the bulk of the MPs are on the cricket ground, watching. Nobody is counting votes. They are counting runs, grimly, with a lump in their throat.

Foreigners think that is funny. If they had any sense at all they would order their own opposing vicious parties to meet on the cricket fields and give politics a rest. Thus the world could possibly become a peaceful pitch fit to bowl upon.

No one will be surprised now to hear that the spirit of cricket even invades the austere law courts. In the Test periods some of the courts don't sit on

Saturdays. They adjourn. To watch cricket? Oh no! No English judge would put it like that! He would say, as one actually did,

'. . . adjourned for reasons which I am sure all of you will appreciate . . .' and off they go, judges, learned councils, scribes, bailiffs, warders with their prisoners still handcuffed to their wrists to watch the nation's Midsummer Heroes defend or attack three upright sticks of wood, crowned by a bail without remand.

The puzzling thing about it all is that the English are quite unaware of what they look like at the height of their cricket ecstasy.

There is the case of Wednesfield, a settlement of nuts and bolts makers in Staffordshire. Its councillors came out in full strength, donning frock coats and top hats to play a comic cricket match. Comic! You see? They don't know they are comic. They believe that only by putting on a disguise while catching googlies or doing a chinaman they become figures of fun. But no medical journal took this case up. To the English it was healthily normal.

Well, I could go on and on thinking aloud but I must come to the end of my story. So I will only tell you the impressions of a friend of mine, a continental professor of medicine. He had come on a visit to Birmingham to study how the hospitals are run here. It was the final day of the Test. As he walked through the corridors of a large hospital he noticed small conspiratorial groups of doctors. In passing he could hear one whisper in a tense tone, '137 for 5.' He was still puzzling over this outrageous fever which normally no human frame could endure when he heard another colleague say, 'Leg caught off stump.' A strange operation this, he thought. The word 'caught' suggested a sinister method of amputation which made him shudder. When he arrived at the operating theatre he wondered for a moment whether his mind had become unhinged or his hearing was playing funny tricks. The surgeons were performing an operation but instead of using familiar words they were muttering through their gauze masks words which sounded like sharp twists, burst stumps and slipping catches. It became truly mysterious to my foreign scholar. When they took him round the wards his eyes popped out when he saw the lame jump out of bed and dance the conga and the deaf and dumb sing 'For he's a jolly good fellow' at the news that Alec Bedser was not out. A nervous shiver caught him. This was uncanny. A few moments later he saw grave relapses of mild cases at the news that Compton was bowled by Lindwall for no runs.

This was too much for him. He dashed out into the street, fearing for his sanity. Yet everything was normal. Outside the hospital, police officers, burglars and pickpockets crowded round the car radios, listening to the commentaries, and crowds in front of radio shops watched tiny, grey figures on a tiny, grey screen. Throughout the country the nation had stopped work, solidly. It was the biggest voluntary paid stoppage in English history.

My continental friend gave himself an injection and then did some quick thinking. He came to the obvious conclusion that, as all *his* reflexes were satisfactory, it was the English who had all gone hopping mad, clinically mad, batty, off their stumps, silly mid-offs all, with a cricket chirping in their bonnets.

With this diagnosis, he rushed back to the continent and published his discovery which only confirmed what foreigners are suspecting all the time: that Cricket is a form of English lunacy, a Midsummer Madness.

The fools. They will never understand. They just won't see that there is method in this English madness. It keeps them sane . . .

*   *   *

above, *Horn Fair on Sussex Downs, 1938. On St James's Day, Ebornoe invites a neighbouring village to play it at cricket. During the match, a sheep is roasted by the playing field. At the end of the game it is sold and the player with the highest score on the winning side is presented with the horns;* below, *A Nice Afternoon's Cricket. Frocester near Gloucester going in to field against an RAF Regiment XI in 1944, with an obviously determined captain leading a motley band including the vicar as umpire and a wicket-keeper who runs the local car hire service.*

above, *Many County and England players took part in a charity match between Major Carlos Clarke's XI and P. G. H. Fender's XI at Major Clarke's residence, 'Ellens' at Rudgwick near Horsham in June 1939. Here we see 'Gubby' Allen playing defensively;* below, *Hugh de Sélincourt.*

above left, *Brian Johnston: 'Johnners' ever cheerful;* above right, *Neville Cardus making a speech at the Cricket Writers' Club;* below, *John Arlott: the voice of cricket.*

above, *Tommy Woodrooffe's sober view;* below, *Freddie Grisewood waiting his cue.*

left, *Percy Fender with his wife at Victoria Station before leaving for Australia in 1928 to cover the MCC tour as a journalist and write a book;* below left, *Jim Swanton sitting by;* below, *Rex Alston.*

above, *Jack Hobbs giving some hints to three of the entrants in the batting competition at the twentieth Annual Children's Garden Party and Market Fair at Duke of York's HQ Chelsea in June 1936;* below left, *Learie Constantine demonstrating the art of bowling;* below right, *'The Don' watches A. F. T. White, captain of Worcestershire, toss the coin at the start of the 1948 Australia tour.*

above, *Seventeen England cricketers led by Len Hutton sail for Australia in* Orsova *for the 1954–5 tour. Colin Cowdrey and Alec Bedser are behind Hutton;* below, *An unusual opening pair. Arthur Morris* (left, *of Australia) and Len Hutton walking out to open the batting for the Authors* v. *The National Book League in 1956.*

above, *Suva (the capital of Fiji) fielding in their match with the West Indies at Albert Park, Suva, 1956. Suva defeated the West Indies, who included Garry Sobers and Sonny Ramadhin;* left, *'Archie' MacLaren quietly watchful.*

ECHOES OF THE GREEN

For a mind programmed to accept as a fact of life the commentary-platoons of the 1980s, it is nigh impossible to capture the consciousness of half a century ago when many thought that first-class cricket could never be a 'live' broadcast commodity. Village cricket was a different matter though. The Leader from the Listener *in May 1930 shows an attitude of the times.*

Running Commentary

Arrangements have been made to broadcast eyewitness accounts of the five Test matches after the close of each day's play; and this reminds us again that first-class cricket does not lend itself to a good running commentary. The thrills are spread out over three or four days, and there could be no guarantee that the time chosen for the broadcast would provide the concentrated excitement which makes the Derby or an International Rugby match as thrilling to the listener as to the spectator. Larwood (or Grimmett) *may* be skittling wickets like ninepins: but also a Hobbs–Sutcliffe, or Woodfull–Bradman, partnership may be in full swing, and however entrancing to the connoisseurs watching, it cannot give the unseeing listener many thrills. But how different cricket broadcasts *might* be! one exclaims, after hearing Mr Archie Macdonell on the joys of village cricket in his talk on 10 May. There you get, as well as the legitimate and anticipated excitements of wickets falling (and on village greens forty wickets may easily fall on a Saturday afternoon), all sorts of unauthorised incidents, unknown at Lord's or the Oval, such as the non-arrival of whole or part of the opposing team and the eleventh-hour recruitment of complete strangers. This kind of excitement, unfortunately, is just what the efficient organisation of the MCC makes impossible: so, for Test matches, we must be content with eyewitness accounts. But, for an afternoon of thrills, why should we not have a running commentary of the last hour in some village match every Saturday? If the experiment were tried, it is highly probable that the annual fixture between, shall we say, All Muggleton and Dingley Dell would prove as popular an item on the programme as the Derby or the Boat Race.

* * *

Six years later, the broadcasting of a village match became a reality.

Two Against Eleven

The *Listener*, September 1936

Cricket, in these days of eleven-a-side matches, has become a much more stereotyped game than it was in its carefree youth, when touring sides would gaily tackle twenty-two of the local worthies or (to go back to the eighteenth century) a grand match would be staged between Three of Kent and Three of England, and would be watched, moreover, by ten thousand spectators. Some of the 'freak' matches of the past must have provided good entertainment: for example, who could have failed to enjoy the great game in which Squire Osbaldeston defeated 'the two best players of Nottingham' by making 84 not out and then dismissing his opponents for the insignificant total of 17 in their four innings? Some of the romance of these early cricketing days will be revived on Saturday, when Ashdown, of Kent, and Wensley, of Sussex, will play against 'an XI of the Isle of Oxney', at Wittersham, Kent. (A commentary on part of the game is to be broadcast in the National Programme.) The match is a repetition of one that was played in September, 1832, when two All-England players, Wenman and Mills, tackled the locals and beat them by 66 runs. Fortunately for Ashdown and Wensley, who will have to share all the bowling, fielding and wicket-keeping while their opponents are batting, the field of play is comparatively small, and this will save them a certain amount of running and will also give them a chance of helping their own scores along by a few vigorous 'sixes'. There should be a good day's cricket, and local opinion seems to be fairly evenly divided on the crucial question of whether the inhabitants of Wittersham and Stone-cum-Ebony (who will provide the Isle of Oxney XI) will be able to avenge their defeat of 104 years ago.

*   *   *

Village cricket is 'pure' cricket in the sense that it represents, for the most part, the game in its original spirit and setting without all the commercial accoutrements that can so easily sully its character in the big-time venues. Each of us has his own view of the game on the green and not all of them are common.

W. A. Darlington, dramatic critic of the Daily Telegraph *for nearly fifty years; Leonard Clark, poetry critic of the* Yorkshire Evening Post *during the 1940s and a poet whose own work enjoyed the esteem of many who find pleasure in a simple reflective poetry of the English countryside; writers and broadcasters Michael Home and C. Gordon Glover who resided north and south of the Fen country; and Hugh de Sélincourt whose book* The Cricket Match *was once described by Sir James Barrie as 'the best book that has been written on cricket or any other game' – all of them in a period of twenty-five years recorded the echoes from their green as they heard them.*

Village Cricket
W. A. Darlington

'Holidays No. 3', August 1936

Till I began to think about it for the purpose of this talk, I don't believe I ever clearly realised what a wide term 'village cricket' can be. Since I was a small boy, I have spent many a happy holiday playing this most delightful kind of cricket, and the variety of conditions under which I have played it or seen it played is really startling.

Let me begin at the bottom, and work up. In the Sussex village where I now spend all the leisure I can, there are not enough inhabitants to run a team. There *is* a village green, and cricket *does* get played on it. But the green slopes at an angle of about thirty degrees to the horizon, and is a small one at that; and there is no village inn. Cricket cannot really flourish in such conditions; and as a matter of fact there hasn't been a game since the village decided that the proper way to celebrate the Jubilee was for the women to play a match against the men.

The only member of my household to take part in this encounter was our 'daily woman'. Unfortunately, she proved rather a weakly woman, scoring no runs and dropping two catches. (Sorry for the pun. If I hadn't been *such* a long way from my audience I shouldn't have dared to make it.) Coming a little further up the scale – but not much – there is the cricket I used to play in Wales during my school holidays. My father had got himself a job in that mountainous country, which was all very nice for him but cramped my style abominably. All the places flat enough to play cricket on had already been used as sites for houses and when I grew old enough to play for the local team I found the conditions were most peculiar.

Only two clubs in the district had proper fields, and these were both so small that there was no room to move the wicket about. Match after match had to be played on the same pitch, which got balder and more dangerous as the season went on. By the time I got back from school, the last blade of grass had disappeared and batting became a real adventure. I often wished that I had the moral courage to go in to bat in a fencing-mask; it would have been a lot more useful than pads on those wickets.

At a neighbouring village, a local bigwig had put a lovely riverside meadow at the disposal of the club. It was delightfully green, but so marshy that the ball wouldn't pitch. So they put down a matting wicket, which was tricky, but mercifully slow.

Hardly any runs were ever made in these encounters. I remember once making a laborious 7, which was quite enough to establish me as a leading batsman, because the side's total was 25 or so.

Not only were the wickets peculiar, but the outfields as well. I once saw square leg make a magnificent running catch on the Aberdovey ground, and instantly disappear as though the ground had opened and swallowed him up. Time passed, and as there was still no sign of him the rest of us organised a search-party. We found him lying among boulders at the bottom of a sort of young quarry about four feet deep. He was bruised and half-dazed, but he still had the ball in hand. Just as one always believes a dying man's last utterance, the batsman took his word for it that he had made the catch, and departed.

You will believe that after an apprenticeship served in conditions as rough as this, I found even the most primitive forms of village cricket as played in southern England comparatively effeminate, but extraordinarily pleasant. One might have to field knee-deep in thistles, and leaning against a cow; but one never broke one's neck.

The atmosphere was different, too. In mid-Wales, cricket was an odd pursuit, imported by the foreign invader and rarely indulged in by the natives. I don't know whether it is still like that, but that is how it was thirty years ago. In England, on the other hand, it is part of the national life. In fact, it is the best understood symbol of the lighter side of rural life.

Say 'Village Cricket' to yourself, and what sort of mental picture do you get? I get an idyllic scene of manly sport and innocent good fellowship. The village blacksmith, a genial giant, is about to bowl to a bowed rustic in braces and corduroys, with one brown pad firmly strapped on to the wrong leg. On the boundary, in front of the village inn, is a row of elderly rustics, each with a fringe of whisker and a mug of beer, telling each other lies about the runs they used to make when they were youngsters.

The captains are the Squire of one parish with an MCC scarf just managing to meet round the place where his waist used to be before it sank without trace, and the vicar of the other, lean and long, wearing a very old county cap.

That is a fancy picture, long since out of date. Village teams nowadays all seem to wear flannels and good cricket pads. Brown pads are probably not made any more, and when I meet village blacksmiths they generally turn out to be undersized men who play darts. But the spirit of the thing is there, the same as ever.

Dickens caught this spirit in his account of the match between All Muggleton and Dingley Dell. In some ways, of course, that is the worst account of a cricket match that has ever been written. Dickens had obviously never played the game himself; and if he had had it explained to him, he had completely misunderstood the explanation. But if he was weak on technical detail, he was strong on atmosphere. The feeling of good fellowship in the *Pickwick Papers* match is the feeling which R. C. Sherriff captured so exactly in his play *Badger's Green*, or which I encountered only last week in a field in Buckinghamshire, when I was playing for Sir John Squire's famous team of authors and things.

But if you're a visitor from London, out for the day, you don't get the full flavour of these village games. That can only be tasted when you are playing for one village against the next, and are admitted into a little world where both sides are old friends and old rivals, where all sorts of private jokes are bandied about, when each side knows the other side's umpire's funny little ways, and can take measures accordingly.

There is another side to this, however. A game between two villages where local rivalry is strong and local feeling runs high can be a very grim affair, if anything happens to upset tempers on either side. One of the most unusual and uncomfortable games I ever played in was a match of this description between two big villages which both had ambitions to be regarded as summer resorts. The rivalry was bitter and both captains had done their utmost to get together the strongest possible XI for the match. To everybody's disappointment, the afternoon turned out wet, and instead of starting at 2.30, the game didn't begin till half past four. (I was playing for the home side, by the way.) The other people won the toss, and batted first, and their star performer, an Oxford blue of that year, made a very fine 50 in quick time. Everybody expected their captain to declare at 5.30 and have a shot at getting us out.

But no, his one idea was to give us, the hated rivals, no chance of winning the match. He went on solemnly batting until we had got the whole side out. We were left with a bare half-hour's batting, and no possibility of either getting the runs or of getting out. In fact, the game was ruined by one man's petty selfishness, and both sides knew it.

Everybody was angry, and our captain was perfectly furious. He called his team round him, and said, 'Look here, I'm going to show this blighter what I think of him. I want you and you' – he picked out his two solidest and steadiest batsmen – 'to go in and stay in. And I want you, if you can, to play out time without making a run of any kind.'

So out the two heroes went, and did as they were told. Every ball that was off the wicket they let alone; every one that was straight they met with completely lifeless bats. It wasn't very interesting as cricket, but it was a most successful comment on the visiting captain's behaviour. He was boiling with rage, but he could say nothing – especially as the Oxford blue and several others of his side were obviously amused and felt it served him right.

The two batsmen played out time safely, but they didn't manage in the end to keep the score-sheet clean, because the visiting fast bowler suddenly lost *his* temper, too, and started to bowl bodyline stuff. In sheer self-defence the batsmen snicked a boundary or two. I think it was the only time I have ever seen a cricketer genuinely annoyed with himself for making runs. You may not believe this, but it is perfectly true. I was one of the batsmen, so I know.

But such incidents are conspicuous by their very rarity, and I have generally found that village cricket is the happiest of all kinds of cricket that are played. And, thank heavens, the wickets – while not as bad as the Welsh wickets I began on – never suffer from the modern disease of being too good. In good club cricket, nowadays, half the side never gets a chance to make runs at all. Either it's an easy wicket, and the first few batsmen make hundreds, or it's a difficult wicket and nobody can stay in. You don't have that trouble in the villages.

Here and there you do, of course. I know three or four pampered village teams which are allowed to play their matches on the private ground of some big country house, on a wicket that a county team might covet. But that hardly counts as village cricket at all, because half the side often consists of distinguished visitors from the house itself.

I was once playing on such a ground when the news came that a certain friend of the family had been chosen to captain England in a forthcoming Test match against a touring colonial team. 'Well,' said the lady of the house superbly, 'he may be captain of England, but he's only twelfth man for us next Saturday.'

* * *

Serious Cricket
Leonard Clark

North of England Home Service, July 1953
I have not played cricket seriously for many years, though I am still able, in imagination, to hit sixes off Trueman and bowl Hutton first ball. When I say 'seriously', I am not quite accurate, for there was an occasion three years ago when I was press-ganged into a side composed of the young ladies and gentlemen of our street, who had been challenged by the young ladies and gentlemen in the next street. I had to take the place of a girl who had defaulted at the last minute, because her mother wanted her to go on an errand. The match, by courtesy of the vicar, was played on his sloping lawn. When it came to my turn to bat, our captain, aged twelve and a half, with all the inspiration of adventuring childhood, declared our innings closed at

twenty-two runs, a prodigious total, no doubt, and enough, as it turned out, to give us the victory. But I was deeply disappointed at not being permitted to acquit myself, and promised myself that I would never play for the team again, even if asked. However, my wounded feelings were slightly assuaged when the other side went in to bat. When their score stood at 6 runs for eight wickets, our captain, for reasons known to himself, took the demon bowler off and put me on. Better still, he directed me to bowl downhill, where my only worry was the number of byes our midget wicket-keeper would concede.

The player who faced me when I was about to make my first delivery was a girl called Jane. I had already decided to bowl a very fast daisy-cutter, as observation had shown me that small boys are unable, owing to a little matter of reach, to do very much with this kind of ball. But here was a lady, and on the grounds of decency alone, I had not the heart. I changed my terrifying run up to the wicket to a middle-aged amble and tossed her up a very slow leg-break. She played the ball by a method entirely unknown to the MCC. For she suddenly changed her stance and turned herself into a left-hander. Before the ball had even touched the ground, she had hit a fearful wallop into a neighbouring garden. Seeing the score now standing at 10, for there had been an agreement beforehand that there should be no sixes, my blood began to rise. 'Women,' I said, 'ever the destroyers of men's fondest hopes.' So I decided to bowl her a fast daisy-cutter. Then I glanced at her again. She looked so young and appealing as she held the bat with one hand and her hat on with the other. Instead, I bowled her a slow, straight underhand, and was promptly 'no-balled' by the vicar's daughter, who was acting as umpire. Good manners prevented me from contesting this strange decision, but quickly I went through all the various balls I could bowl. It would have to be a daisy-cutter. The trouble was that, for the remainder of the over, though I could bowl it remarkably effectively all along the ground, I could never bowl it straight. But in the end I got her. Off one of my widest balls, which everybody else would have left alone, she was stumped, and retired, I regret to say, with her tongue out, to the other side of the lawn.

My analysis, at this stage of the proceedings, read, 'One wicket for 6 runs.' I could see our captain frowning at me; he had not forgotten that four, nor the disgrace of that no-ball. I was terrified lest he might take me off, but the sound of a tea-trolley being wheeled out from the house seemed to soften him. He graciously allowed me another over.

My next opponent was the owner of the wickets. This put me in a frightful quandary. I argued to myself that if I got him out there was always the danger he would remove his property and not allow a second innings. He was a miserable-looking boy, who played cricket, I believe, more as a business than anything else. I could see the glint of professionalism behind his spectacles and sensed an attitude which said, 'Don't you dare to hit *my* stumps.' To some extent I could see his point and decided to hit as small a portion of them as possible. So I bowled him a ball which Heaven permitted to be straight; he did not even see it. It hit the middle stump right at the bottom and the bails toppled off. Then, with a sudden burst of anger and displaying more temper than was seemly in the presence of the vicar, the wretch turned round, raised his bat, and clouted the wicket-keeper. Both boys then burst into tears, he flung the bat as far as he could, grabbed up the wickets, and left the ground before tea could be served. My analysis now read, 'Two wickets for 6 runs.' The match was over and our street had won.

But there was a time when I also played cricket 'seriously' with grown-up men in a country village. On Friday evenings, the list of the team used to be pinned up in the bow window of 'The George'. I can still see that list. My name was invariably last for I was still 'the boy'. Although I was a neat and nippy fielder, I have an inkling that I was chosen each week because of my ability to play the piano, a very necessary accomplishment when a cricket team makes its headquarters at an inn.

Our oldest and fiercest rivals resided in a village some six miles away. Our match with them was such an important fixture in the calendar that a whole day was devoted to it. We went to them this year, they came to us next year, and so on. If we visited them, it was an occasion for two brakes; for wives, sweethearts, and other supporters travelled with us. We flattered ourselves that they came to watch us play. The truth was that we were given a magnificent lunch and tea for nothing and that there were six 'pubs' on the way back home.

The fixture was always played on August Bank Holiday and in the Squire's park, for he it was who financed the away team and provided the lunch and tea. I played in six of these matches, but the one I remember best of all has never found its way, alas, into the romantic pages of *Wisden*.

We left our village when St Ethelbert's clock was striking nine; this meant it was ten o'clock. The two brakes, bulging out with bodies, baskets and cricket gear, and drawn by two chestnut horses, left 'The George' to the accompaniment of the cheers and catcalls of those unfortunates not privileged to watch us defeat our opponents. After about one and a half hours' somnambulistic wandering through orchards and barley fields and along dusty lanes we reached the enemy's camp. Wickets had already been pitched in the Squire's park. The Squire shook hands with us all and told us we were in for a beating. Round the park we could see the ladies in their multicoloured Edwardian dresses, shading themselves with tiny, frilled parasols. Our opponents won the toss, decided to bat, and before one o'clock were all out for 36 runs. In spite of the words of praise and anger muttered under his breath by the Squire, their wickets tumbled before the inspired bowling of our two stalwarts, Philip Harper, aged fifty-two, and Henry Mare, aged fifty-five.

Now 36 was much lower than the usual run of scores in local matches and we thought we had the match in our pockets. For had we not got young

Philip Harper, who could stay in for hours? And his father, who was good for a dozen or so? And Renton Evans, the schoolmaster's son on holiday from his public school? Best of all, we had Randall Jones, our umpire. Yes, we would win this year or, in Henry Mare's words, 'We got 'em on the 'op, my lads.'

But we had not reckoned with the Squire. We had forgotten that he had been educated at Oxford College and was as crafty as a fox. However, we walked up to the big house for lunch, which was laid out for us on the lawn. Will such mountains of food ever be seen again? For there, on half a dozen white-clothed trestle tables, were huge rabbit pies, boiled hams, and chicken, with enough lettuce to provender an army. Then the Squire and his butler brought round mugs of cider. Never have I drunk such an earthly version of heavenly nectar. It was a hot day and we drank as much as we wanted. What we did not know was that the cider was very old, that it had been laced with rum that morning, and that the Squire had given strict instructions to his team that they were to drink only one mug per man. My recollections of what happened after the gargantuan feast was over are slightly muddled. But they are not half as muddled as those of other and more mature members of the team. I know that old Philip drank seven mugs and that Vernon Thomas, our wicket-keeper and the mildest of men, managed to get down four and a half. We had to stop Randall Jones from drinking the stuff two mugs at a time, one in each hand.

Round about half past two we began our innings. I have never seen such an exhibition. To begin with, Sam Baxter, our captain, completely changed the batting order, so that within ten minutes we had three wickets down for no runs. Then our umpire, Randall, enlivened the proceedings by giving the next man out lbw, even though no appeal had been made. Old Philip tied himself into knots because he would insist on putting his pads on the wrong way round and was bowled first ball. Young Philip, coming from the Pavilion, made a slow procession right round the ground before arriving at the wrong wicket. Then, to top everything, the umpire, Randall, held up the match because he decided he needed a chair to sit on. He laboriously dragged the chair from one wicket to the other at the end of each over, under the impression that there was now only one umpire officiating. Young Philip trod on his wicket. Alfred Hosgood, the blacksmith's apprentice, hit out at everything and, when he was finally bowled neck and crop, said that he had seen three balls and, by some error of judgement, had clouted the wrong one. The schoolmaster's son, after hitting one beautiful boundary, collapsed in the middle of the pitch, and had to be assisted off. For the rest of the match he lay with his head in one of the ladies' laps plaintively moaning, 'Let me be – I want to die.'

By half past three our score stood at 25 runs for eight wickets. It was now my turn to bat and I had drunk just enough cider to give me the confidence of a Hammond. I disdained pads and gloves, informed the soporific company that destiny had chosen me for this particular moment, and then, grabbing hold of someone else's bat, marched out into the sunshine as if I owned the park, the players and everything else. I took guard and awaited the arrival of the first ball. It came floating through the air as big as a football, but I could not understand why it had a ring round it. I took a mighty swipe and, more by luck than judgement, hit it straight up into the air immediately above my head. The fielders rushed in to make my exit absolutely certain. I shouted to Silas at the other end to come for a run, but Silas refused to budge. The ball went so high into the summer sky that even Randall, the umpire, joined the company that was trying to catch it: but fortune was on my side. Instead of landing into a safe pair of hands, it dropped right on top of Silas's head, who had suddenly decided to run and was now standing by my side. He was carried off unconscious. We still had 11 runs to tie, twelve runs to win and last man in.

The last man was Joshua Ruddock, the village undertaker. Now Josh was a good husband and father but he had never made more than three runs in any match in which he had played. I waited anxiously for Josh to appear but there was no sign of him. The fielders began to get impatient. The Squire was grinning all over his face. I saw lots of movement on the boundary and much scurrying about, but Josh did not join me. He could not be found. In the end, they had to send out search parties to look for him and, eventually, discovered him snoring like a pig under a great ash tree at the end of the park. They did all they could to wake him, but cider and summer had conquered. Every time they got him to his feet, he fell down again. They fastened his pads on, put a bat in his hand, pointed him in the direction of the wicket and gently propelled him along towards it. They shouted at him and told him he would never play again unless he batted, but poor old Josh was past it. They left him sleeping under the ash tree, still with the bat in his hands and the pads loosely dangling on his legs.

And that is how our rivals won the August Bank Holiday match that year by 11 runs. I still have the score-book that records the eventful occasion. It makes very interesting reading. I am given 'Not out—0', and opposite the name of Joshua Ruddock appear the words, 'Unable to bat—0'. For all I know, Joshua may still be sleeping there, but old Philip, Henry Mare, Sam Baxter, Silas, and Alfred Hosgood are certainly playing cricket elsewhere. And Randall Jones, I am quite sure, will be umpiring.

*   *   *

Village Cricket Sixty Years Ago
Michael Home

Home Service, January 1959

Sixty years ago, every village near us in Breckland had a cricket team. How ours was raised was usually a miracle. The labourer, as he was then known, had no Saturday afternoon off, and only rarely would a man be let off. We at least had a nucleus. Our vicar – 'the Reverend', as we knew him – was a useful bat and a good wicket-keeper. His son, Lance, who was up at Cambridge, would play for us as often as he could and he was a fine hitter and a terrifyingly fast bowler. There was my father – something of a stonewaller – and my elder brother, until he left home, and my very young self. The balance had to be made up out of a pool of about eight, and often, as late as on a Friday night, not more than three or four would seem to be available.

Except for the Reverend and Lance, and myself after I went to Thetford Grammar School, no one wore flannels. Sunday best, and shirt-sleeves, was the rule. Trousers were held up by braces or those elastic belts with snake-head fasteners. Boots were just boots, though some of the younger men wore tennis shoes. My father, always ingenious, wore thick carpet slippers with an outsize in tintacks driven through the soles. To shield our eyes against the sun we wore ordinary caps, though the Reverend generally sported a panama and Lance a college cap. At the first game I remember, some of the players wore bowler hats. It was a windy day and a hat was blown on the stumps, and there was a lot of argument as to whether or not the owner was out.

We first played in the park, which had a reasonable outfield, but many grounds on which we played had their far outfields rough and uncut. It did not pay to drive a ball along the ground: the art was to hit high and handsome. If a ball landed in tall weeds or a clump of nettles we ran till 'Lost ball!' was called, and the total went up by six. As for the pitches themselves, once a farm roller had done its work in spring, the only preparation was to cut and mark out. Shooters were plentiful and it took some pluck to stand up to a really fast bowler.

'How do he bowl?' would be asked about someone with whose bowling we were not acquainted. If the reply was that he 'wholly cut 'em down', my young heart would sink into its boots. Underarm bowling was still common enough in the 'nineties and some of it could be pretty fast too. An Ellingham bowler known as Plumpicker took more wickets than anyone in our parts. It was the low trajectory that beat you, and the speed with which the ball left the pitch: plus, of course, a most devilish accuracy. Then there was the new 'break' bowling. Caston had a man – I believe his name was Bailey – who could bring a ball in a good six inches from the off, and I remember how we were flummoxed the first time we played *him* at Caston.

What about batsmen? There, the question would be, 'Do he play strooks?' Of our team, only the Reverend really played strokes, though my father had one of his own invention. It was probably some ancient ancestor of the cut, for he would poke at a ball on the off, hoping to nudge it through the slips. The rest of us had only the good old principle of, 'Here comes a ball: let's try and hit it.' If the bat was straight it was wholly by chance and never design. And some of us *could* hit it. I have known a bowler, playing out of his class, as he thought, in village cricket, say despairingly that it was no use bowling straight, for the straighter the ball the further it was hit. One of the best hitters was Lewis Savory of Breckles. Pitch him up anything on the leg and it was almost a certain four or six. No apparent effort; just natural timing and an uncommonly good eye. I remember as if it were yesterday how I, too, began to be a player of 'strooks'. It was about sixty years ago, a wet Thursday afternoon, and I had been given permission for the first time to use the school library. Almost the first book I picked up was a manual of cricket by W. G. Grace and I can still feel the flash of revelation when I began to be aware that varying sorts of balls should be countered by various things called strokes. In less than no time I was going forward with a straight bat. I even learned to cut a ball. As a climax, there came a day in the park when I overheard two of our men discussing me as I was going in. 'He oughta make a few. He've wholly larnt to handle a bat.'

For an away match on a Saturday morning the start might be delayed if we were still a man short, but when we did set off it would be in our big cart: two in front, two behind and the communal cricket bag as well. The rest would go in the vicarage wagonette, the Reverend's coachman driving. John Balfour, village schoolmaster and scorer, always went in the wagonette, as did the umpire – George Adams, or Jimmy Thompson, or, much later, Monkey Downes.

· Downes was a mole-catcher; a shortish man with a fringe of whiskers, a simian upper lip, and a twinkling eye. He always stood umpire in his Sunday black, a bat, as a sign of office, in his hand. It was Downes who once made a famous quip about the weather. We were playing Ellingham away and only fanatics like the Reverend and my father would ever have set out. It rained cats and dogs all the way and it was still raining as hard as ever when we had had tea. Then the Reverend took a look out from the flap of the big tent.

'I don't know, Downes, but it looks to me as if it's going to clear up.'

'Ah, sir,' Jimmy said, 'that's what the davvul told Noah.'

Umpires could be match winners in those days and woe to an opposing player who played 'strooks' or whose flannels hinted that he might become a bit of a nuisance. If a ball struck his pad or he flashed at something on the off, up would go the umpire's hand. If he was not to be run out, he had to be in by the length of a street. The man most umpired out was Saunders, known everywhere as the Ellingham Stonewaller. Perhaps there was some reason for it, since he took his guard with the bat about six inches from the stumps, the bat then upright close to his right leg. And there he would stay immovable till a bowler sent down a rank bad ball.

Jimmy Thompson was the hero of one of the few pieces of umpiring out that I ever remember connected with our own team. Jimmy was a postman and one day when he had a letter to deliver at an outlying cottage Wretham way, he took a short cut through some Wretham woods. The Wretham agent for Squire Morris was a bully, and it so happened that he saw Jimmy and came galloping up on his horse. Jimmy was ordered to get back to the road.

'You can't order me about, sir,' Jimmy told him stoutly. 'I'm on the Queen's business.'

'Queen or no Queen, out of here you get!' the agent roared at him, and he shepherded Jimmy till he was off Wretham land and back on the road.

It was some time later when we played Wretham at Heathley and the agent was playing. He and Rowley, their vicar, were their two best bats: Rowley a stylish left-hander and the agent rather a showy bat who had a liking for anything wide on the off. He cut at such a ball, missed it by inches and was staggered to hear Jimmy call, 'Out!' There hadn't been an appeal, but that was nobody's business.

'What d'you mean, out? I wasn't near it by a mile.'

'You're out, sir,' Jimmy hollered. 'And, Queen or no Queen, out you go!'

Extras were often plentiful on our pitches. Even an agile long-stop, stockings stuffed with grass, could not stop them all. All ground fielding was tricky, for the ball did queer things in hard or rough outfields, and the body was often safer than hands. But I cannot remember a real casualty. There were occasional hold-ups when a batsman got a crack on the inside of a right knee. Most of us preferred to use only one pad as giving greater mobility, and the pads were so old and pliant that they were little more than an ornament. If a ball struck a pad it was the batsman's fault. He had a bat to see that it did not. As for gloves, they were unknown, and a rap on the knuckles was just the luck of the game.

Most bowling then was either medium or fast and the only really slow bowler I ever played against was Squire Morris of Wretham. He was a tall, stout, cumbersome man who always put himself on for a few overs when we played on his park. He would take a very slow step or two and then a high-tossed ball would come slowly down towards you. The first time I ever played against him – I was about fourteen at the time – I walked up the pitch and hit him full-toss for two. I did it a second time and then, at the end of the over, the Reverend, who was at the other end, had a quiet word with me. 'Michael, I think you'd better stay in your ground.'

I was far too young to appreciate the fact that Squire Morris's bowling was only a kind of interlude. He would give himself an over or two, be duly gratified if he flummoxed a batsman or even miraculously took a wicket, and then would take himself off. After all, it was he who provided the small cask of ale for the men and the stone-ginger for the boys; and the really good tea.

Tea was usually taken at about half past four: plenty of home-made bread and farmhouse butter and good plain cake. Then we would be at it again. There were never great scores, perhaps, but there was always keen cricket. Scoring was artificially slow because there were rarely boundaries and everything had to be run out, and there would be much blowing of bellows after a four or six. The Wretham ground sloped well down and away towards the church, and in one match a Wretham bowler had the bad luck to give my father a fast full toss on the leg. It left the bat with the crack of a pistol and he and Master Lance actually ran eight till my father virtually collapsed. It was the longest hit I ever saw and it took two relays to throw the ball in.

Our matches were battles of wits. Men had played against each other for years and strategy was what we called in Norfolk accordin-*ly*. The only one who always suffered from nerves was John Balfour. Even when you were in the field you could hear him groan when a catch was dropped or his chuckle when one was held. And a match did not end on a Saturday evening. It was something to be talked about during the week, though by Tuesday the list – as we called it – would be up in the little reading-room for names to be put down for the following Saturday's match. The Reverend's name would always head it, with Master Lance's if he were at home. Then would come my father's, and at intervals during the week he would be looking at that list to see how it was filling up. So the wheel came full circle to another Saturday morning. Maybe we were still a man short, yet somehow the miracle was always happening.

*   *   *

The Truth About Village Cricket
C. Gordon Glover

July 1955
England and South Africa meet at Headingley, Leeds, this week for the fourth Test match, the big battalions of cricket opposing each other in the trimmed and tailored solemnity of the Great Occasion. On Saturday, some thousands of other cricket matches will start round about two-thirty in the afternoon. Stumps, and beer, will be drawn at seven. Rooks will have racked the summer afternoon in an infinity of immemorial elms; doves moaned; cow-shots from cricketing cowmen sailed over the heads of cows; bees buzzed in the bonnets of innumerable umpires; and a whole regiment of fast

bowlers been declared by old gentlemen on benches to be serving up dolly-drops compared with the cannon-balling blacksmiths of their young day. In fact – the enduring ceremony of village cricket.

Now what, you may well ask, has village cricket to do with Test cricket? Both, after all, obey the same laws and are governed by the same conditions. Is there a parallel? A violent distinction? Does every village cricketer carry an England cap in his jacket pocket? What, in fact, *is* village cricket?

I am sufficiently a Philistine to say that there has been a great deal too much about village cricket. Squire, cobbler, parson, ploughboy, yellow-flannelled poet! True democracy! Flash of willow, sting of red leather on horny palm – all that! The buoyant brotherhood of a pastime 'not so much a game as a way of life'. That was Sir James Barrie.

It is only fair to say that, in many respects, Sir James was perfectly right. But what a way of life! Barring croquet (a game unexampled for malice and ferocity), I doubt if there is anything to touch true village cricket. And it might be healthy to cut right through the moan of doves in immemorial elms, and look at village cricket with affectionate honesty. 'There's a breathless hush in the Close tonight . . .' And over many and many a village green. Let us take the lid off it and ascertain the cause.

Take, for example, this game – or annual 'Derby' – between Great Muttering and Doggerel Green, adjacent villages which are about as friendly towards each other as a pair of puff-adders. One 'breathless hush' is due to the fact that the beetle-browed fast bowler smoking them down from the duck-pond end is not a Muttering man at all, but a week-ending Minor Counties player whom Muttering – and that is Muttering all over for you – have thought fit to play.

Doggerel themselves are a 'breathless hush-up' anyway, and wear the self-righteous, cocky air of men who, by playing clean, seem to have the game very fittingly in hand after the hush-making incident of the stumping of the Minor Counties player just before the tea interval. It was painfully plain from the Pavilion steps to see what had happened. Mr Minor Counties (who had hit forty-seven runs in twenty-three minutes) was seen to play the ball down towards third man, watch third man leisurely field it, and then, perceiving no run, stroll forth to pat the pitch.

The Doggerel wicket-keeper was then observed to make agitated semaphore for a quick return, and, having received it, remove Mr Minor Counties's bails. That was a breathless hush for you, all right! But it didn't last long. The brows of the Minor Counties man were stag-beetled when he returned to the Pavilion. But this, after all, is village cricket, and a 'Derby' match to boot, and wicket-keeper had the ancient laws behind him, if not the accepted ethic, when taking his dramatic action.

The scowling, ginger-haired harpy, petulantly sloshing teacups about in that enamel basin, is Greta Botherington. She is one of the 'ladies' without whom, of course, there would be no teas. She is also the wife of the Doggerel

Green 'lion', a radio personality who cannot play cricket for little apples, although, he declares in his biographical dossier, it is his prevailing passion. Village cricket, I may say, is full of these.

Mrs B. is in a rage because she has come a cropper over the tea rota. She has swapped dates with Madge Prowell under the impression that today was the date of the jolly 'President's XI' game – and she loves making lavish little *moues* at the President's wealthy cricketing friends over the teacups.

Madge Prowell is the smug-looking brunette eating chocolates under one of the immemorial elms. She has collared the 'President's XI', and knew it all the time! Both ladies, like all ladies in any way attached to village cricketers, will be buttered up no end by the President at the Annual General Meeting and thanked for their buns and co-operation.

The Annual General Meeting of any village cricket club – and I have attended a few – runs very much to pattern. The Secretary will resign, the younger lads will be glowered at for doing no work on the ground, and somebody-or-other will 'come out with it straight, Mr Chairman' and decline to serve upon any committee which includes 'certain parties'.

The 'certain parties' – and no club is a club without them – will then march off to The Cricketers Inn and darkle in a corner. It is unfortunately the general rule that the 'certain parties' who are always either taking, or giving, offence are first-class cricketers whom the team can do neither with nor without. I hold it to be true that the 'jolly band of brothers' spirit on the village green is as mythical as the famous blacksmith bowling in his braces and being invisible to the batsman as he pounds up a one-in-four hill. If these things were true, then village cricket would be too good. No match would be a human occasion which did not contain at least one act of open defiance in the face of an umpire, and at least one upraised finger of dismissal which turned itself half-way into a bee in the umpire's right ear. This is village cricket.

I am assured by old-timers and by many a writer who has wool-gathered among the flannelled figures moving in the long, blue shadows of evening that things used to be otherwise. Wagonettes, rosy-faced farm-hands, googly-bowling curates, pins of brown beer, mighty hitters, gamekeepers who could turn the ball a foot – all that. But I doubt it, for there can be no subject on which more wishful mush has been written than the Sacred Squares of the Doggerel Greens of England.

Yet, withal, we continue to play village cricket and to love it. There is still the thrill as the first sound of bat on ball echoes down from the nets on an April evening, still the headiness of the green incense that rises from the new-cut pitch, still the eager, older eyes cocked upon the youngsters as they take their first stand.

The brown boots, waistcoats, and braces of other days have gone. Village cricket is mighty respectable these days. Even grey flannels can raise a frown. The hard-hitting blacksmith – if ever he existed – is now replaced by the wiry technician from Pest Control. The country parson is a rare bird upon the field today. And the wicket itself rarely displays the picturesque and hazardous evidence of cattle which have paused in passing. And these things are probably all to the good, if it is a game of cricket and not a comic charade which is required. Nevertheless, let us be honest about the matter. Village cricket seldom was, seldom is, and seldom will be the nursery of Test cricketers. It is a law – and a pretty astringent one – unto itself. Picturesque possibly, hot-tempered certainly, but a piece of sacrosanct, buttercuppy mumbo-jumbo, not at all!

*   *   *

Hugh de Sélincourt, educated at Dulwich and University College, Oxford, schoolmaster, drama and literary critic for several London newspapers before turning to full-time writing, must be one of the few village cricketers to find themselves in the writings of satanist Aleister Crowley. The rituals of black magic seem far removed from those of the game on the green, yet who knows what sinister forces the captain of Storrington (the Tillingfold of his cricket fiction) had at his command!

Cricket on the Green

Hugh de Sélincourt

August 1935

Village bowling had better not be taken too lightly. I've played many a good game with old Joe, who tossed up with a funny low action an innocuous-looking slow just asking to be beaten out of the ground. He had a large, kind face palpably innocent of guile, and invariably chewed a succulent piece of grass. Oh! I've seen him do damage. One over I shall never forget against the General's team – our game of the season. A really class batsman came hurrying in – with 'Oh, this will be jam!' written all over his face. The first ball he took a dip at – he couldn't help himself: it simply asked for it – and he missed it: stumped with a furious appeal but he'd shuffled back and was rightly given *not out*. Along came the next. It went for six, thudding on top of a tea-tent. (We are done proud in this match.) Joe's large smile faded: you could see him thinking – 'Will this gawdy toff fall into the old trap same like Bill Hawkins?' – and down came a more tempting one, tossed a little higher, tossed a little slower. Swish went the bat with violence through the air: well across it, exactly like Bill Hawkins, down went the wicket quite gently. Came in a man with a great cricket name, growling it was nonsensical to treat what was obviously good bowling in that reckless fashion. The first ball he played back to with elaborate caution and missed: it nearly bowled him. The second ball he treated, if possible, with even greater respect; he touched it with the edge of his bat and gave me a simple catch at slip. Sam Bird, our umpire, a great philosopher, who had heard the incomer's comment, was doubled up with mirth. He managed to say to me, 'There's more ways of being nonsensical than one. Fair beats the band, that does,' and then recalled to the dignity of his office, he announced loud and clear, 'Gentlemen, the ball is over!' What old Sam Bird doesn't know about cricket isn't worth knowing. It's in his bones, the game. The village is lucky which has a man who knows as much about the game as old Sam: and you can meet them everywhere, though like other worthies they don't believe in 'pushing themselves forrard'! It's good to get them talking: I often have. Our Test Match Selection Committee could learn – but let me keep from any painful topic. All I mean is they know their own minds, these old chaps: and they know cricket.

Over-confidence can be a worse snare even than nervy diffidence. A team with nineteen consecutive wins on their little fixture list came to play us. Let us call them the Haberdashers. They came a winning side, in two large charabancs bringing their girl-friends with them. Their manner before the game was the manner of conquerors. They'd come to put us through it. We ached to beat them. We won the toss, but alas! wicket after wicket after wicket fell in a dreary dismal procession. They changed their bowlers: must make some sort of a game of it. The score crept up – to a miserable total in the fifties, but something to bowl against. They reversed their batting order, and the tail batsman thus promoted played with reasonable care. The others didn't. Their fixed wish was to hit the old fellow into the pond. Nine sixes would do it – an admirable idea, no doubt: but they couldn't bring it off. The old fellow wasn't born yesterday: it was slaughter. They made 23, tried to skittle us out and failed and got really wretched. I was glad they had brought their girl-friends with them. They were in need of a little comfort on the drive home.

*   *   *

Hugh de Sélincourt broadcast on cricket with regularity during the early 1930s, delivering both talks and summaries. The pity is that so much was not retained. Happily, a few summaries survive.

MCC *v.* Cambridge University
Hugh de Sélincourt

Regional Programme, June 1937

The Cambridge team have every reason to be well pleased with their day's cricket, for twice they were in a very bad position and on each occasion they fought back hard, showing real grit, and emerged in the end in a stronger position than anyone would have thought possible.

Compton and Aird, the overnight not-outs, opened with the score at 73 against the bowling of Rought-Rought and Fraser, a slow left-hander from the Dominions; and almost at once Aird was dropped at mid-off off Fraser, a bad miss as the pair took the score to 178, very slowly but very surely – 56 in the first seventy minutes – until just before luncheon when Compton, attempting a fourth run from a hit by Aird, nearing his 50, was run out. Aird, totally unprepared for such keenness and swiftness, sent Compton back when he was in the middle of the pitch; he slipped over in turning and was put out – a piece of forlorn bad luck as he was batting beautifully, had scored 80 and looked set for his century.

After lunch the MCC appeared to have Cambridge comfortably in their pockets but suddenly and surprisingly collapsed against the bowling of Hunt and Fraser. The remaining six wickets fell in half an hour for 21 runs. Good work, of course, for the Cambridge bowlers and fieldsmen, helped, one must confess, by lamentable batting on the part of the MCC.

Aird was beaten by a faster one from Fraser he tried to chop; Pearce hit wildly across a half-volley from Hunt; Fraser brought off a neat 'caught and bowled' to get Lord Tennyson. He thought it a bum-ball but the umpire did not. Smith was nicely taken in the deep by Rought-Rought – a well-judged running catch; and Hunt had Powell and Peebles; Hunt in the whole innings taking five for 51.

Cambridge, with an unexpected lead of 19, opened shakily. The pace bowlers were soon taken off, and Sims and Peebles had them so very groggy that it looked terribly like another collapse. But they stuck to it with magnificent pluck. Four wickets fell for 49; then Pawle, the top scorer in the first innings, and Studd dragged the score to 90. Another wicket, the sixth, fell at 99 – at a quarter to six. And then Rought-Rought joined Pawle, and Rought-Rought stopped. More than that, he attacked the bowling, taking no risks, in a courageous and refreshing manner. Their partnership showed the freest and best batting of the day; both of them brought off rattling good shots all round the wicket. They have taken the score to 152 for six from 99 for six – most invaluably – Rought-Rought not out 30, Pawle not out 46 – and Cambridge leave off 161 runs on with four wickets in hand – a position on which they are most warmly to be congratulated.

In the end Cambridge lost by seven wickets after the pitch improved on the last day and Compton and Edrich shared a stand of 103.

*   *   *

MCC *v.* Oxford University
Hugh de Sélincourt

Regional Programme, July 1937
Oxford started off this morning at a great pace against the bowling of Allom and Sims. Whetherly, who had gone in yesterday evening to fill up the bad last five minutes of the day, shaped quite unlike the usual '11', his number on the card – he scored, as a matter of fact, even faster than Mitchell-Innes, who was not at all slow – amongst other admirable shots lifting Sims, and later Compton, effortlessly into the grandstand for six. He and Mitchell-Innes put on 132 in sixty-five minutes – a marvellous rate of scoring – before Mitchell-Innes put a sharp one into the hands of Jehangir Khan at short leg off Edrich, whom he had been cutting and gliding like a master. His 84 was a fluent, stylish innings, beautiful to watch. Two for 38 – three for 170.

Then, at length, Owen-Smith was put on to bowl leg-spinners from the nursery end. They span, too, wickedly, with a definitely diabolical variation of pace. In his first two overs he took four wickets for two runs. He clean bowled Whetherly, who had made 63 and was trying for his fourth six off a sinfully tempting ball; he got Kimpton and Grover stumped, and he got Singleton lbw. Owen-Smith is having a pretty good match when you come to think of it – a dashing 168 not out with the bat, and then this remarkable bowling feat which changed the whole course of the match.

Oxford were all out by the luncheon interval for 233, or 249 behind the MCC total of 484. Scott, Darwall-Smith and Macindoe made some nice hits, but they could do nothing really against the bowling of Sims – 3 for 38 – and Owen-Smith – 5 for 33. The follow-on was not enforced, which was a great pity. It would have been far better practice for the Oxford team to have been hard up against it, and, if possible, to have pulled through, than to be thus played with, with all the rigour of the game gone.

Ballance and Singleton did most of the bowling, and till tea-time they bowled very well. After tea they and Mitchell-Innes were mercilessly hit by Edrich and Compton, Owen-Smith and Jehangir Khan who was missed at the wicket and at long on. Eventually Wyatt declared – 488 runs on – leaving Oxford an hour's play.

Barton and Dixon opened well until Barton, who had made 30 by some excellent cricket, put a bumper from Allom into Edrich's hands at silly short leg. Mitchell-Innes survived a confident appeal from Allom for lbw off his first ball – it must have been a near thing – and was again nearly bowled by the very next ball; but after that he played his own lovely game. Owen-Smith bowled Dixon for a patient dozen, and then – as in the first innings – Whetherly came out for the horrid last minutes. And he survived, opening again tomorrow, as he did today, with Mitchell-Innes not out 23, himself not out 5, with 407 runs to make and with eight wickets in hand.

As was to be expected, Oxford were never really in the hunt and lost decisively by 226 runs.

*   *   *

For the 'Saturday Talk on Sport' on 2 July 1938, Radio Times *provided the background: MacKinnon of MacKinnon, the thirty-fifth Chief of the Clan MacKinnon and the oldest clan chieftain living, who celebrated his ninetieth birthday in April last, is one of the only two survivors (with the Rev. E. E. Ward) of the famous match between Oxford and Cambridge played in 1870. Cricket-lovers will remember that Oxford had three wickets left and required only four runs to win. MacKinnon of MacKinnon, who was in the Cambridge team, will describe to listeners how Cobden, the Cambridge bowler, achieved the miraculous.*

Before that happened, Kenneth Rankin presented a historical survey of the Varsity match.

Cobden's Match and Memories of other Varsity Matches

MacKinnon of MacKinnon and Kenneth Rankin

National Programme, July 1938
It's rather the fashion nowadays to run down the Varsity match, and to say that, like a certain periodical, it's not as good as it used to be. The play, we are told, is poor, the matches dull, the performers themselves compare very unfavourably with the great ones of the past, and nothing exciting seems to happen in the way it once did.

It's quite true, in one respect at least, that things have altered, for if a man nowadays misses a catch, he may have all manner of excuses but he can't very well equal a famous one of the long-ago and excuse himself on the grounds that he was 'looking at a girl getting on to a drag', for drags are very few and far between, and the bus-conductor's remarks about legs not being mere ends apply to everybody nowadays, Varsity cricketers included, I suppose.

When it comes to comparing teams and personalities, the moderns don't really come out of it so very badly. What some people are apt to forget is that a good many of the great ones of the past didn't reach their best till after they had come down. For instance, it might perhaps surprise you to hear that Duleepsinhji's record at the Varsity was far superior to his famous uncle's, or that C. B. Fry, though he did get 100 against Cambridge in 1894, was then a far better soccer player and long-jumper than he was a batsman.

But now for a bit of history. Today's match is the hundreth of the series, though the first match of all was played a hundred and eleven years ago, when in 1827, it was poetically stated – as far as I remember:

> Keen to win the laurel,
> Oxford under Wordsworth mustered
> Cambridge under Jenner clustered
> Met in friendly quarrel.

That particular match, like some of the other earlier ones, lasted only two days, and was drawn. So, too, were those in 1844 and 1888 – but here rain played its part, and it is a point upon which past generations can heartily congratulate themselves, that it was not until 1899 that a match was drawn because too many runs were made. Of course a drawn match can be just as exciting as anything else and, as it's nicest to talk about exciting things, do you remember C. K. H. Hill-Wood and E. T. Benson, the last two Oxford men, keeping their wickets up as the minutes slowly ticked away in 1928, or F. G. H. Chalk and V. G. J. Jenkins, the Rugby footballer, defying an apparently victorious Cambridge attack on a wet wicket in 1933? Grand finishes both these were, and so, from a Cambridge point of view at least, was the one in 1891. They had a whale of a team on paper, with S. M. J. Woods as the leading man, they had won the two previous matches very easily, and this year after Oxford had followed on they only had a matter of 90-odd runs to get. But G. F. H. Berkeley bowled magnificently and eight wickets were down with the runs still unmade. Down the steps rushed Woods, with no gloves or pads, one crack, and the match was over.

Another game that Cambridge remember with particular pleasure was that of 1905. They won by 40 runs at the end, but at one time in their second innings all seemed lost, for with six wickets down for 77 against W. H. B. Evans they were still 24 behind. But then H. C. MacDonell and L. G. Colbeck put on 143 most brilliantly, and when Oxford went in with 164 to win, Morcom and Napier – what terrors they were to Oxford – bowled irresistibly and the Dark Blues were all out for 123. Next year Cambridge won again, and M. S. Payne began the match with the most amazing innings. He actually made 64 in the first half-hour, during which time the bowling screen was moved twice. We don't see very much of this nowadays.

Oxford's answer to the 1905 match would probably be that of 1896. First of all they very nearly had to follow on against a total of 319. I say 'very nearly' because in those days the side that was 120 or more behind *had* to follow on, whether the other side liked it or not. Frank Mitchell, the Cambridge captain, *didn't* like it, and told E. B. Shine to bowl away twelve runs, which he did by sending down three high fast full pitches to leg. Three years previously, Cambridge had tried the same perfectly legitimate dodge, though nothing much had been said. This time there was a terrible rumpus, and they were hissed and hooted by the MCC members as they went back into the Pavilion. Time, and an alteration to the laws, proved that Mitchell was right, but the demonstration had upset his team and at the close of play eight wickets were down for 154. Eventually, Oxford had 330 to win, a lot for the last innings. They started badly, but G. O. Smith, the famous centre-forward, and Oxford's last choice for the match, played the innings of a lifetime. C. C. Pilkington, H. D. G. Leveson-Gower (his captain) and G. R. Bardswell gave him splendid help. Smith was caught at slip for 132, but Oxford won by four wickets, which was a great performance with so many runs hit.

The most exciting thing in all cricket is a hat-trick, and the bigger the game the bigger the excitement. The hat-trick's been done four times in the Varsity match, and each time, oddly enough, by a Cambridge man. In 1926 it was R. G. H. Lowe, in 1911 it was J. F. Ireland. He was captain that year and his final victim was his fellow Marlburian, R. O. Lagden, the rugby international. P. H. Morton did it in 1880, and ten years before that came the second most famous hat-trick in all cricket history. I say the 'second most famous' with all deference, because I think everyone is agreed that the most famous of all was J. T. Hearne's for England against Australia at Leeds in 1899 when he got rid of Hill, Gregory and Noble in his three consecutive balls. But for sheer drama, this particular one in 1870 takes the palm.

It has inspired reminiscence and controversy from that day to this; it also inspired one of the most unforgettable sentences in all cricket literature. 'Nobody', says the original Badminton, 'could quite realise what had happened for a second or so – But then – up went "Bos" Absolom's hat, down the Pavilion steps with miraculous rapidity flew the Rev. A. R. Ward, and smash went Mr Charles Marsham's umbrella against the Pavilion brickwork!'

Cobden's hat-trick will never be forgotten. Tonight I am a very honoured person because I am here in the studio with MacKinnon of MacKinnon who played in the Cambridge side on that famous occasion, and today is still not out with ninety to his credit.

Perhaps you will be good enough, sir, to tell us what you remember of that historic finish?

MacKinnon of MacKinnon:
Well, I have come up once again to see the Oxford *v.* Cambridge match. I am sorry the match has started on a Saturday this year, and I extend my sympathy to those country parsons who, in consequence, may have been prevented from being present on the first day.

Now Mr Rankin has asked me to say a few words on a famous Varsity match. The year was 1870, which was a very interesting one to me, for I took my degree at Cambridge, I was elected to the MCC of which Club I am now the Senior, out of 6785 members, and also I played in the Cambridge XI that year, which beat Oxford so dramatically.

I will now tell you briefly the story of that match. The game had gone very evenly up to the end of the second day, when the captains agreed the match should be concluded, in order to enable Oxford to win. At that period, the game stood like this, Oxford having three wickets in hand, four runs to get, and the last over of the day, of four balls, was to be bowled. The spectators began to leave the field. It was, to their minds, a foregone conclusion.

At that critical moment, Money, our captain, a lob bowler, put on our fast bowler, Cobden. By the by, why aren't there lob bowlers nowadays? A little bird has whispered to me that neither Bradman nor Hammond know how to play them. Was not the Varsity match of 1875 won by a lob bowler? When Cambridge, towards the end of that match, wanted but 14 runs to win, and had three wickets to fall, Sammy Ridley, captain of the Oxford XI – a lob bowler, put himself on, and took two of the last wickets and so won the match for Oxford by 6 runs, the pluckiest thing ever done in cricket, to my mind.

Now to revert to the 1870 match. Cobden bowled his first ball to Hill, who was well in, and who scored one run from it, thus getting to the bowler's end. That left three wickets, three balls, three runs. Cobden then delivered his second ball, and Butler was caught by Bourne at mid-on. With his third ball he bowled Belcher middle stump. That left the same three runs, one ball, and one wicket. The last man, Stewart the wicket-keeper, then walked to the wicket. He passed close to me in the field, and was as white as a ghost. His captain, Pauncefort, had given him a little brandy, and told him on no account to lift his bat from the blockhole, an injunction rather difficult to follow, you will all admit. He did lift his bat, and the match was over. Bowled middle stump.

Now, in the course of sixty-eight years, I have told this story to a good many of my friends, and very few have told me correctly the number of runs we won by. I won't worry you all by guessing at this, and so will tell you we won by two runs, and I will leave it to you to work it out.

As one, of many instances, of interest shown in this match in succeeding years, may I mention that two years ago I had a letter from a friend of mine, bearing the honoured name of Lyttelton, Bob Lyttelton, asking me if I could tell him whether the ball which bowled Belcher ran straight through to the wicket, or off his legs. Well, as you will understand, after an interval of sixty-eight years, one's memory is slightly defective, but as my position in the field was that of long-stop, I answered to the best of my ability and recollection.

It has been said that Cobden won this match by his bowling at the end. But in my opinion other factors have to be taken into account. William Yardley made the first century ever recorded in a University match, to be repeated, curiously enough, by another Yardley last year, though no relation. Credit must also be given to the Rev. E. E. Ward, the only other survivor of the two teams, along with myself, and who I hope is listening to me and who, in the two innings, took nine of the Oxford wickets, all but one of the best. I may add that the ball with which Cobden performed the hat-trick was presented to him, suitably inscribed by the MCC, and was kept by him at his home at Capel Curig until a few years ago when he returned it to the MCC, and it now reposes in a glass case in the Pavilion at Lord's, adjoining the urn containing the famous ashes brought home from Australia by Ivo Bligh's team in 1883.

Now the moral, which I would wish to point out to all cricketers, particularly the young, is this. Never, at a critical part of a match, be despondent, or lose heart, but persevere to the end, and it may be, another Cobden will be found up your sleeve.

*   *   *

That charismatic broadcaster Freddy Grisewood, whose accomplishments ranged from singing the solo bass part in George Henschel's Requiem *at the Queen's Hall to playing cricket and tennis for Worcestershire, invited Sir Walter Monckton, holder of innumerable distinguished offices, to the studio for the programme 'The World Goes By' in July 1941. He asked him to give his memories of two days of July cricket in which he played. The match was described as the most famous in the history of school cricket since the MCC went up to Rugby in Tom Brown's schooldays, just a hundred years earlier.*

Fowler's Match

Sir Walter Monckton

Home Service, July 1941

I am all for talking about cricket, but I should prefer to tell you about games in which I played a more triumphant part. I remember, for instance, a game for Jack Squire's Invalids on New Year's Day on Hambledon Hill with snow on the ground and a matting wicket. We started that game just as hounds were meeting on the same spot. That was the right sort of cricket for me. Cricket without screens – and I was even allowed to bowl. Or I should like to tell you about games at the Oval when year by year I kept wicket for the Bar against our friends, the Barristers' Clerks. I might even tell you of the occasion when I kept wicket for the Harrow Wanderers at Ascot. We lost by 36 runs and I let 39 byes. That day I was struck in every part of the body except the hands.

But I should have spared myself a recollection of Fowler's match. Still, it was as exciting a game of cricket as any of you could wish to see. Of course, schoolboy cricket is not first-class, but it does rouse first-class excitement . . . It is thirty-one years ago this month that I made my nought in Fowler's match, and I don't suppose anyone will mind my releasing the news now. I shall never forget the breathless excitement of the last half-day of that great and unexpected victory of Eton over Harrow.

We Harrovians started the match with high hopes; we had a good side, seven of them Old Flannels, that is, they had played against Eton before, and had got over that first schoolboy nervousness at Lord's. We had not been beaten that season. We had won against Eton in 1907 and 1908. 1909 had been a draw. I shudder to think what Harrovians would have said to you had you told them on that first morning that Harrow would not beat Eton again at Lord's. But a Cassandra – among cricketers who had risked that prophecy – would have been right.

Guy Earle, the Harrow captain, won the toss and we went in first and made 232. Eton started their first innings by five o'clock. When stumps were drawn for the day at 6.30 owing to bad light, Eton had lost five wickets for 40 – and I regret to admit that 8 of the 40 were byes. Next morning Eton did even worse in the second half of their first innings and were all out for 67. So we had a first innings lead of 165. They followed on and in spite of a real captain's innings by Bob Fowler, the Eton captain, who got 64, with one wicket to fall Eton were only 4 runs ahead. But their last pair, and especially John Manners who made 40 not out, hit gallantly and put on about 50. Even so, Harrow were left only 55 to get to win. So hopeless, said the *Times* report, was Eton's position at the end of their second innings that many Etonians had left the ground. I believe John Manners' family were among them. But against a strong batting side, Fowler had what I suppose was the greatest triumph of his short life. With the first ball of the innings he clean bowled Wilson. Harrow were all out for 45. Fowler took eight wickets for 23 and so won the match for Eton by 9 runs. No one on the Harrow side reached double figures. This was a day when we all made our ducks together. I was in the fashion all right going in fourth wicket down and being ignominiously bowled for nought by a slow full pitch. I can still remember my left leg going towards mid-on – the short, jabbing motion which failed to connect, and the long walk back to the Pavilion. Our last man in, Alexander, made 8, and with O. B. Graham made a brave last-wicket attempt to save the day. They put on 13 and we only needed another 9 to save the match.

After the game, the Etonians were naturally shouting for their men to come on the balcony. To quote *The Times* again, 'Most pardonable pandemonium reigned for fully half an hour.' Before Fowler went out to get the cheers he so well deserved, he and Tufnell put their heads into the Harrow dressing-room and said, 'I say, this must be rotten for you fellows' – only they didn't say 'rotten'. The excitement on the ground and on the Pavilion steps was worth watching – even to a Harrovian. I found some slight consolation myself in the sight of Alfred Lyttelton, ex-Colonial Secretary, seizing A. J. Balfour's top hat and hurling it into space.

*   *   *

Harold Hobson, the eminent drama critic of the Sunday Times *for thirty years and a shining example of how a career can be attained against crippling adversity – he was struck by polio at the age of seven – came to the microphone several times during the war years to talk on cricket and cricketers, and in so doing lightened the burden of the times for all who heard his drily humorous comments.*

It Isn't Cricket
Harold Hobson

July 1942

The other evening I came out of my office in Westminster with one of my colleagues, and we found that two people had left their cars parked so close to his that he couldn't get out. We pushed and pulled a bit, but couldn't move either of them. The brakes had been left on. We tried the doors but, of course, they were locked. My friend was rather annoyed, and said, 'It's most inconsiderate to leave cars like this. It isn't cricket.'

Now, he's not at all a sporting man. He just wanted to get back home to his fire-watching. Yet it didn't strike me as in any way odd that he should say, right in the middle of London, 'It isn't cricket.' But if he'd said, for example, 'It isn't tiddly-winks,' or even, 'It isn't Association football,' I should have been astonished. In fact, I might even have been mildly alarmed.

I've always taken it for granted that people use the phrase 'It isn't cricket' because of the very high standard of sportsmanship that cricketers usually show. I've taken it as a sort of tribute to cricket's distinguished moral reputation. But so far as I can make out, I've been wrong. Cricketers may be a more saintly and scrupulous lot than the players of other games, like croquet, for instance, and ludo; but that isn't the reason we say of anything that's slightly off-colour, that it isn't cricket.

No. It's because of a man called Fellows. Harvey Winson Fellows. *Winson,* not Winston. An old Etonian. A fast – a *very* fast bowler – and a big hitter. Grace reckoned that he had once hit a ball further than any other man who ever stepped on to a cricket field. It was on the Christ Church ground at Oxford, and it went 175 yards – a hundred and seventy-five yards – before it struck the earth. It went thirty-five yards further than the best hit Grace himself ever made.

That's a long time ago of course – nearly ninety years, but Fellows was only about thirty at the time and he lived till after 1900. Many people still alive must have known Mr Fellows quite well. Some of them might even be listening at this moment. If they are, I hope I shall do no injustice to the memory of their old friend.

He was legal adviser to the MCC, and a member of the Club till he died in 1907. So his interest in cricket was lifelong. And yet I can't help feeling that he didn't take his own playing very seriously, though when he was a young man he'd practise bowling at a single stump in the meadow at his home for hours. But he never became attached to any regular team. And he played only a few times each year. He turned out for the Gentlemen against the Players, and it was largely because of him that when he played the Players had to follow on for the first time in the history of the game, and were beaten for the first time by an innings.

But his chief games were for the I Zingari XI.

He'd a very peculiar way of delivering the ball so that it hummed through the air like a top. His speed was colossal. I admit that doesn't give a very good idea of how fast Fellows really was, because 'colossal' can mean pretty well anything you like it to mean. Let's get at it this way. There was a man called Jackson. He played for Notts. In an old print a player is coming back from a match with a black eye, and a damaged arm and leg. A friend stops him, and asks, 'Good match, old fellow?'

The cricketer says, 'Oh yes, awfully jolly.'

The friend goes on, 'What did you do?'

And the cricketer answers, 'I had an over from Jackson. The first ball hit me on the arm, the second had me on the knee, the third in my eye, and the fourth bowled me out.'

Well, that was Jackson. And Fellows was supposed to be faster.

Then there was Marcon, a friend of Fellows. They were at Eton together, and made their first appearance at Lord's on the same day. Marcon took nine wickets, and Fellows five. Marcon needed two long-stops, a wicket-keeper was said to be quite useless to him, and at Oxford he broke a man's leg with one of his deliveries. Fellows was said to be as fast as Marcon.

He was said to be as fast as George Brown, of Hampshire and Sussex. Brown's stumper used to put a sack of straw inside his shirt to protect his chest. At Lord's, a man tried to stop a ball from Brown with his coat. It went right through the coat, and instantaneously killed a dog on the other side.

So I think we can take it that Fellows bowled pretty fast.

At the same time, he had great stamina. When he played for the Gentlemen of England against the Gentlemen of Kent in 1849 he bowled unchanged right through both innings. He was under five foot ten, yet he weighed thirteen stone four.

There were queer things done in cricket in Fellows' day. You had to be fairly bright in the uptake, or you came down a peg or two. It wasn't at all uncommon, on the morning of a big match, for a message to arrive for the best player in one of the teams, saying that his wife was dangerously ill, and he must go to her at once. It generally turned out to have come from the backers of the other XI. The wicket-keeper would sometimes suggest to the batsman that there was a spot outside his crease that might prove his undoing. If the batsman was foolish enough to step forward to pat it down, off came his bails in an instant.

Yet nobody ever suggested that Fellows didn't play fair. Some batsmen thought him too fast for safety. The famous Fuller Pilch, of Kent, once or twice played him at Lord's with his head turned away. But nobody said he wasn't fair.

Yet it was about Fellows that that phrase 'It isn't cricket' was first used. It happened like this.

There was a clergyman, the Rev. James Pycroft, who wrote a book called *The Cricket Field*, which was published in 1851. Pycroft had a terrific prejudice against overarm bowling. He thought it was ugly; he thought it was inaccurate; he thought it was dangerous. He wanted to go back from round-arm bowling to underarm bowling. He maintained that underhand bowling was above board, and that overhand bowling was – well, it was really underhand.

Now Fellows, in the days of his greatest speed, kept his arm so low that some people said he bowled underarm. But gradually he raised his arm higher, though no higher than the rules of that time allowed. But naturally Pycroft didn't like it. And he said so, in his book *The Cricket Field*. These were his words, 'Why, then, we will not say that anything that that hardest of hitters and thorough cricketer does *is not cricket*, but certainly it's anything but play.' There you are, you see – Isn't cricket. Millions of people who have never heard of Fellows know what you mean when you say, 'It isn't cricket.'

I never knew Fellows. I've never known anyone who knew him, and now, I suppose he's pretty well forgotten, but in a sense he's on somebody's lips every day, and on everybody's lips sometime or other. And that's more than can be said for some *very* eminent people. But I wonder whether he himself realised it. I wonder if he knew that the words, 'It isn't cricket,' all arose out of him. And if he did, I wonder if he was annoyed, or secretly rather proud.

I'd *like* to know.

The last time I spoke about cricket I had some very interesting letters from listeners, especially from listeners in the Orkneys, and Bradford, and Sutton-in-Ashfield, all telling me things I didn't know. And so I'm wondering now whether anyone who knew Mr Fellows as an old man can tell me what he felt about Pycroft's remark.

*   *   *

H. D. G. Leveson-Gower, former President and Captain of Surrey and Chairman of the England Selection Committee on several occasions, looked through his scrapbook and talked about cricket and cricketers in 'Tonight's Talk' in 1947.

Cricket Scrapbook
H. D. G. Leveson-Gower

Home Service, January 1947

As by a happy chance I am opening my 'Cricket Scrapbook' on the eve of one of those famous encounters, England *v*. Australia, it would, perhaps, be suitable to this occasion if I start with one or two reminiscences of Test cricket. It was as far back as 1880, when the Australians were on a tour in this country, that a fortunate idea occurred to C. W. Alcock, the then Secretary of the Surrey County Cricket Club, that there should be a game late in the season between England and Australia.

The match took place in September, and the three Graces – W. G., E. M., G. F. – were in the England side. It proved a great success, for the public had the chance of seeing the Australians, and the cricket authorities of studying their ability, bearing in mind the possibility of a challenge in the near future to the supremacy of English cricket. It was the sensational victory of the Australians by 7 runs in the 1882 game that made it quite clear that Australia's cricket in the future must be treated very seriously. It is to the result of this Test match that the origin of the mythical 'Ashes' can be traced. It was said that English cricket had been cremated at the Oval.

From that time on, there has been a succession of Test matches, both here and in Australia, and I can remember some very exciting finishes; for instance, in 1902 the Australians won by 3 runs at Manchester, and England won by one wicket at the Oval. Surely that was good enough for anyone! I have often been asked, and the question is so often put, 'How do you compare players? For the sake of argument, W. G. and Bradman?' The answer is, 'You just can't compare them.' One star differs from another in glory, and you must take players during the time that they played. Could anyone have excelled W. G. in his day? Could anyone have been better than Hobbs in his time? Or Bradman today? And it's the same with all of them. But I must put one higher than all others – W. G. Grace – and that is entirely because of his length of service. Do you know that he made a thousand runs in May when he was forty-seven? Another instance, he played for the Gentlemen against the Players in 1865, and forty-one years later, when he was fifty-eight, I asked him if he would play in a Gentlemen and Players match at the Oval. At first the answer that came out of that famous beard was, 'No'; but I said, 'Oh, yes, you will, and I want you to play for one particular reason. And that is that your birthday happens to take place during the match.' To this he replied, 'Snipe!' At which I pointed out to him that my nickname happened to be 'Shrimp', not 'Snipe'. 'Well,' he said, 'they both begin with "S" and they're both something to eat.' Then he went on to say, 'But, you know, my birthday is on the third day, and the match might be over on the second.' But he did play, and he got 74. And it is for that reason, length of service, that I must put W. G. by himself as the greatest cricketer of all time.

Close on fifty years ago, the President of MCC, the Hon. Alfred Lyttelton, asked me whether I would be prepared to manage the MCC team to play at Scarborough during the Scarborough Festival the following year. Those of you who have been to Scarborough know that Mr C. I. Thornton was the founder of the Festival, and one of the greatest hitters of his time. He batted without any pads on; at least that was the story, but on closer investigation it would be found that underneath his flannels he had shin guards and pads.

C. I. Thornton very often used to hit the ball into Trafalgar Square (at Scarborough, it is just outside the ground). On one occasion a lady on a cricket ground in the south (I think it was Canterbury) came up and said, 'Are you Mr Thornton?' 'Yes, madam,' was the reply. 'And you are the great hitter who hit a ball into Trafalgar Square?' 'Yes, madam.' 'Do tell me whether you were playing at Lord's or the Oval?' 'At the Oval, madam, and the ball went via Westminster!' The Australians, ever since they toured this country, have never missed playing at Scarborough against Lord Londesborough's XI, C. I. Thornton's XI, and, in later years, my XI.

I come to Surrey, my own county, where I have had the honour of occupying the posts of Treasurer, Captain and President. Whilst I was playing for the county, among the players was that grand little batsman, Bobby Abel. He had a most kindly disposition, and always said 'Thank you kindly, sir' to any question you might put to him. Here is an incident. I took the Surrey team to watch a performance at a music hall. One of the star turns was a lady of ample charms, but rather scantily attired. I asked Bobby if he admired her. 'Thank you kindly, sir, but I wouldn't like to play a fast bowler in that costume.'

While I was actively engaged in cricket with Surrey I became a member of the Selection Committee. Of course we made mistakes – that, I understand, is the reason why there is indiarubber at the end of our pencils and bumpers at the end of motor cars. During the time I was on the Selection Committee, I received a good many letters – mostly anonymous. Here is one of them. 'Dear Sir, – Unless you play So-and-So in the next Test match, you will be shot outside the Oval.' Well, So-and-So did not find favour with the Selection Committee and he did not play. After the match I received a bulky package; I opened it, and inside there were a dozen 'In Memoriam' cards, edged with that black which was so prevalent in the Victorian age, and this letter: 'Dear Sir, – You didn't take any notice of what I wrote; I am sending you a dozen memorial cards which you can send to your friends – they will need them, and I have some more as well – in order that they might be present at the final stages of your life.' Well, they didn't get my ashes that time.

I should like to say just one word about the value of cricket and Test matches. You cannot always win – you very often lose; and that applies to both sides. Surely the cricket teams which go overseas from this country and the return visits do a tremendous lot of good. They must. In 1947 – the season which is just approaching – we shall have the opportunity of welcoming back Hammond and the members of the MCC team. I should like to congratulate Hammond very much indeed on having joined that select band who have made over 50,000 runs in first-class cricket – a distinction which he thoroughly deserves. We shall welcome them back, as I say, for they went out not only as cricketers but ambassadors. What the results of the remaining Test matches will be, I know not, but I am convinced that just as the Australian Services delighted the British public in 1945, so this MCC team has given pleasure to the Australian public.

I seem to see the end of a splendid match. The umpires have doffed their white apparel, but the spectators linger on; they are loth to leave. They crowd round the Pavilion. They want to give vent to their delight and their thanks to the players who have given them that pleasure. I should like to linger on. I want to vent my pleasure and delight in these memories of cricket which my scrapbook has offered me. They mean much to me in the late autumn of my life. Cricket is a great game. Long may it continue a game. Test matches are great encounters; long may they continue tests of friendship and goodwill.

*   *   *

A CATCH OF COMMENTATORS

For many, the identity of cricket is reflected in the commentary. And the commentators have become just as much 'the personalities of the game' as the players on the field. Even though 'Jim' Swanton, Rex Alston and John Arlott have all now vacated the seat behind the microphone, the strength of their appeal was such that their names will always be synonymous with broadcast cricket. Jim, slightly pontifical, summarised superbly with cultured charm and dignity; Rex, urbane, tenor-voiced, quick and expository; John, uniquely observant, unrivalled in phrase, the very voice of the game.

Meet E. W. Swanton
Jacob de Vries

Sports Service, October 1968

Swanton: I only had an interest in cricket because my father happened to be very interested in it. He was the Treasurer of his own local cricket club which was at Forest Hill, which was a good club in those days and I think still is, and he really led me on. He made me a member, for instance, of Surrey County Cricket Club when I was only fourteen and I still am a member and cricket was in my blood from that time onwards.

de Vries: And you played at school, did you?

Swanton: Yes, I did. I was at Cranleigh and I didn't play with any very great success. We were chiefly a rugger school but even so I didn't seem to do particularly well there. I did in fact play in the XI but my cricket developed later on.

de Vries: You left school and went into journalism almost immediately. How did that come about?

Swanton: Well, you know, one rather fell into these things. I was supposed to be able to write English and my father had some sort of entrée into a place called the Amalgamated Press, which is a sort of factory for an enormous number of papers of all sorts, and I worked there. Started at twenty-five bob a week.

178

de Vries: What were the sort of things that were expected of you?

Swanton: Well, I subedited. Incidentally, I think that writing is a matter of practice and sweat. Talent is a thing that I think can be developed by practice and by going hard at it. Oh, I subedited various things. There was a paper called *All Sports* which was dead, I think, rather before you came on the scene, Jacob, and I worked for that and I also pretty soon began freelancing for the *Evening Standard* and for other papers as well.

de Vries: What was your first real big cricket assignment?

Swanton: Well, my first big cricket assignment I suppose was after I became a member of the *Evening Standard* staff and they allowed me to write cricket, which they did from 1928 onwards and my first Test match was in 1930, the second Test at Lord's. It was a four-day Test match and it was the first four-day Test there had been at Lord's incidentally. England made 425 in the first innings and Duleep played a wonderful innings of 173 and everyone thought that England ought to have declared before nightfall on the first day – so little did they know about how to wage that sort of match, so little did they know about Bradman. It was always said that Archie MacLaren – I wasn't a member then so I can't vouch for this quite – but Archie MacLaren was striding up and down the Long Room saying Percy's mad, he ought to declare. In fact, England went on, we lost nine wickets overnight, we went on batting even the next day and made 425 and then Australia replied with a little matter of 729 for 6. The Don made 254 of those. I remember the Saturday very well, this was the Saturday the King came on, that's George V of course, and he inspected the troops and the score was 161 for none and the next ball Ponsford was out and Don Bradman came in, and I very well remember at the close of play he himself had made 155 – at which Woodfull had just got out – so the England bowlers took a bit of a bashing. The next day the Don went on and made 254 and they made 729 for 6. Everybody made runs that got in and then we had a very long rearguard which didn't look like being very successful until Percy Chapman was joined by Gubby Allen, now the Treasurer of MCC. 'Percy', when he made none, was dropped in the covers. I can see now Vic Richardson, I think it was, and Ponsford, neither of them went for a catch and it simply fell between them, and after that 'Percy' played very finely and very glamorously and Gubby Allen, who hadn't bowled very well and had been picked as a bowler, played extremely well, made 57, I think, and in the end it looked as though we were going to save the game. We didn't quite do that but there was a great thrill at the end because Walter Robins got a couple of very quick wickets and another catch was dropped. I think the Australians' score was 20 for 3 [22 for 3, in fact], they had to get 72 to win and eventually they did win in the evening sunshine of the fourth day. The sun had shone all through the match, the crowds were absolutely enormous and the cricket was vintage, but then you see there were some tremendous players, Hobbs, Woolley, Hammond, Duleep, Hendren, Chapman, and the Australians had Woodfull, Ponsford, Bradman, Kippax, McCabe, Richardson.

de Vries: This is really cricket ideally as it should be, isn't it?

Swanton: Well, I always think that people come to watch batsmen and it is batsmen who give glamour to the game and of course batsmen flourished in that match – and fielding too, there was some wonderful fielding.

de Vries: Sporting journalism in those days was rather different from what it is today, wasn't it?

Swanton: Well it was, yes. Different sort of people were at it and of course their approach was slightly different too. I wonder how many of those people listening now remember reading, for instance, Howard Marshall, who was a very fine writer, incidentally, one of my predecessors on the *Daily Telegraph* on cricket and rugby football; a dear old chap called Leo Munro, who was also cricket and rugby football for the *Daily Express*, rather different in style from the average *Daily Express* technique and method today. A chap called Colonel Philip Trevor, CBE – the CBE was always put in – who was also the cricket and rugger correspondent of the *Daily Telegraph*, Bertie Henley of the *Daily Mail* who, incidentally, was the dramatic critic as well as the cricket writer, that was quite a common thing in those days you know. I think perhaps we worked harder. I must mention to you one enormous man for whom I had a very great respect. Stewart Caine, who was Editor of *Wisden*, the sort of man whom any young man would look up to . . . I was an early member of the Press Club and I used to listen in great awe to Stewart Caine.

180

de Vries:	Bernard Darwin you haven't mentioned yet.
Swanton:	No, well I didn't come to know Bernard very well until later. He is without question to my mind the father of sporting journalism. He was a fine golfer himself but he could write about any game and did in fact write quite a bit about cricket and wrote a book about W. G. Grace, whose picture we're looking at over there on the wall, Jacob. There was nothing better than Bernard's writing about almost any subject – I mean he was one of the foremost essayists, I suppose, of his day, wasn't he?
de Vries:	I think essayist is the right word.
Swanton:	Yes, he was a reporter too, though.
de Vries:	Oh yes, indeed. I mean, he wrote most beautifully but gave the facts as well.
Swanton:	Yes. I feel the job of anyone like myself who is privileged to be able to write about games is primarily as a recorder of events. As a reporter, one tries to give the picture of the thing and that's what Bernard of course did in his superb prose. I mean, one lags thousands of miles behind him but I sometimes think now how shall I approach this? I think perhaps, how would Bernard have done it? You've got to keep your reader entertained, haven't you? It's no good filling him in with an awful lot of technical stuff and jargon; particularly in cricket there's tremendous jargon. I think the BBC's slightly responsible for some of it, Jacob. I don't know whether you'd agree with that, but I think that a good bit of it is beyond the comprehension and the interest of the average reader. I think Bernard Darwin's philosophy on that was – he said he always spread the golf rather thinly over the bread.
de Vries:	I'm rather amused that you should say that the BBC is responsible for the jargon because you've had quite a lot to do with cricket broadcasting on the BBC, Jim. When did you first start the broadcasting side of it?
Swanton:	Well, I first operated for Empire Service in about 1934, but I didn't start doing any outside broadcasts until 1938 – that was just before I went to South Africa with the MCC, that was my first real broadcasting assignment.
de Vries:	You went out quite independently, didn't you?

Swanton:	Yes, I did. I went out as a freelance really, on a shoestring with Wally Hammond's side in 1938. I went with a very small BBC contract, a very small contract from the South African Broadcasting Corporation, and a little writing for the *Field* and for the *Sporting and Dramatic News*.
de Vries:	And then your broadcasting in South Africa during that tour expanded. Instead of fifteen minutes you had initially, it grew to two hours a day?
Swanton:	Yes, it did grow to two hours. Then when the last Test lasted for ten days, I was paid by the day, so I was rather pleased.
de Vries:	This was the famous timeless Test in Durban, wasn't it?
Swanton:	Yes, it was, which ended in a draw.
de Vries:	So you came back with a profit?
Swanton:	So I came back with a small profit and a great profit in terms of experience.

*   *   *

Rex Alston
Brian Johnston

'Meet a Sportsman' – *Roundabout*,
Light Programme, June 1961

Johnston:	Now Rex, you must have been asked many times how does one become a BBC commentator. How did you become one?
Alston:	Well, I think probably my background is a bit unusual for a commentator. My father was a parson, he was a bishop in Manchester. I was a schoolmaster at Bedford; I married, I had two children and we lived in Bedford and then during the war there was suddenly a knock at the door at lunchtime one day and there was a BBC Billeting Officer saying the BBC were coming to Bedford and I wondered is

there anything in this for me. Well, I applied and what do you think I became? I became a Billeting Officer, but not for very long, Brian. I then became an announcer, I was drafted to Manchester and while doing announcing there I had the idea that I might become a commentator because I knew something about sport.

Johnston: Now you're being very modest, and don't be modest in this programme. Tell us what you actually did in sport before you went to the BBC.

Alston: Well, I was fond of all games, I was quite a decent cricketer, quite a decent rugger player, I got a half-blue as a sprinter at Cambridge against Oxford and was good enough to beat the two Oxford men at any rate but Harold Abrahams was a bit too fast for me. Then I played Minor County cricket for Bedfordshire and a lot of club cricket, and I played rugger for Bedford and the East Midlands and I played a certain amount of club tennis, I suppose. I was a reasonable sort of eight-handicap golfer, so an all-rounder but not any high spots.

Johnston: You've done all these sports on the air – which is your favourite one?

Alston: I think if I was told that as far as broadcasting was concerned I had only one sport for the rest of my life, it would have to be cricket.

Johnston: Well, tell us some highlights then.

Alston: Well, there are so many. You see, I've been to every Test match I think in this country since the war and two foreign tours. I think probably the tensest day was in 1953, the Lord's Test match, the fifth day, the day that goes down in history as Watson's and Bailey's day, when they saved the show against the Australians against all odds. I think that that was the most exciting.

Johnston: Now like all of us, things must have gone wrong for you. Can you tell us any amusing incidents?

Alston: Yes, I remember at Lord's once, I was very busy concentrating on Ken Barrington batting away and I wasn't quite sure how to describe a certain shot, so I said, 'Well, at the end of the over we'll ask Jim Swanton what he thinks about Barrington.' Well, there were two or three more balls and then I turned round to ask Jim what he thought and there was nobody there at all, just a little notice, 'Slipped out for a minute.'

Johnston: Very awkward. Now Rex, at the end of this month you are retiring from the BBC staff regretfully. First of all, has it been worthwhile – the job?

Alston: Very much so, I've enjoyed it enormously. I've been frightfully lucky, I think, to have had the chance to see all these things, to have had the best seat, but one of the things that sticks out in my mind is the letters you get. You get a certain amount of rude ones, of course, but you also get some very complimentary ones, and those especially from blind people. You know, one realises after what they have written how frightfully important it is that one should give absolutely one's best to those who are listening, especially to the blind people.

Johnston: Rex, what are you going to do in retirement?

Alston: Well, I'm hoping to go on broadcasting, Brian. I'm going to do a great deal of writing but I've got a large garden at home in Surrey near Shere. I love gardening and I shall spend a bit more time there. I hope to play a bit of golf, see a bit more of my wife and children and even grandchildren, 'cause I'm a grandfather, you know.

Johnston: You are?

Alston: Yes indeed.

Johnston: This business of the grandfather. I must explain to anyone who has never seen Rex, he looks a great deal younger than a great many people who aren't even fathers. Therefore, may I say thank you very much, Rex, for allowing us to meet you in *Roundabout*, the very best in your – what's obviously going to be a very busy – retirement and may I many times in the next few years have the pleasure of saying 'Over now to Rex Alston'.

*　　　*　　　*

John Arlott

Brian Johnston

One Hundred Years of Australia,
Thirty-four Years of Arlott, August 1980

Johnston: Well, John, you made what I consider a very courageous decision to leave what is a most marvellous scene and that is the cricket arena. Now what made you make that decision?

Arlott: My age really. I don't think I get any better. In fact, I think I get a bit slower and no brighter and while I think I can still do the work, write a copy and do the commentaries, I find the travel an awful bore and an awful drag. It's one thing to do commentary and then go and write your newspaper report, but then it's altogether a different thing when at ten to seven you go out with 250 miles to drive home.

Johnston: There are two points there: you're younger than me so you make me feel a bit guilty, and of course you do this newspaper as well. Which will you look back on with the greatest pleasure, the newspaper side or the broadcasting?

Arlott: Broadcasting without a doubt. I couldn't believe it possible when it first happened and I still sometimes wake up in the night and think, 'Well, how on earth did all this happen?'

Johnston: I don't really remember the first time that you really felt that you were a regular member. Was it in that first Indian tour that you became a regular member?

Arlott: Oh no, in 1946 I was just doing little bits to India every day, and then towards the end of the season as one went round to county matches the regions then would give you a quarter of an hour, a half-hour, so I had the chance to learn as people don't nowadays. They simply don't get the chance we used to get on commentary.

Johnston: I think one of the strengths, if we've got a strength, is the complete contrast between us all. Going back to when you started, I mean you had dear old Rex with you then?

Arlott: Rex, Jim Swanton, Alan McGilvray, Ken Ablack, Charles Fortune. I never dreamed that a bunch of men so assorted, so different, could work together year in, year out, and it's nearly twenty-five years I suppose and I don't think I've

185

ever known a row and I don't think I've ever known anybody play anyone else a dirty trick, and everybody has been generous and if you realise that we're like all broadcasters, exhibitionists, I think you begin to understand how much that means, and I'd like to really thank all the people who've created that atmosphere in which it was possible to work so happily.

Johnston: I suppose the person who's rubbed off on most of us, and he certainly did with me because he's the one I listened to, was Howard Marshall.

Arlott: You see, I never heard him. Mine, I suppose, is a funny upbringing as far as radio is concerned, because until I came to work in it I really never heard anyone. My father made crystal sets – we used to listen on earphones when I was young. But then after that I was out in the evenings. When I left home I was in digs where there was no radio to listen to, so I don't suppose I heard Howard Marshall more than once in my life until I heard him during the war.

Johnston: There's this tremendous contrast, isn't there, between us and the Australians? They're very down-to-earth, they score and they don't do what we call 'colour'. Did this develop with the English people since the war?

Arlott: It's a strange thing, isn't it, that there is a natural English characteristic about commentary and yet we're all so different. I'm not quite sure what it is, perhaps it's more emotive, less objective. Certainly it's more subjective than Australian commentary which aims at complete precision.

Johnston: Yes, you see I think we're lucky that we're allowed our heads and we've got a sense of humour, and we pick up things which are part of a cricket match in addition to what's actually going on on the pitch.

Arlott: Well, it's a very human activity, isn't it? And, of course, for six hours any cricketer is going to show more of his character than, for instance, a soccer player will in an hour and a half, and I think one comes to appreciate them as human beings.

Johnston: I just wondered, is one tempted to build their characters up rather like Neville Cardus has undoubtedly built up one or two of the famous older characters? Do we tend sometimes to build a character up?

Arlott: I think there's a tendency that way. You see, I wonder how much of it is due to the fact that most of us did a great deal of commentary on county matches when you could be on half an hour in the morning, half an hour in the afternoon, half an hour in the evening. You'd do an hour and a half a day. It's nearly as much as anybody does on a Test match, plus you did a couple of summaries as well and you were doing this constantly and county cricket is such an intimate game, you can't help but be near the players.

Johnston: Well, that was it, one stayed in the same hotel, had breakfast with them. I suppose breakfast is a great testing time. One used to sit at their tables and talk.

Arlott: Especially on Sundays when breakfast used to go on for three hours while they all sat and went through every Sunday paper and passed comment on everybody who had succeeded and everybody who failed and there was a certain spirit – composite spirit of the people who are in what Brian Sellars used to call 'the circus'. But one did come closer to the players than, for instance, one tends to do on those big impersonal Australian grounds with very strict people who say the media mustn't go near the players.

Johnston: Do you think we've missed out on not being first-class cricketers first?

Arlott: I'd have given my ears to be. I think it's important that one must have played. I don't think you necessarily have to have played well so long as you know what all the problems are. My word, I know what all the problems are. I've failed at everything, batting, fast bowling, slow bowling, finger spin, loose spin. I even tried to keep wicket once.

Johnston: Oh, did you? Well, that I did, but I also tried the bat and failed that. Do you ever sometimes reflect like I do – I know you've got a great many other interests professionally and privately – but do you feel sometimes that a bit of wood and a bit of leather and here we are earning not a bad living, let's face it, just talking about it?

Arlott: Well, it's as Len Braund said to Fred Tate when Fred broke down after missing that tragic catch in the Old Trafford Test in 1902; Len clapped him on the shoulders and said, 'Go upstairs and get your money, Fred, it's only a game.'

Johnston: Yes, and one spends one's life watching it and talking about

187

it, so looking back is there any one particular thing you pick out, any special memory, any special person you would like as your model cricketer? Any match about which you say, 'I'd love to watch that game again and again'?

Arlott: I don't think I would. You see, it's one great picture, one great way of life to me. I'm very, very, very fond of Leo Harrison who probably taught me more about cricket than anyone else and is one of the best friends I've ever had in my life. I'm very fond of Basil D'Oliveira. Now that may be a bit more seeing my own credit in him – very proud to have brought him over. But I think the greatest thing that happened to me was when the Cricketers' Association elected me their President. That was the greatest honour they could conceivably have paid me because no one's admitted who is not a current county player and when they elected me to that I thought, well, it's almost as good as being a player.

Johnston: Well, I think that was wonderful. It was wonderful for you and incidentally it was very good for the radio and everything else to come to a commentator and say, 'Come on, you look after us.' And I gather you're going to go on doing that.

Arlott: Absolutely, I shall continue to do, yes.

Johnston: And when we start next year, God willing, can we picture you sitting at home perhaps just listening to us?

Arlott: You can indeed and you may even get a few rude telegrams.

Johnston: Oh, I hoped you were going to say, 'You might even get a few sweets or cakes sent from Alderney.' Any chance of that?

Arlott: Well, it is possible, but you're more likely to get a bottle of champagne, I think.

Johnston: Ah, that's the stuff. Well, John, obviously we're going to miss you terribly. We shall be thinking a lot of you listening to us and I know I'm speaking for millions and millions saying thank you very much for all you've done, and when I do my dinners and things I say to other people that you, I think, have done more to bring cricket into every home in the North of England right down to the south-west tip than any other person I know . . .

Arlott: That's very kind and it's very generous. I don't think you can even guess how much I've enjoyed it. I must pinch myself to believe it, it's been wonderful.

*   *   *

John Arlott was a founder panel member of the ever popular Any Questions *which Freddie Grisewood chaired for so many years. When the veteran Grisewood announced his retirement from the national forum of radio in 1968, Arlott declared, 'He is, for me, the last of the Edwardian gentlemen.'*

Grisewood, once described as 'a lean John Buchan-ish figure of tremendous distinction with a rich tranquillising voice', started his broadcasting career as a professional singer in the embryonic days of the Corporation. Older listeners will remember the stories he devised of 'Our Bill', the Oxfordshire rustic, and this talk, broadcast in 1934, illustrates vividly an amused interest in arbitration between warring factions. Grisewood was, of course, to demonstrate his own skill at 'diffusing the barbs' in later years.

The Whole Duty of a Cricket Umpire
Freddy Grisewood

October 1934

We were in the throes of an unprecedented summer. Day after day the sun had blazed down upon our brown land – until the earth showed great cracks in its surface, and in some neighbouring villages the lack of water had become a serious menace. Our garden had become a very Sahara – plants were flagging for want of water, and although we carefully drenched some of our more precious possessions, we were knowledgeable enough, under Bill's guidance, to use the water-can very sparingly. 'Once you starts to water,' said Bill, 'you 'as to keep on a'waterin'. Fur better to keep the 'oe a'movin' the soil round the roots.'

So the days Bill visited us during that summer were given up to a general tidying – there was little or nothing else that we could do – and we waged an intensive and highly successful war on the weeds. 'You only 'as to cut 'em in this weather,' was Bill's advice, 'an' you won't 'ear from them no more,' which was perfectly true.

In our leisure times, and they were many, our conversation turned to cricket. Bill, on the subject of our national game, was *laudator temporis acti*! 'Cricket ain't wot it 'ad used to be,' he said, 'they makes the pitches too good for one thing. I went to Cheltenham some years back to see the county play against they 'Orstraylians. Call it cricket – I've never sin the like in all my natural. It were more like that there croquet game than cricket. They 'it the ball – when they 'it 'im at all – all along the ground, never raised 'im once they didn't. They kept a'messin' about keeping it out o' their wickets wi' their pads. I'd 'ave 'ad 'em out quick if I'd been standin' at umpire.

'But nobody didn't seem to take no notice o' that. You'd 'ave thought as they was all used to it. Well that wouldn't 'ave done fer us. If the ball 'its you on the leg in our matches there's a roar as you can 'ear a mile off, an' if it's not your own umpire as 'as the say, out you 'as to go. You see, sir, it be all in the game – but there they was with the ball fair rattlin' up against their pads an' ne'er a one said anything. I don't call that cricket, do you, sir?

'An' as fer that pitch – I 'ad a close look at it when they players 'ad gone in fer their lunch – it were a lovely bit o' turf, sir, more like a bowling green nor anything else. T'wasn't no good for cricket. All the time I were a'watchin' I never see a ball go a'flyin' over the batsman's 'ead – like it 'ad ought to. They be the sort o' balls to get the wickets. The batsman, if 'e ain't afeared, 'as a sort o' slash at 'em an' very like tips one into the long-stop's 'ands. Many's the good batsman 'ave I sin get out like that. But you couldn't do nothin' like that on that pitch at Cheltenham – it were terrible dull.

'There were only one man as played proper at all – an' that were that Jessop. By goy, 'e didn't stand for no nonsense! 'E 'it the clock tower once, ever such a crack – came a' jumpin' out at the ball like a tiger. 'E didn't set no store on all their twisters an' things, treated 'em all alike, 'e did. Ah, 'e were a fair treat to watch. When 'e come out I come away. I couldn't abide to watch no more.

'But we 'ad used to 'ave some fine games in this village afore the war, sir, when Master Fred 'ad used to live 'ere. You never knewed 'im, did yer? 'E 'ad used to be captain o' our side, an' there weren't many places as could do no good again' us – not in those days. But there's a lot more in village cricket than you'd credit, sir. I see as they 'Orstraylians 'a' brought a team over this year – that Bradman – they do say as 'e be a wonnerful bat like but . . .

'You can talk about your Bradmans and your Hobbses and the like – and I ain't a'sayin' but what they don't cut a lot of runs – but that's in this 'ere 'igh-flown sort o' cricket, but when it comes to the real thing, cricket as 'er 'ad ought to be played, on the village green with Squire standing the tea, and "The Spotted Dog" nice an' 'andy in case any of the players gets a thirst – then there's only one chap on the side as counts at all – an' that's the umpire. Many's the time I've seen a good umpire put out a side quicker'n any bowler can – an' easier, too, 'cos when it comes to it 'is word be law, an' if 'e says you're out, out you 'as to go: an' if 'e's the village blacksmith it ain't no manner o' good you tryin' to argue! The only thing as you can do is to lay for 'im on a dark night an' 'it 'im with something an' clear out quick – but you 'as to be smartish then, an' take good care as you don't miss.

'O' course there be all sorts o' umpires, an' each one 'as 'is own way o' doin' things, but there's *one* match as stands out in my mind clear as daylight, an' one umpire as I'd stand a drink to whenever I sin 'im! An' that were Joe Allen as used to be postman in our village. 'E weren't much to look at, were Joe, but 'e 'ad a proper spirit to him – that 'e 'ad – an' wouldn't stand for nobody creatin' at 'im, not for a minute. Ah! a rare 'un 'e were for a cricket match. I've known 'im run the last three miles o' his round of a Saturday so as to be in time to stand umpire. Folks used to know when there was a match on 'cos they used to get their letters so quick.

'We was friendly with nigh all the neighbouring villages – our chaps used to go and help 'em in their football and cricket matches – but there were one place as we never set no store on at all – that we never. Us couldn't abide 'un. And that were Slopton-on-the-Wyre, about ten miles away. Us always used to say as no good ever came out o' Slopton, an' by goy it were true, too! Whenever any o' our little 'uns 'ad used to be naughty, their mothers 'ad only got to say, "Look 'ere, if you don't be'ave yourself I'll take yer to Slopton," and that stopped 'un proper.

'Us didn't have no more to do wi' 'em than us could 'elp. But us allus 'ad a cricket match again' 'em. 'Twere an old custom as 'ad started when us were friends an' 'adn't died out. But o' course there were ever such a bitter feelin' about this 'ere match, an' 'twere allus a ding-dong struggle.

'To give 'em their due, there was one thing as they *could* do – an' that was to play cricket. The year I'm a'talkin' about the match was on our ground. For weeks us 'ad worked in the evenings on the pitch, 'an many's the chap as let 'is allotment go to blazes 'cos 'e were puttin' in all 'is spare time on the cricket ground – but us didn't worry much about that, times weren't so 'ard in those days as they be now, and us only cared for one thing, an' that was to beat those danged Slopton folk. Us 'adn't got a very strong side, neither, that year. Us 'ad some smartish bowlers, but with the exception o' Master Fred we 'adn't got many as could cut more than a few runs apiece.

'Us used to meet in "The Spotted Dog" in the evenings, arter us 'ad put in a bit o' work on the wicket, an' talk about our chances. O' course, Ol' Joe was allus there – you couldn't keep 'im away from anything to do with cricket, even tho' it were only talkin' about it. An' he allus used to say: "You leave it to me, masters! I'll win this 'cre match for yer, you see if I don't!"

'Well, at last the day come, an' us all come back early from the plough an' such – us were allus allowed off early that day, 'cos of this 'ere match. An' us all got into our whites – Master Fred 'e were ever so okkurd about us all wearin' whites. Us 'ad used to play as us was, but 'e very soon stopped that, an' wouldn't let Tiny Wells wear 'is bowler 'at when 'e were a'playin' until Tiny bowled so many wides without 'un as it were dark afore the first innings were over. So 'e 'ad to let 'im wear it again. Tiny never couldn't bowl without 'is 'at on. I believe 'e used to go to bed in it, 'cos I've never seen 'im without it. 'E were a good bowler, were Tiny. Used to make the ball come straight up off the pitch, an' if the batsman were a'roachin' forward to 'im 'e used to get it under the jaw! 'E frightened many a one out like that. They 'ad used to come in all full of swank, an' start as if they were goin' to set about the bowling, but after they'd had a couple o' smacks under the jaw from Tiny they were fair muzzled, an' the only thing as they wanted to do was to get out, ah, an' quick. An' us used to see about that all right.

'About two o'clock all they chaps from Slopton comes along in a great big horse chara. Motors were scarce in those days. An' they all looked swollen-headed as if they 'ad won the match already. They was all turned out ever so smart, with blazers an' caps an' all. An' the whole village seemed to 'ave come wi' 'em – some on bicycles, and others in traps an' the like. You never see such a crowd – all a'singin' and a'laughin' – they didn't laugh much when the time come for 'em to go home again, though! But I'll come to that later.

'We was all a'standin' there, with Ol' Joe, who 'ad just finished 'is rounds. The captains, Master Fred an' their chap, tossed up, and Master Fred wins the toss an', o' course, 'e put 'em in – us allus did that 'cos there's a smartish little place one end o' the pitch as is just right for Tiny's bowlin' – that was what us 'ad been workin' at all these 'ere weeks – an' it didn't allus last for more than one innings – but that was generally enough.

'Their first two batsmen as come in were great strappin' chaps – one 'ad a sort o' felt 'at on 'is 'ead. They takes guard, an' the chap with the 'at stands up to Tiny's first over. 'Is 'at didn't stay on 'is 'ead long arter that though, 'cos the first ball as Tiny bowled knocked 'is 'at off – an' they run two byes afore us could get after it. The very next ball as Tiny bowled 'it the chap in the windpipe an' very nigh strangled 'im! It was ever such a long time afore 'e could get 'is breath again – an' arter that 'e didn't seem to care much about cricket at all! 'Cos when the third ball come along 'e steps off the square leg or somewhere, an' the ball never rose a inch but run along the ground an' cut 'is middle stump a'flyin'! You never 'eard such cheerin' in all your natural, and Squire's daughter 'er split 'er gloves a'clappin'. Well that were one on 'em gone, an' a good 'un, too, from all accounts.

'The next chap in were their captain, an' Ernest, our wicket-keeper, shouts out, "'Ere's a watty-'anded 'un, you'll 'ave to cross over!" An' so 'e were, too. An' I 'as to go long leg instead of third man. 'E looked a tough customer, an' 'e never flinched at all when Tiny's first ball at 'im went past 'is ear'ole like lightning – and the next one 'e 'it smack into the pond an' nigh killed one o' Mrs Hunt's pet drakes as was 'ocklin' about there! An' all they Slopton folk sets up such a roar as you could 'ear it a mile off. The chap at the other end was one of those as never moved 'is bat at all – kept it in the block-'ole and just let the ball 'it it, or 'im, but us couldn't get 'im out, try as us would. An' all the time their captain were a'pilin' up the runs, an' things weren't lookin' at all bright for us. So arter a bit, Master Fred 'e chucks the ball to me an' sez, "'Ere, Bill, you 'ave a go! Us can't get 'em out with good bowlin', maybe a bit o' bad stuff'll do the trick!" Well I ain't much of a bowler – I ain't as young as I were – but I takes the ball and goes on from the end where Ol' Joe was umpirin'. 'E weren't 'alf mad, weren't Ol' Joe, 'cos there 'adn't been no appeals against either of the batsmen.

'Well I bowls a ball or two quiet like, just to try an' entice their captain to 'ave a go, but 'e plays 'em back nice as nice all along the ground. The third ball as I put down swerved a bit an' 'it 'im on the leg. It wasn't anywhere a'nigh the wicket, but Ol' George, who were a'standin' at point, sings out, "'Ow's that?" Up goes Ol' Joe's 'and – an' 'is face were a picture – "Out!" 'e sez determined like. "What did you say?" sez their captain, "I don't think I 'eard you right." "OUT!" yells Joe, "an' out you goes!" An' 'e 'ad to go. As 'e were a'goin' Master Fred come along an' sez, "That were a rummy decision o' yourn, weren't it, Joe?" "That may be, sir," sez Joe, "but it were the first chance I 'ad at 'im!"

'Well, we goes on a'bowlin' an' a'fieldin', an' in the end us manages to get 'em all out, but not afore they'd made 92 runs – which were a smartish total for a village cricket match, an' us weren't too sure as 'ow we could cut as many as that. But, 'owever that might be, we was more than ready to 'ave a go at it.

'Master Fred went in first, wi' Ol' George (as keeps "The Spotted Dog"). Ol' George were one o' the fattest chaps as ever I see – 'e weighed nigh on twenty stone. 'E goes in an' takes guard from Joe, an' 'e looked like a great big 'aystack a'standin' there. The bowler at Joe's end 'as one look at 'im an' turns to Joe an' sez, "'Ow be I to bowl – I can't see the wickets?" "You stop your rattle," sez Joe, "an' get on with your bowlin' – if it 'its 'im in front, it's leg afore, and if it 'its 'im be'ind, it's a wide!" So the bowler don't say no more, but walks to the end of 'is run – an' you never sin such a long run as 'e took – 'e were very nigh lost in the brambles o' the mound at the far end o' the ground. 'Twere as long as the length o' a cricket pitch, were 'is run, that I knows 'cos I measured 'im.

''E comes a'gallopin' down to the crease, an' the ball fled out of 'is 'and and right over the long-stop's 'ead, an' goes to the boundary for four byes. Ol' George grins, an' sez, "That's easy! Gie us some more like that, master." An' the next one as comes down 'e snicks over slip's 'ead for another four. Well, we yells a bit, you know, an' the other folk don't like that at all.

'Well, to cut a long story short, us got 92 runs the same as them, an' 'ad lost all but one of our wickets. Master Fred were still in, an' there were only Bob Belcher to come, an' 'e were an oldish man as 'ad been still from cricket for three years, and us couldn't look to 'im for much.

'There were a silence like death when 'e walks in. Master Fred comes out to meet 'im, a'smilin', an' sez somethin' as none of us could 'ear, but I sin Ol' Bob grin a bit, an' nod 'is 'ead. 'E takes guard from Ol' Joe, an' the bowler as was on first goes back to 'is brambles – an' then somethin' 'appened as I never sin afore or since! Just as soon as 'e turns round an' begins 'is long gallop up to the wicket, dang me, if the two o' they batsmen don't start a'runnin'. The bowler, 'e stops short, fair mazed, an' their captain shouts: "Run 'em out, Ted!" An' sure enough, the bowler throws at the far wicket – never 'it 'im though. Up goes Joe's 'and, an' "No-ball!" 'e sez, as loud as the Crack-o'-Doom. An' by goy, it were too – an' us 'ad won the match. You never 'eard such a row as there was, in all your natural. 'Course, they sez as it weren't fair, but Ol' Joe 'ad 'em proper. What they sez was that the ball weren't in play afore it were delivered, an' Joe sez, "An' what about our Bill 'ere this arternoon? 'E were backin' up an' were out o' 'is ground, an' the bowler, instead o' bowlin', knocks the bails off, an' Bill were given out? If that's fair what we done's fair too, an' in any case your bowler threw at the wickets 'stead of bowlin', an' anyone knows as that's a no-ball." Ah! an' they 'adn't nothing to say to that.

'An' so you see Ol' Joe were right when 'e said 'e'd win the match for us – an' that's a thing I shall never forget!'

*   *   *

The doyen of cricket umpires in Britain was, for many years, one Joe Filliston. In 1961, approaching his own century, he was interviewed by Kenneth Pragnell.

Umpire Reaches His Century

Pragnell:	Today I'd like you to meet 99-year-old Joe Filliston. First life member of the Association of Cricket Umpires and born in 1862, the year when Lincoln was President of the United States, the Civil War had been on one year, Queen Victoria was on the throne here in Great Britain and W. G. Grace was a mere toddler of fourteen years of age. What is your first memory of the time when you were born?
Filliston:	Well, I was always very fond of cricket. I used to make my own balls and tie them up with string with brown paper and make cricket bats out of egg chests – shape 'em.
Pragnell:	You didn't have much money in those days?
Filliston:	No.
Pragnell:	Not only are you a remarkable man but the thing that amazes me – you've still got your own teeth.
Filliston:	I won't part with them. I've still got wonderful health and while I've got them few teeth left I won't part with them.
Pragnell:	Has anybody ever tried to make you part with them?
Filliston:	Well, they did – but I wasn't that way inclined.

Pragnell:	Now I understand you're a family man – you have a daughter and a son. How old are they?
Filliston:	My son is about, is sixty-six, my daughter is about sixty-four.
Pragnell:	Have you grandchildren?
Filliston:	Yes.
Pragnell:	Great-grandchildren?
Filliston:	My eldest grandson's daughter, Joanna, two years old.
Pragnell:	Where is your son now, is he still in Britain?
Filliston:	No, he's retired and he's just enjoying himself.
Pragnell:	But in this country?
Filliston:	Yes.
Pragnell:	Was he a keen cricketer?
Filliston:	He was on the staff at Lord's. He left to play football for Charlton Athletic, centre-forward.
Pragnell:	So sport has always been in your blood.
Filliston:	We've always been in sport, yes.
Pragnell:	A few moments ago I mentioned W. G. Grace being fourteen when you were born. Did you ever play with the great W. G.?
Filliston:	Yes, I played with Grace at the Crystal Palace. I was then playing for the Kensington Wanderers and there was another great bowler who used to play, used to be the oboe player at the London Pavilion, the name of George Clegg. He turned down the county of Yorkshire. He was a Yorkshireman.
Pragnell:	What other famous cricketers did you play with at that time?
Filliston:	Well, there was 'Plum' Warner, Bosanquet, the googly bowler, and O'Brien was playing for Middlesex. He was a very big hitter, and Albert Trott . . . when they were playing for Middlesex . . . Albert Trott had a bat and it was too light for him – he wanted to hit one over the Pavilion so I put some tea-leaves in his bat and he wanted to know how I'd done it. And he obtained his ambition.

Pragnell: By hitting it over the Pavilion?

Filliston: Yes.

Pragnell: What about the great 'Ranji', did you ever meet him?

Filliston: 'Ranji' I first met at Fenner's at Cambridge. I was then playing for Ely City, Cathedral City.

Pragnell: As a spin bowler?

Filliston: Yes. Spin bowler . . .

Pragnell: How remarkable a cricketer do you think 'Ranji' was?

Filliston: Well, he was a man of a style of his own on the leg side. He could take them off his face and get square leg hits for four. People tried to imitate the same things and spoilt their cricket career.

Pragnell: Whom did you used to play for?

Filliston: I used to play for several clubs in the Lancashire League, the North Staffordshire League and the Durham League. I also played for Staffordshire County. I headed the amateurs for two years in the North Staffordshire League.

Pragnell: When did you retire from this cricket?

Filliston: Well, I was playing up to – I was about sixty-four.

Pragnell: Sixty-four?

Filliston: As a professional.

Pragnell: Yes, that's thirty-five years ago, in fact.

Filliston: Yes, and then I took up umpiring for the Honourable Artillery Company for some few years, and several other clubs. London University I've umpired for, the BBC and many clubs, too numerous to mention.

Pragnell: But don't you find it tiring standing at the wicket?

Filliston: I enjoy every moment, and when a man gets 50 or 100 I'm getting them myself.

Pragnell: Do you ever try bowling now? I presume you'd bowl these tweakers, wouldn't you?

Filliston: Well, I did. I once played for the MCC against Patcham Priory from Brighton some few years ago. They asked me to go on to bowl. I got three wickets for three runs and a thing I've never done before in my life, I bowled underhand spinners.

Pragnell: But you still got three wickets?

Filliston: I got 3 for 3.

Pragnell: Now what has made your life obviously as happy as it is? I mean, you're a very cheerful man, at the age of ninety-nine. What do you think is the great secret in your life outside of the love of cricket?

Filliston: Well, people often ask me, what's the secret of your 'long livity'. I don't even know the answer to it – it's just a coincidence. I've always liked me beer and I've always liked me pipe and I've lived in an ordinary manner. I haven't done this and I haven't done the other like people say they are for 'long livity'. I'm just an ordinary man.

Pragnell: You've had a warm heart and a free life. You've done what you wanted to do. This is the great secret, do you think – doing what you've wanted to do? In your case, cricket?

Filliston: Well, there's one thing I never did, I never worried myself over anything. It's got to be got over and that was that.

Pragnell: Now we're looking forward to your 100th birthday next February. Are you going to have any special celebration for this?

Filliston: Well, there may be a few old-age pensioners invited to a certain place. Just to celebrate the event, but they are all junior to me by twenty years.

Pragnell: Just one final question. What do you think of modern cricket as compared with the cricket when you were in your heyday before the turn of the century?

Filliston: Well, they've certainly got better wickets than when I used to play. Prepared wickets. In my day it was watered and rolled only, and you could still get your fifties on 'em – I got fifties and 100s too. But today there are what are called billiard-table wickets. The cricket is just the same now if they played it in the right spirit but they've departed from that.

Nearly three years later, Kenneth Pragnell again brought Filliston to the microphone. By now, Filliston was 102 but still hale and happy to recall the great names of the past.

Pragnell: There have been a lot of criticisms about Grace, the sort of man he was. You were somebody who knew him and played with him. What is your real opinion?

Filliston: Well, my opinion, he was like old Johnny Douglas, a basic soldier on the field, and a very nice man when he was off. Very affable, both of them. But very strict on the cricket field which it ought to be.

Pragnell: A good captain?

Filliston: Yes, good captaincy, yes.

Pragnell: What about Sir Jack Hobbs, did you know Sir Jack at all?

Filliston: Well, Jack Hobbs during the First World War, there was me, Jack Hobbs, Jack Elson, Bob Abel, coaching the boys at Westminster School, and occasionally 'Plum' Warner come behind the nets and wanted some coaching in his officer's clothes.

*   *   *

R. C. Robertson-Glasgow, 'Crusoe' to all who knew him and many who did not, played in that never-to-be-forgotten match in 1925 on the Taunton cricket ground when Jack Hobbs beat W. G. Grace's record of 126 centuries. Speaking in 'I Was There', he recollected the excitement, shared by half England, as Hobbs equalled the record on one day and beat it on the next.

When Hobbs Beat Grace
R. C. Robertson-Glasgow

General Overseas Service, February 1951

It was twenty-six years ago and on a sunny Saturday at Taunton, a market town in Somerset, when Jack Hobbs, playing for Surrey against Somerset, equalled the record of the great W. G. Grace. Grace had made 126 centuries, and Hobbs had had a very long chase after it. In this match he was destined to equal that record and (though few thought it at the time) to pass it as well.

I was playing in that match for Somerset, one of the unfortunate bowlers, and I cannot say I remember the match in anything like its entirety. I do not think many people do. It comes back rather kaleidoscopically and always

199

Hobbs, Hobbs, Hobbs comes back most in the memory. And all the excitement comes back with it.

On 20 July of that year 1925, Hobbs had reached 125 centuries, and he just made 105 in that famous fixture of the year against Kent at Blackheath when, somehow, he got a bit stuck, not unnaturally, for he could not go on making hundreds for ever, and that was his twelfth of the season, anyhow. And he made, I think, 50-odd against Nottingham and 50-odd against Gloucestershire at Gloucester; and he made 49 against Middlesex, and 1 at Brighton – being lbw to the great Maurice Tate – and 30 odd against Leicestershire. And the newspapers kept coming out with posters – what fun those posters were in those days, too! – saying, 'Hobbs fails again.'

I suppose it must have got on Hobbs's nerves. It would get on anybody's nerves in the end.

However, there came now his great chance, and on the lovely little ground at Taunton the boundaries are fairly short, so there was a better chance than on some grounds. So here we are – Taunton, 1925, 15 August, Saturday morning. But, at first, no innings by Hobbs. Somerset won the toss and in we went, and, I am sorry to say, rather quickly out we went. We made about 160-odd, for which there was very little excuse on the best of wickets.

So, somewhere about tea-time, in Surrey went, Hobbs and Sandham, the great pair; and in the very first over by Robertson-Glasgow there was a loud groan from the crowd when Hobbs hit up a catch to cover-point who accepted it gratefully. But, unfortunately for Somerset, it was a no-ball. Groans and groans for this catch changed into cheers of relief. What did Hobbs look like at the start of this innings? I can tell you, very well. Great player though he was, he was obviously very anxious. He batted extraordinarily well; with his style he could not do any other. He was always, to me, the greatest player of the lot. But he was for him almost scratchy, and when he had made 7 he popped up a ball – from me it happened to be – and it should have been caught at mid-on, but I do not know what happened with mid-on. He was what you might call basking in vigilant content.

And then when he had made 30 or so, there was a very, very confident appeal for lbw from the same bowler who suffered from the lack of vigilant content. But the umpire thought otherwise.

Sandham had gone when he was 13 and Hobbs had been joined by that magnificent batsman, D. J. Knight, an England player who had made his name before the war and had played for England against the Australians about four years before this. He batted beautifully, and he got into the thirties and was going very well indeed. Well, these two got into a muddle over a run. They were both in the middle of the pitch – an unenviable position for both – and Knight, most unselfishly and quick-thinkingly, too – just had time to pass Hobbs in the middle of the pitch, so that he was out and Hobbs was not.

Then came Tom Shepherd, who could hit or defend, both extraordinarily well. That great left-hander, Jack White of Somerset and England, found a beauty for Shepherd, and out went poor Tom for nought. This was a tremendous batting side and in came Jardine – D. R. Jardine.

And so evening drew on, three or four wickets down, and Hobbs still going on fairly strongly. He had been in, as a matter of fact, only for two hours and twenty minutes. On Saturday night he was 91, not out.

Monday morning was a great scene: Taunton had never seen anything like it, I imagine. There were many farmers there – large men taking up a good deal of room – Jack White's father amongst them; he always came to watch, never spoke much but watched every ball very carefully. There were reporters, newsreel men, a movie camera on the little tin roof of the Pavilion. There were no BBC commentaries in those days. And one reporter, a very old friend of mine, came up and said, 'Oh, for Heaven's sake let Jack do it.' But we had no intention of letting him do it.

Out Hobbs came, and Jardine was his partner. He was run out after Hobbs was out. Jardine and Hobbs, no unillustrious pair, were they? Well, three singles to Hobbs, Bridges and Robertson-Glasgow bowling. Then a no-ball from Robertson-Glasgow. Whuff! That was hooked for four like a flash by Hobbs. That made him 98. And then I remember he went in, and, for some whim or other, he changed his bat – brought out another one. Then Bridges was bowling: Hobbs got a single and Jardine a single. There was Hobbs: 99. There was an utter silence. Then up ran Bridges, who bowled a good enough ball and Hobbs turned him round for a single: it glided short-leg, and Hobbs was home!

And here I must just quote from a contemporary report, 'Tremendous cheering, of course, greeted the accomplishment of the feat. Indeed so pronounced was the enthusiasm that the progress of the game was delayed some minutes, while at the end of the over all the players in the field shook hands with Hobbs, and the Surrey captain brought out a drink for the hero of the occasion, who raised the glass high and bowed to the crowd before partaking of the refreshment.'

Jim Bridges got Hobbs out, by the way, and well he deserved his wicket: caught wicket for 101. So Grace's record was equalled and the crowds, a lot of them, melted away. The reporters melted away, and the cinematographers removed from the little Pavilion. And then Somerset in the second innings did something to redeem their shocking failure in the first, and we made 374 – a pretty decent total. And so, on the last day, Surrey were left 180-odd to win, which meant something that nobody had really thought of – that was that Hobbs could also beat Grace's record, in the same match.

You should have seen Hobbs in that second innings, he was a beautiful sight: no longer anxious, no longer scratchy. I bowled him, I remember I bowled him a ball that in the first innings he would have been perfectly happy to prod for nothing – he cracked it past cover-point like a shot out of a gun, for four. Well, we knew where we were, then. We knew that Hobbs was in full cry, and although he was forty-two – a very young forty-two, let me tell you – he was still in his prime and still the greatest batsman to me, even then, the greatest batsman in the world.

Sandham was batting very well, as he always did (never forget Andy Sandham got his 100 centuries in cricket, too), but he played a good second fiddle to Jack Hobbs, and Jack went on, and bowlers came and went, but nobody could get him out.

Well, Hobbs got that 100, and almost as soon as he had got it Surrey had won the match by ten wickets. How wonderful to equal Grace on one day and beat him on the next! And it was Hobbs's fourteenth century for that summer.

*   *   *

The amiable exterior Robertson-Glasgow presented to the world disguised bouts of severe melancholia and, tragically, he took his own life. A dominating figure in South African cricket in the first two decades of this century, Aubrey Faulkner suffered from the same affliction with the same sad end. After the First World War he had settled in England and opened a School of Cricket which was responsible for bringing to the fore several players of subsequent renown. In September 1930, in what was probably his last broadcast, Faulkner conversed with Jack Hobbs, who had announced his retirement from Test cricket.

Hobbs Retires from Test Cricket

Faulkner:	Well, Jack – we're terribly sorry you've played your last Test match. What do you feel about it all yourself?
Hobbs:	My feelings are mixed. Of late years Test match cricket has taken a lot out of me. I really started off this season not wanting to play. But I was persuaded to start again – and I am disappointed I did not do better. I was ever so keen on justifying my inclusion.
Faulkner:	I wouldn't bother, Jack. Considering everything, you did your share. Haven't you any regrets at retiring from international cricket?
Hobbs:	Yes – many. It's not comforting to feel I will no longer be a power in the land. I have found personal success very

gratifying. I think it's going to be hard for me to drop out of it all. However – I can't expect anything else. Others greater than myself have had to do the same kind of thing in the past.

Faulkner: Still, it's all very sad, Jack. What a pity we can't stay young! These young fellows today don't know how marvellous it is to be young enough to get on with things. Are you hopeful about England's chances in Australia in 1932?

Hobbs: Not very. Two years ago things looked far more promising. Our young amateurs are not somehow fetching up as they should. And England needs young amateurs of the highest class. They help to knit a team together. They can adopt an attitude towards the game which we professionals dare not. The game is our living. We are bound to take it seriously, perhaps too seriously at times.

Faulkner: Should Australia be stronger in 1932 than they are now?

Hobbs: Yes – much more so. For, besides their present fine young men, they have several more good young fellows coming along to the front. And cricketers develop so fast in Australia. I expect the hot sun, and the free lives they lead, are the cause. Besides that, it is easy for their young men to develop their shots on the good, even-paced wickets in Australia. Confidence is more quickly gained than in England.

Faulkner: That's so. What made you take up cricket as a profession?

Hobbs: I was always mad keen on the game. My dad was groundsman at Jesus College, Cambridge, and he too was keen. Tom Hayward was my hero in those days. As kids, we all worshipped him. Our family had no money – therefore, I couldn't afford to play the game as an amateur. But I was determined to become a player all the same. The offer from Surrey was a godsend to me. I can still remember my excitement when it was made.

Faulkner: I expect you can. Were you ever anxious concerning your future after you had once taken the plunge?

Hobbs: I was a little scared when I got up to the Oval. There seemed so many great players on the staff. I began to wonder how I would ever get my chance. At that time I never dreamt I would ever play for England. Even playing for Surrey appeared a pretty mighty task.

Faulkner: Isn't it funny to look back? I expect though you soon settled down and began to model yourself on someone?

Hobbs: Yes. I studied Tom Hayward's methods. I found him a great source of inspiration. It was a wonderful experience watching him bat in matches, and also later on when I used to go in first with him. He made the bowlers – especially the fast ones – look so simple. It gave me great confidence. Hayward was truly a wonderful batsman.

Faulkner: Are you superstitious, Jack?

Hobbs: In small things, yes. I like to play in certain caps. I always put my pads and gloves on in a certain order – right pad always on first. I dislike, too, being on the figure 9. I am glad also to get off 13. I never mind being on 99. I see you're smiling at my funny ways.

Faulkner: Not a bit of it. I haven't yet met a cricketer who hadn't some peculiar fancy of his own. At any rate, your peculiarities don't seem to have handicapped you much. When do you consider you were at the zenith of your career?

Hobbs: About 1914. I lost a lot through the war. I felt on the top of the world just before it. The bowling was good – yet I always had a feeling I could cope with it. I got an immense amount of satisfaction out of my cricket in those days. We batsmen all seemed more up against it then.

Faulkner: How do you account for the large scores of today?

Hobbs: First and foremost, I blame the super wickets we now play on. They give the bowler no help. They are fast without being lively. Then, too, the art of defence has improved out of all knowledge. Pad play has been brought to a fine art. Bowlers don't get the chances today they did twenty years ago. On more 'sporty' wickets batsmen would be induced to have a go for the bowling more. Nowadays, we can sit back and wait in confidence for the runs to come.

Faulkner: What do you consider the outstanding features in present-day county cricket?

Hobbs: I think too much cricket is played. Also, too many teams start off playing in each match with the idea of not losing it. Most of us players become tired out long before the end of the season. We are unable to put the little extra amount of vim into our cricket we would like. I expect many of us become stale without realising it.

Faulkner: Is the present slow batting due to less enterprising batsmen, or better bowlers?

Hobbs: Neither. It is due to the amount of negative bowling which takes place. Most bowling is just short of a length – and practically every team has an in-swing bowler or two. These place several men on the leg side. If a batsman commences to open out, he is soon bottled up by these leg-theory merchants.

Faulkner: Are you ever anxious when taking your first ball?

Hobbs: Not particularly. I'm only anxious when preparing to go in. At that stage I dislike being talked to. But as soon as I get on to the turf I am all right. When I arrive on the wicket I see if there is any damp on it. I always like making my first run quickly. I've never yet bagged a pair. I don't want to now. I play back rather than forward, as I like getting a good look at the ball at the commencement of an innings.

Faulkner: Which type of bowling do you mostly like playing?

Hobbs: This all depends on what mood I am in. But no matter how I feel, it is the ball that goes away from me to the off-side which is always the most difficult to cope with. I often wonder why bowlers don't spend most of their time developing this type of ball. The ball which comes into a batsman is far easier to watch than the other one.

Faulkner: Which innings do you consider the best you've ever played in a Test match?

Hobbs: Taking everything into account, such as the state of the wicket, and the importance of the occasion, I should say my second innings in 1926 against the Australians at the Oval was my greatest. The wicket was really bad before lunch, but I did my best to make the Australians think it was really not very difficult.

Faulkner: You succeeded, Jack. I saw every ball bowled to you, and chuckled with glee at your cunning. I can honestly say, though, that I saw through your scheme. And I have never ceased admiring you for it. I bet you got a heap of satisfaction out of it all. Which do you think were the three greatest Test innings you have seen?

Hobbs:	Without doubt, Charlie Macartney's century at Leeds in 1926, when he got a hundred before lunch, was one of them. For sheer audacity I have never seen its equal. Then, too, there was Bradman's amazing 300, also at Leeds, this year. And finally, Herbert Sutcliffe's 160-odd at the Oval in 1926. You remember, when he and I were lucky enough to help England out of her tight corner. I've never seen Herbert's courage and fighting qualities more splendidly in evidence. I will always regret that our partnerships in Test matches are now a thing of the past. He is a great Test match player. It's as good as a tonic being in with him.
Faulkner:	Whilst we are on the question of Sutcliffe's attitude towards Test matches, perhaps you'll say what part you consider temperament actually plays in the game.
Hobbs:	A tremendous lot. I would even say that no man can hope to reach the top unless he possesses both technique and temperament. The one is of little use without the other. I have seen this over and over again. Temperament is a funny thing; you've either got the right one or you haven't. And if you haven't, well – big cricket is not for you. This is what Test match selectors are always up against.
Faulkner:	Do you think that final Test matches (now that you haven't to play in them any more) should always be played to a finish?
Hobbs:	Yes, I certainly do. After all, a Test match is a test of something. There should be a definite end to it. I don't find them boring, because everything that takes place must have a direct bearing on the finish. Then, too, if a game is played out, the best team ought to win. And isn't this what a Test match is really for?
Faulkner:	I agree. But I don't think either of us will be popular for saying so. If these long Test matches are continued with, strenuous efforts will be made in England, during the next few years, to unearth young players with the right Test match temperaments. Can you offer any suggestions which will help to further this end?
Hobbs:	I think trial matches should be perserved with. Big matches are the only means of summing up a player's temperament. But I don't favour the idea of all the best players in England being on the one side in Trial matches. These games should be something like North *v.* South, or East *v.* West. Or sides

might possibly be drawn from, say, the first, third, fifth and seventh teams, etc., in the Championship and pitted against sides drawn from the second, fourth, sixth and eighth teams, etc. This ought to ensure that all promising young players would play in at least one Trial match each year.

Faulkner: Have you any message for young fellows just entering first-class cricket?

Hobbs: I would advise them not to become too depressed over their failures. Remember the good days – and forget about the bad ones. It's useless worrying oneself to death. Besides, what's the good of it? An optimist will always go farther at cricket than a pessimist. I would also say, don't become over-confident. There is a lot to learn about the game. I'm still learning about it myself. At the beginning of an innings I would advise young players not to cut or pull too much. Play straight-bat shots for a while. And, above all, always make the most of opportunities. They don't come every day.

Faulkner: Splendid, Jack. You make me feel I want to start cricket all over again. What are your own plans for the future?

Hobbs: I hope to play one more season for Surrey – possibly two. After that, I'm not quite sure. Several attractive coaching jobs have been put up to me. I don't fancy the idea, though, very much. I don't expect I will ever be able to break away from the game entirely. Goodness! – it seems funny even thinking about the time when I will not be taking an active part each season. But I mustn't grumble. I've had a good innings. I will have a fine time to look back upon.

Faulkner: You're lucky. The majority of us are not so fortunate. I suppose you've had shoals of letters over your retirement from Test match cricket?

Hobbs: Yes. I've spent many nights, lately, trying to catch up with my correspondence. I am astounded at the public's kindness. I shall always remember how sympathetic everyone has been to me. I can't thank the public enough . . . But I think it is time now to say 'Good night'. I will say so for both of us. Good night, everybody.

*   *   *   **